The U.S. Geological Survey Bird Banding Laboratory: An Integrated Scientific Program Supporting Research and Conservation of North American Birds

By Gregory J. Smith

Open-File Report 2013–1238

U.S. Department of the Interior
U.S. Geological Survey

U.S. Department of the Interior
SALLY JEWELL, Secretary

U.S. Geological Survey
Suzette M. Kimball, Acting Director

U.S. Geological Survey, Reston, Virginia: 2013

For more information on the USGS—the Federal source for science about the Earth, its natural and living resources, natural hazards, and the environment, visit http://www.usgs.gov or call 1–888–ASK–USGS.

For an overview of USGS information products, including maps, imagery, and publications, visit http://www.usgs.gov/pubprod

To order this and other USGS information products, visit http://store.usgs.gov

Suggested citation:
Smith, G.J., 2013, The U.S. Geological Survey Bird Banding Laboratory: An integrated scientific program supporting research and conservation of North American birds: U.S. Geological Survey Open-File Report 2013–1238, 88 p., http://pubs.usgs.gov/of/2013/1238/.

Contents

Figures

The U.S. Geological Survey Bird Banding Laboratory: An Integrated Scientific Program Supporting Research and Conservation of North American Birds

By Gregory J. Smith

Abstract

The U.S. Geological Survey (USGS) Bird Banding Laboratory (BBL) was established in 1920 after ratification of the Migratory Bird Treaty Act with the United Kingdom in 1918. During World War II, the BBL was moved from Washington, D.C., to what is now the USGS Patuxent Wildlife Research Center (PWRC). The BBL issues permits and bands to permittees to band birds, records bird band recoveries or encounters primarily through telephone and Internet reporting, and manages more than 72 million banding records and more than 4.5 million records of encounters using state-of-the-art technologies. Moreover, the BBL also issues bands and manages banding and encounter data for the Canadian Bird Banding Office (BBO). Each year approximately 1 million bands are shipped from the BBL to banders in the United States and Canada, and nearly 100,000 encounter reports are entered into the BBL systems. Banding data are essential for regulatory programs, especially migratory waterfowl harvest regulations.

The USGS BBL works closely with the U.S. Fish and Wildlife Service (USFWS) to develop regulations for the capture, handling, banding, and marking of birds. These regulations are published in the Code of Federal Regulations (CFR). In 2006, the BBL and the USFWS Division of Migratory Bird Management (DMBM) began a comprehensive revision of the banding regulations.

The bird banding community has three major constituencies: Federal and State agency personnel involved in the management and conservation of bird populations that include the Flyway Councils, ornithological research scientists, and avocational banders.

With increased demand for banding activities and relatively constant funding, a Federal Advisory Committee (Committee) was chartered and reviewed the BBL program in 2005. The final report of the Committee included six major goals and 58 specific recommendations, 47 of which have been addressed by the BBL. Specifically, the Committee recommended the BBL continue to support science, conservation, and management of birds through the use of banding and banding data and that the BBL be managed by the USGS and located at the USGS Patuxent Wildlife Research Center (PWRC) in Laurel, Maryland. Recommendations that have not been implemented include those already addressed by other organizations, as well as lower priority, such as developing a BBL business plan.

The comprehensive review and recommendations of the Committee, the response of the BBL to address the Committee's recommendations, and other improvements to its operations have positioned the BBL to provide a high level of service to the banding community. As new technologies are developed and incorporated into BBL operations, further efficiencies are expected to enable the BBL to continue to meet emerging scientific needs.

Introduction

Comprehensive Review of the Bird Banding Laboratory

Bird banding and marking are scientific methods used to determine location, range, population size, migration, behavior, and other parameters for avian species and specific populations. First determined as a Federal responsibility for migratory birds in 1920, the BBL was originally located in Washington, D.C., and was later moved to the Patuxent Wildlife Research Center (PWRC) in Laurel, Maryland, during World War II. Bird banding and the U.S. Geological Survey (USGS) Bird Banding Laboratory (BBL) have become critical assets for managing waterfowl and other migratory gamebird populations, assisting in the recovery of Federally endangered and threatened species, supporting ornithological research activities, and promoting the conservation of migratory birds.

The BBL provides bands at no cost to permitted banders in the U.S. and Canada. Currently (2013), approximately 1,630 Master Banders hold permits and approximately 5,050 banders hold subpermits. The BBL issues approximately 1 million bands and receives about 100,000 reports of banded birds or encounters each year. The BBL manages the banding data for Canada as well, and the database now includes more than 72 million banding records and 4.5 million encounter records. These data complement the related databases managed and analyzed by the USGS PWRC that include the North American Phenology Network with 6 million records and the North American Breeding Bird Survey with 78 million records. Having these large-scale databases within the USGS and associated with USGS landscape assets, such as the USGS Landsat 8, creates scientific synergy for avian ecological research that is available nowhere else.

Over the past 93 years, the BBL has evolved to keep pace with the increased volume of banding data produced by the banding community, has improved the variety of bands available to support a wide array of banding projects, and has adopted new technologies that will allow for improved management and analysis of data and address new research challenges. As a scientific agency, the USGS has supported an integrated scientific approach to meet the emerging challenges and demands of the scientific community.

To address challenges to meet emerging scientific needs and advances in technology, in 2005 the Directors of the USGS and USFWS chartered a 14-member Federal Advisory Committee to define a vision for the BBL over the next 10 to 15 years. This independent committee and a subcommittee charged with writing a report met seven times from 2005 to 2006. The committee produced a published report, Haseltine and others (2008)—U.S. Geological Survey (USGS) Circular 1320—that resulted in two primary recommendations:

1. "…the primary role of the BBL should continue to support the use of banding and banding data by researchers and managers engaged in science, conservation, and management of birds…"

2. "…the BBL be managed nationally by USGS Headquarters as a research and operational support unit and provided with resources appropriate to its national and international functions…" and "…continue to be physically located at the Patuxent Wildlife Research Center…"

This independent committee, chartered under the Federal Advisory Committee Act (FACA), recognized the importance of BBL responsibilities as part of the scientific community and as part of a scientific agency, the USGS. Moreover, the Committee also saw the benefit of the continued institutional organization of the BBL as a national research and operations program managed nationally and physically located at the PWRC. Committee membership represented a diverse array of nongovernmental organizations, professional societies, universities, and U.S. and Canadian agencies. The time, funds, and expertise dedicated to this review, report, and recommendations were substantial, and the findings and recommendations chart a course for the BBL for the next 10 to 15 years.

Purpose and Scope

This report provides a comprehensive synthesis of the changes and new procedures implemented by the USGS Bird Banding Laboratory in response to the 2008 report issued by the Federal Advisory Committee (Haseltine and others, 2008) to define a vision for the BBL over the next 10 to 15 years (see appendix 1). It describes the response of the BBL to the recommendations of the Federal Advisory Committee as well as the integral scientific role of the BBL in the avian ecological scientific enterprise.

Bird Banding Laboratory Stakeholders

The bird banding community is a diverse constituency representing a variety of interests and activities. The major stakeholder groups represented in the BBL Federal Advisory Committee included:

- The Ornithological Council
- The U.S. Fish and Wildlife Service
- Cornell Laboratory of Ornithology
- The Institute for Bird Populations
- Colorado State University
- Canadian Wildlife Service
- National Audubon Society
- Ducks Unlimited
- The Wildlife Society
- North American Banding Council
- The Conservation Fund
- Pheasants Forever

The composition of this community has changed in recent decades, from a preponderance of private citizens banding birds as an avocation to a much larger representation by agency biologists and academic research scientists. At this time, the bird banding community is nearly equally divided among three general stakeholder groups that are enumerated below.

Bird Management and Conservation Agencies

The BBL has a long history of direct communication and involvement with the four Flyway Councils and their associated joint technical committees. The Flyway Councils are composed of representatives from each State wildlife management agency. Although, whereas they were initially developed to coordinate the management of waterfowl and other harvested game bird populations, in recent years they have added nongame sections to their technical committees to address the regional management of all groups of birds. The BBL sends representatives to the Flyway joint technical committee meetings each winter to provide annual updates on BBL activities, and is regularly involved in regional banding-related issues for game and nongame birds. Given the importance of banding data for the management of migratory game bird populations, the BBL has a staff biologist position that is dedicated as a liaison with the Flyway Councils in order to provide a direct communication link with the BBL and to facilitate issuing permits and permit authorizations needed to conduct the required management and conservation activities.

In addition to working with the Flyway Councils, the BBL also regularly communicates with Federal agencies involved with bird banding activities. The BBL has a long history of supporting bird banding on USFWS wildlife refuges, primarily for managing migratory game bird populations, but also for conservation of nongame birds. The banding and marking of birds is integral for the conservation and recovery of Federally listed endangered and threatened species, and the BBL has actively supported these activities for decades. In addition to the USFWS, the BBL supports banding activities on lands managed by the U.S. Department of Agriculture (USDA) and Department of Defense as well as wildlife management activities conducted by Animal and Plant Health Inspection Service (APHIS). A BBL staff biologist also serves as a liaison with these Federal agencies.

Research Scientists

The BBL has supported a wide variety of ornithological research activities for decades. With recent advances in marking technologies, scientists are increasingly requesting BBL permits to conduct cutting-edge research on many aspects of avian ecology such as using satellite transmitters to track bird movements over large landscapes and small data loggers to remotely record information on activity patterns, physiological condition, and other aspects of avian biology. In addition to these types of projects, bird banding and marking are also essential in various studies of avian behavior, ecotoxicology, and population dynamics. These studies require an array of permitting and auxiliary marking authorizations that are provided by the BBL and are considerably more complex than traditional banding studies.

Most of these research scientists are associated with academic institutions. These research activities are also conducted by Federal government agencies including the USGS, the USDA, The Smithsonian Institution, and the USFWS. In addition, nongovernmental organizations, State wildlife agencies, and even private consulting firms are now (2013) involved in research activities that are supported by the BBL.

Avocational Banders

Citizens who conduct banding as an avocation remain an important component of the banding community. These banders continue to provide data on the changing status of and trends in bird populations across the U.S. and Canada and to document the movement patterns of birds across the continent. Some banders conduct research that is published in the peer-reviewed literature, and many contribute to local and regional publications. These banders are becoming increasingly involved in collaborative projects designed to address large-scale conservation concerns, such as the Monitoring Avian Productivity and Survivorship (MAPS) project coordinated by the Institute for Bird Populations, which obtains data from hundreds of avocational banders and Project Owl-net designed to improve our knowledge of the migratory movements of small owls.

Avocational banders have traditionally been associated with one of the three regional bird banding associations—the Eastern, Western, and Inland Bird Banding Associations. As funding allows, the BBL participates in the annual meetings of these associations to provide updates on BBL activities and to receive input from these stakeholder groups.

Recent Bird Banding Laboratory Advancements and U.S. Geological Survey Investments

Highlights of recent BBL advancements include:

- The conversion of 4.5 million paper and microfilm encounter records to digital format, an investment amounting to nearly $1 million and resulting in the availability of most reported band encounters in electronic format (2010).

- The launch of a new Internet-based band-reporting program allowing bands to be reported online rather than through the costly toll-free telephone system (2012).

- A new data system that allows for recapture information to be incorporated in the BBL database. This system is essential for the analysis of new, more sophisticated capture-recapture data to assess the population dynamics of sensitive species such as the American Black Duck and Laysan Albatross. Studies are currently underway to provide USFWS managers with cutting-edge information (2013).

- The complete transformation of the 72-million-record dataset to a relational database that supports detailed scientific analyses (2006).

These recent transformations to more scientifically and technologically advanced systems have supported the scientific community and avian research in addition to meeting the regulatory needs of migratory bird harvest programs. BBL integration into major ecological events such as the Deepwater Horizon oil spill disaster and Hurricane Sandy continue to drive innovation in banding and encounter data management and analyses. Since 2000, more than 1,500 scientific publications have used BBL data and capabilities to continually improve the state of our knowledge about migratory bird populations in North America (see appendix 2).

In addition to the two primary recommendations, the Committee developed six broad goals for the BBL. These six goals were broken down into 23 objectives, with 58 specific recommendations as to how to achieve those objectives (see Appendix 1 for a complete listing). The five highest priority objectives out of the 23 are identified and the actions taken by the BBL to address the specific recommendations to meet those objectives are as follows:

1. To ensure a continuing and adequate supply of high-quality, Federally issued numeric bands of required sizes, materials, and types.

   BBL actions: Currently (2013), the BBL maintains a 2-year supply of all band types including hard-metal bands, representing an inventory of approximately $350,000.

2. To improve mechanisms for verifying, accepting, storing, and managing bird banding data.

   BBL actions: The BBL has converted to an entirely electronic processing system for banding data through the use of the BANDIT software. It is continuously improving the data-quality-control processes to more efficiently handle large volumes of data without sacrificing data quality.

3. To accommodate recapture data.

   BBL actions: The BBL has developed the software and data architecture to store and facilitate the analyses of recapture data, beginning with the long-term population monitoring data for breeding Laysan and Black-footed Albatross as a prototype and expanding this system to address emerging studies of the American Black Duck.

4. To ensure through the permitting process that banders know how to safely handle birds, collect data accurately, and maintain birds in humane and healthful conditions.

   BBL actions: The BBL implemented an electronic permit renewal process in 2011 that has greatly reduced the time required to renew banding permits. Its permit office, which handles more than 7,000 permit actions annually, is continuously improving the efficiency of its operations. Knowledge of the safe and humane handling of birds is one of several important factors used during the evaluation of permit applications.

5. To encourage the development of banding programs in Latin America and the Caribbean.

   BBL actions: Currently (2013), the BBL is closely coordinating with the Mexican government concerning the development of a Mexican bird banding program. It remains actively engaged in efforts to develop bird banding programs throughout the Western Hemisphere.

Of the 58 specific recommendations, 47 have been addressed and operational efficiencies have been greatly improved. Highlights of these 47 actions include—

- The BBL now maintains a 2- to 2.5-year supply of all band types.

- The BBL has worked closely with the banding community to create new band sizes in demand such as 1D (for shrikes and other passerines), 5A (for wood ducks), and 9A (for eagles).

- The BBL has developed a new Web site for reporting of auxiliary marker sightings.

- The BBL data-management system is now (2013) regularly modified to improve the automation and efficiency of banding data processing as new needs are identified.

- The BBL is working cooperatively with the USFWS to develop a prototype recapture database for Albatross and the American Black Duck. This new system will be used to manage recapture data collected by banders and will include changes to the BANDIT software.

- A new Reportband (*http://www.reportband.gov/*) Web site for reporting encounter data was released in 2013. This Web site allows immediate feedback to the reporter provided that the banding data have been submitted, and promotes the use of Web-based maps to improve the accuracy of location information and improvements to other data-quality-control processes.

- In 2012, the printing of Certificates of Appreciation for band reporting was automated; the certificates are now are sent electronically, substantially reducing costs of postage.

- With funding obtained through the American Recovery and Reinvestment Act (ARRA), approximately 4.5 million hard-copy records were converted to digital files.

- The BBL is currently (2013) working with the USGS Core Science Systems to provide public access to U.S. banding data through the BISON Web site. In fiscal year 2013, data files will be transformed to the appropriate format for BISON (*http://bison.usgs.ornl.gov/*).

- A new streamlined form, which has been well received by the banding community, was recently (2013) created for the permit-renewal process.

- In January 2013, an agreement was signed between the USGS and the Canadian Wildlife Service (CWS) detailing the joint operation of, and listing the roles and responsibilities of, the U.S. and Canadian banding offices.

Of the 58 specific recommendations, 11 were only partially addressed, for practical reasons, as follows:

- **Recommendations 1.3.b and 2.1 f:** Build capacity to store data from nonstan¬dard bird markers.

  BBL response: The BBL did not address this recommendation because a new international program, Movebank (www.movebank.org), has been created specifically to manage these data. BBL actions in this area would be a duplication of effort.

- **Recommendations 2.2.a, 2.2.b, and 2.2.c:** These three recommendations focused on developing and maintaining metadata associated with banding data.

  BBL response: The BBL recognizes that metadata provide value in describing datasets. However, metadata are not widely used by the public and many large data systems do not have metadata files. With respect to gaining operational efficiencies and science support, the priority of these recommendations is low.

- **Recommendation 3.1.b.** Develop a system to notify banders when their data are accessed so they have the ability to contact the person who downloaded the data.

  BBL response: The Privacy Act precludes implementation of this recommendation.

- **Recommendation 3.1.c.** In consultation with banders and users of banding data, review and revise the current policy for use of band¬ing data, and require all data users to agree to this policy.

BBL response: Because BBL data are in the public domain, BBL cannot legally restrict their use. The BBL and CWS have revised their data-release policies that provide voluntary guidance on the use of banding data, but all data maintained by the BBL are openly available for public use.

- **Recommendation 3.2.a.** Maintain an up-to-date Web site with resource information (including links to other Web sites) on best practices for data collection and data analysis.

  BBL response: This information is already available through a variety of other Web sites.

- **Recommendation 4.1.c.** Develop an online, self-administered test to ensure that banders applying for permits are aware of and under¬stand relevant regulations, animal welfare concerns, the banders' Code of Ethics, methods for coding and recording data, and other matters that do not require physically handling a bird.

  BBL response: The North American Banding Council (NABC) has assumed responsibility for implementing this recommendation.

- **Recommendation 4.1.d.** Use the permit renewal process to ensure that banders continue to be aware of current banding standards and practices.

  BBL response: Implementation of this recommendation would require a change in the Federal regulations that apply to bird banding and migratory bird permits. Action on this recommendation is not anticipated in the foreseeable future.

- **Recommendation 6.2.a.** Develop a business plan for the BBL.

  BBL response: The BBL will develop this plan when business plans at the Mission Area and Region are finalized, and can provide context.

Permits

The BBL permit office handles more than 7,000 permit actions annually (new, renewed, inactivated, and modified authorizations) and issues 50 to 100 new Master permits and 200 to more than 300 new subpermits annually.

Evaluating applications for banding permits requires careful consideration with respect to the requester's banding experiences and his or her qualifications for the humane capture and handling of birds as well as the public benefit from the proposed banding activities. This evaluation has become more important in light of increased public concern over animal welfare issues in general and the specific effects of bird banding activities on migratory bird populations.

Of the 273 permit requests received during 2008-12, approximately 16 percent were not issued. The reasons for denying banding permit applications fall into three categories that have existed for decades:

1. The applicant lacks the necessary banding experience for the requested authorizations (unqualified).

2. The applicant's proposed banding project(s) are insufficient to support issuing a permit. In most cases, the proposed projects are vague or lack sufficient scientific merit. In a few cases, they unnecessarily duplicate existing banding projects (poor justification).

3. The proposed banding activities are already covered by an existing Master permit and the applicant can conduct these activities under that permit. An example would be a graduate student working on a USFWS wildlife refuge who can conduct the proposed project as a subpermittee under the refuge permit. In these cases, although the Master permit application is denied, the applicant can still conduct the banding activities (existing permit).

In some cases, enthusiastic avocational banders propose to capture and band thousands of songbirds annually in order to monitor migratory events at known concentration locations. However, these "high-volume" banding activities typically contribute little new knowledge of the status of migratory bird populations while extremely low encounter rates of these banded birds provide very few insights into avian movement patterns. In contrast, banding activities in support of wildlife management programs, such as waterfowl banding, provide essential data in support of the missions of Federal and State wildlife agencies while banding by the research community results in hundreds of peer-reviewed publications annually that greatly expand our ornithological knowledge. As recommended in the Committee report, the focus of the BBL has been to support the banding programs of scientists and managers while placing less emphasis on new "high-volume" banding operations that have limited scientific potential.

Funding

The BBL continues to improve operational efficiency and serve the banding community despite relatively "flat" funding over several years (fig. 1). Salaries have been the major

expense (fig. 2) despite a reduction in BBL staff from 21 full-time equivalents (FTEs) and 3 contractors in 2007 to 15 FTEs and 2 full-time contractors in 2013. The smaller staff continues to effectively manage both the U.S. and Canadian banding programs, which have not diminished in size and scope.

To compensate for this "flat" funding and reduced staff, the BBL has implemented many operational efficiencies during the past decade that have allowed many functions to be automated. With 47 of the 58 recommendations of the Federal Advisory Committee implemented, the BBL has done a credible job modernizing its operations while maintaining cost control. Moreover, the USGS has been able to opportunistically invest in advancing the technology through specific initiatives, such as digitizing encounter records by using funding provided by the ARRA.

Conclusions

The U.S. Geological Survey (USGS) is a nonregulatory and noncommercial scientific agency that acquires, analyzes, synthesizes, and disseminates data for the benefit of the Nation. The North American Bird Banding Laboratory at the USGS Patuxent Wildlife Research Center (PWRC) manages bird banding activities and data that are essential to Federal and State regulatory decisions supporting bird conservation. A 2005 comprehensive review of the Bird Banding Laboratory (BBL) reaffirmed its mission to continue to support science, conservation, and management of birds at the PWRC under USGS leadership.

As a major program of the Nation's largest water, earth, and biological science and civilian mapping, the BBL and its operations have greatly benefitted from new technologies and research activities within the USGS. Moreover, USGS science continues to guide and direct the use of cutting-edge banding and marking techniques to improve the management and conservation of migratory bird populations.

Under USGS scientific stewardship and by making effective use of its capabilities, the BBL has increasingly focused on providing data to diverse scientific partners through greater accessibility of the more than 72 million banding records. The USGS has established expertise in collecting and curating large databases for understanding our natural world, such as imaging produced by Landsat, real-time streamflow data, and the Breeding Bird Survey. By following this model, the BBL has coupled banding data with stable-isotope analysis, satellite telemetry, and other research tools to provide the critical capabilities needed to understand changes in bird populations and migration in the context of ecological change at the landscape level.

Scientific research is inextricably coupled to the mission and functionality of the BBL. The strong, impartial scientific role of the USGS in supporting natural-resource management decisions makes it the appropriate organization to manage bird-banding operations.

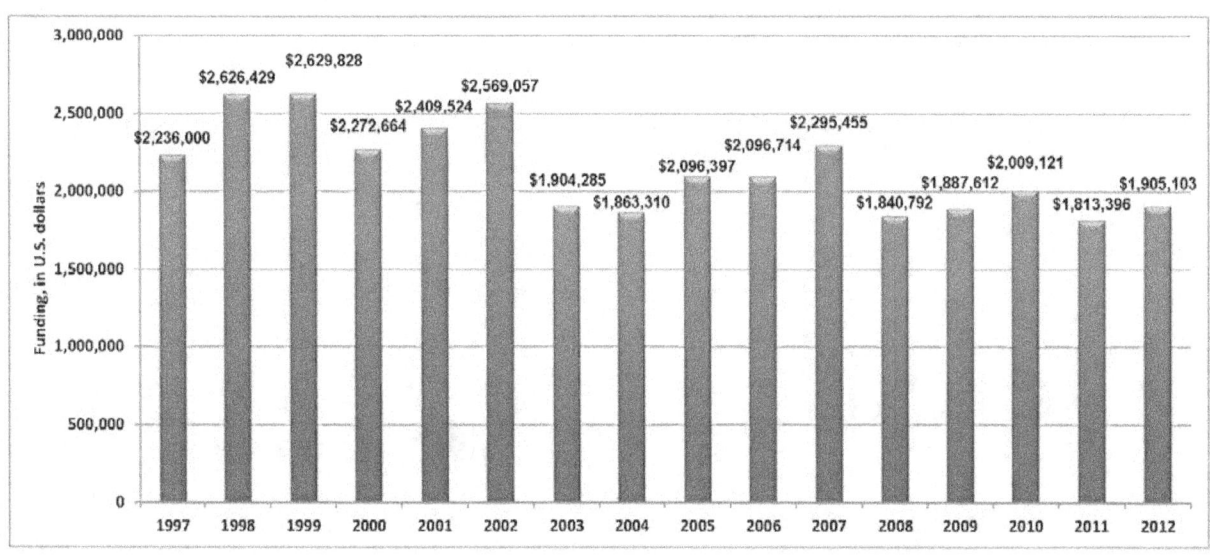

Figure 1.   U.S. Geological Survey Bird Banding Laboratory funding, fiscal year (FY) 1997 to FY 2012

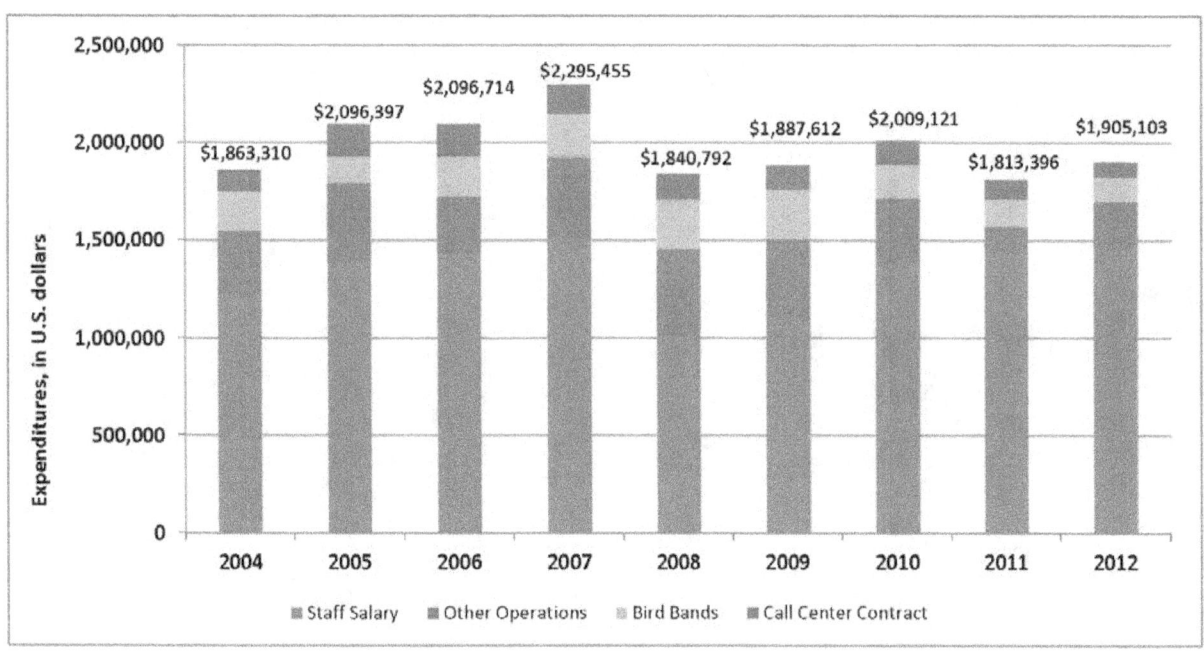

Figure 2.   U.S. Geological Survey Bird Banding Laboratory funding and expenditures from fiscal year (FY) 2004 to FY 2012.

Appendix 1.   Summary of Bird Banding Laboratory Activities in Response to the Recommendations of the Federal Advisory Committee Act Report

In this document, the objectives and recommendations were taken "as written" from the Report of the Federal Advisory Committee on the Bird Banding Laboratory [U.S. Geological Survey (USGS) Circular 1320 by Haseltine and others (2008)]. Actions taken by the Bird Banding Laboratory (BBL) to address these recommendations are provided in bold type below each recommendation.

Acronyms and abbreviations used in this appendix are as follows:

AFRING	African Waterbird Ringing Scheme
AOU	American Ornithologists' Union
BBL	Bird Banding Laboratory
BBO	Canadian Bird Banding Office
CFR	Code of Federal Regulations
EURING	European Union for Bird Ringing
FGDC	Federal Geographic Data Committee
FAC	Federal Advisory Committee
FY	Fiscal year
IOC	International Ornithological Congress
GPS	Global positioning system
LEMIS	Law Enforcement Management Information System
NARA	National Archives and Records Administration
NABC	North American Banding Council
PWRC	Patuxent Wildlife Research Center
USFWS	U.S. Fish and Wildlife Service
USGS	U.S. Geological Survey

Objective 1.1:   Ensure a continuing adequate supply of high-quality Federally issued numeric bird bands of required sizes, materials, and types.   `HIGH PRIORITY`

Recommendation 1.1.a. Develop procedures to ensure that an adequate supply of high-quality bands of all types, materials, and sizes can be maintained in a timely manner and at a reasonable cost. These should include greater diversification of band suppli¬ers and development of in-house quality controls through random checks of bands.

- The BBL currently maintains a 2- to 2.5-year supply of all band types.

- The BBL has developed a band quality-control plan that is followed for each shipment of bands received from the suppliers. All problems identified during the quality-control process or through reports from banders are resolved through communication with the suppliers.

- Following USGS acquisition guidelines, one company currently supplies bands for the BBL.

Recommendation 1.1.b. Establish processes to determine the need for new band types and sizes, and ensure that appropriate band types are both available and used for each species (for example, ensure that hard-metal bands are available and used on species that regularly outlive aluminum bands, and that appropriate bands are available for birds that frequent salt-water environments).

- The BBL maintains in-stock hard-metal bands for sizes 2 and above.

- New band sizes that have been recently created include 1D (for shrikes and other passerines), 5A (for wood ducks), and 9A (for eagles). The BBL works with the banding community to identify the need for new band sizes and then creates bands to meet these needs.

Objective 1.2:   Facilitate coordination of auxiliary markers.

Recommendation 1.2.a. Ensure effective coordination of the use of auxiliary markers amongst banders—regionally, nationally, and internationally—within the Americas. Develop tools, such as Web sites and Web-based databases, where projects can be registered to facilitate coordination. The tools should allow users (banders, public reporters, researchers, wildlife managers, and BBL staff) to independently send and retrieve information. As much as possible, implement through delegation to partners with expertise in particular bird groups, with BBL providing oversight for the resolution of disputes or other problems as required.

- Auxiliary marker information is coordinated between the BBL and Bird Banding Office (Canada) on a regular basis. For species of birds with hemispheric distributions (shorebirds), the BBL has partnered with the shorebird community to develop a unified marking system. Similar coordination occurs with the waterfowl management community, which is responsible for the marking programs for this group.

Recommendation 1.2.b. Require that all auxiliary marker data submitted to the BBL be in a format that can be incorporated into the BBL database so that the BBL can build an accurate, complete database. There are some species for which auxiliary marking is the primary and most effective way of collecting information. For these birds it is essential that the data be submitted in a specified format.

- Current versions of the BANDIT software store auxiliary marker data in standard formats that are automatically submitted to the BBL with the banding data.

Recommendation 1.2.c. With regard to encounters of auxiliary markers, the BBL should: (1) emphasize maximum automation with little or no direct staff involvement, (2) focus on putting reporters directly in touch with banders to transfer and receive information, and (3) require large-scale marking projects (at a minimum) to assume responsibility for managing and coordinating their encoun¬ter data and (or) commit resources (for a Web developer) to BBL to offset costs incurred for these activities. To accomplish this, the BBL should: (1) provide a communication mechanism for informa¬tion to be submitted by, and be available to, reporters of auxiliary marking encounters ("sightings"); (2) develop tools, such as Web sites, list servers, and Web-based databases, where auxiliary marker projects are registered, and reporters can be directed to file their sightings and obtain information about marked birds; and (3) design systems to accept all sightings of auxiliary-marked birds from the public and provide some level of feedback to the reporter, regardless of bander and (or) BBL interest.

- The BBL has developed a Web site for reporting of auxiliary marker sightings and is currently working to improve the automation for processing these data. As more auxiliary marker data are submitted through BANDIT, the BBL will be in a better position to begin implementing automated feedback systems to the reporter of marked birds.

Recommendation 1.2.d. Ensure banders and BBL can receive auxiliary-marking encounter information. Report to banders those auxiliary marker encounters that can be unambiguously linked with a unique band number and for which the bander who placed the auxiliary marker has an interest in knowing of public sight¬ings. Encounters of markers that are not linked with a unique band number, or even to a specific bander, should be made available for consideration on a Web site or list server.

- The BBL has dedicated a staff position to providing reports of marked birds to the banders and dealing with related issues. Efforts to improve the efficiency of this process are ongoing.

Objective 1.3:   Accommodate new methods and technologies for marking birds.

Recommendation 1.3.a. Remain cognizant of the development of new bird-marking techniques and technologies, including appropriate evaluation of their impact on bird welfare, and ensure that information on their safe use is accessible and appropriately dis¬seminated.

- The BBL is in regular communication with the banding community concerning the use of new technologies for marking birds.

Recommendation 1.3.b. Build capacity to store data from nonstan¬dard bird markers, including data collected by automated means, such as satellite transmitters, if such centralized data storage is not otherwise available. Emphasis should be placed on data that may contribute to the management and conservation of birds through integration or coordination across projects.

- Movebank is an international program coordinating the storage of data collected through us of satellite transmitters, data loggers, and other automatic recorders. The program is based in Germany but accepts global data from these sources. There is no need for the BBL to duplicate or compete with these efforts.

Objective 1.4:   Encourage development of new methods for capturing and marking birds in ways that improve bird welfare.

Recommendation 1.4.a. Develop appropriate guidelines that encour¬age banders to evaluate and develop new and innovative methods for capturing and marking birds. Encourage submission of reports on injuries or mortalities related to new methods, with clarification that banders will not risk permit revocation or suspension if mortali¬ties or injuries occur, provided that appropriate guidelines are followed. However, restrict the use of capture methods or markers based on potential impacts only when those impacts are serious, long lasting or permanent, well documented, and unequivocal.

- The BBL continues to provide guidance on the development of innovative methods for capturing and marking birds, and encourages the reporting of these studies in the peer-reviewed literature. Authorization of these experimental techniques is always done with appropriate concern for the welfare of the birds.

Recommendation 1.4.b. Develop mechanisms, potentially through partners, to gather information from banders on bird welfare issues associated with particular capture or marking methods.

- The BBL supported efforts by University of Connecticut researchers to document potential animal welfare issues associated with use of radio transmitters on birds. Results of this study were presented during the 2009 American Ornithologists' Union meeting in Philadelphia, Pennsylvania.

Objective 2.1:   Improve mechanisms for verifying, accepting, storing, and managing bird banding data.
HIGH PRIORITY

Recommendation 2.1.a. Improve the efficiency of submitting banding schedules through use of appropriate Internet technol¬ogy, and an automated system to vet submitted data for accuracy. This should include flags in the database that indicate the level to which data have been vetted, as well as user-friendly automated procedures to communicate with banders regarding questionable data and to receive input from banders. Inform banders that they have the primary responsibility for verifying data, initially through programs provided to banders (for example, Band Manager, Bandit, or MAPSPROG), and then subsequently through responding to automated reports from the banding office. Minimize the need for personal interaction between BBL staff and banders regarding questionable data.

- This is an ongoing process that is conducted with the release of each new version of the BANDIT software, which is shifting more of the burden for data quality control to the bander.

- The BBL data-management system is regularly modified to improve the automation and efficiency of banding data processing as new needs are identified by BBL staff.

Recommendation 2.1.b. Accept location information, including GPS data, to a higher level of precision than currently required by the BBL. The BBL should always require that the cooperator report the actual level of precision of the location data.

- BANDIT software currently allows banding data to be submitted at several levels of precision, including exact coor-dinates obtained from GPS systems.

Recommendation 2.1.c. Collect and store auxiliary marker data, including appropriate metadata describing the types of markers used.

- BANDIT software has been modified to store and automatically submit auxiliary marker data with the banding data.

Recommendation 2.1.d. Ensure that all digital data, including archived data, are maintained in an appropriate, up-to-date format so that they will not be lost as technology changes.

- The BBL follows USGS and Federal data-storage and -archiving standards to ensure that these data are maintained in up-to-date formats.

Recommendation 2.1.e. Allow for flexible timing of submission of banding schedules as appropriate to meet the needs of the BBL and banders.

- BANDIT software currently allows banders to submit their data electronically at any time, including making multiple submissions per year.

Recommendation 2.1 f. Build the capacity to store data from nonstandard bird markers, including data collected by automated means, such as satellite transmitters, if such centralized storage is not otherwise available. Emphasis should be placed on data that may contribute to the management and conservation of birds through integration or coordination across projects.

- Movebank is an international program that coordinates the storage of data collected through us of satellite transmitters, data loggers, and other automatic recorders. The program is based in Germany but accepts global data from these sources. There is no need for the BBL to duplicate or compete with these efforts.

Objective 2.2:   Develop appropriate systems to store and maintain metadata associated with banding data.

- At this time (2013), the BBL has not taken action on the recommendations for this objective.

Recommendation 2.2.a. Use FGDC (Federal Geographic Data Com¬mittee) metadata standards, as appropriate, for all metadata associ¬ated with banding records.

Recommendation 2.2.b. Consult with appropriate experts to determine the types of metadata about the context of banding (for example, project objectives, methods, effort, and so on) that could and should be stored centrally and how they should be recorded.

Recommendation 2.2.c. Develop a system to accommodate the metadata recommended in 2.2.b by providing training and educa¬tional materials and user-friendly tools for metadata submission in order to encourage banders to submit such data.

Objective 2.3:   Accommodate recapture data.   **HIGH PRIORITY**

Recommendation 2.3.a. Develop an automated system for sub¬mitting, vetting, and accepting all recapture data into the BBL database, and encourage all banders to submit recapture data, including historical data, through this system, unless it is already being submitted through another program such as MAPS. Concur¬rently, require banders to submit metadata associated with the recapture programs under which those recaptures were recorded (again, unless it is already being reported), as recapture data with¬out associated metadata are of questionable value and can easily be misused.

- The BBL is working cooperatively with the USFWS Region 1 Migratory Birds Management Office on a project to develop a recapture database for albatross data collected from the northwestern Hawaiian Islands. Additionally, in FY 2013 the BBL will begin to create a system to manage recapture data collected by banders. This process will include modifications to the current BBL data-management system as well as major changes to the BANDIT software to allow for the proper management and submission of these data to the BBL. The changes to the BBL data-management system should be completed during FY 2013, whereas a new version of the BANDIT software may be released during FY 2014 to allow banders to begin submitting their recapture data to the BBL.

Objective 2.4:   Create an archive for storing voluntarily submitted ancillary and associated data.

> **Recommendation 2.4.a.** Develop automated systems for submission, vetting, and acceptance of voluntarily submitted ancillary data (and associated metadata, including information on data quality control), noting that the responsibility for data quality control resides with the bander. Remind banders that these data will be available to the public.
>
> - The BANDIT software allows for the management of these ancillary data. Some data-quality functions have been incorporated to improve the vetting of some of these fields, but better data-quality-control procedures need to be developed before these data will be of sufficient quality to be submitted to the BBL. Improvements to these data-quality-control procedures is an ongoing process with each new version of the software.

Objective 2.5:   Continue to improve the efficiency of methods for receiving encounter information to enhance the quality of informa¬tion received and reduce the costs of processing encounters, while encouraging greater reporting.

> **Recommendation 2.5.a.** Develop and promote Web-based, auto¬mated reporting of band recovery data, with appropriate checks to ensure that all required data are submitted, and provide immediate feedback to the person reporting the band. Offer finders the option of an electronic or paper "Certificate of Appreciation."
>
> - A new Reportband (www.reportband.gov) Web site for reporting encounter data was released in 2013. New functions of this Web site include providing immediate feedback to the reporter as long as the banding data have been submitted to the BBL, use of Web-based maps to improve the accuracy of location information, and improvements to other data-quality-control processes. In August 2012, the BBL shifted to entirely electronic Certificates of Appreciation, a step that improved the availability of these certificates while substantially reducing costs to the BBL.

> **Recommendation 2.5.b.** Begin to include a Web address on bands to enhance Web-based automated reporting of recovery. Promote Web reporting to reduce errors and costs; however, in the near term, continue to support the use of toll-free numbers for report¬ing bands. Investigate the costs and benefits of an automated telephone system to capture data using touch-tone technology that could simultaneously handle English, French, and Spanish, to reduce the costs of processing calls.
>
> - All bands procured by the BBL now have the Web address printed on them. As supplies of older band types are depleted, only Web-address bands will be supplied to banders in the future. Use of the 1-800 telephone number to report bands continues, but because of the complexity associated with obtaining this information, converting to an entirely touch-tone system is not feasible at this time (2013).

Objective 2.6:   Ensure the preservation and eventual computeriza¬tion of historical (nondigitized) banding data currently stored at the BBL.

> **Recommendation 2.6.a.** Arrange immediately for proper physical storage of the original records (in consultation with the National Archives and Records Administration) to ensure that they are adequately protected and do not deteriorate.
>
> - The BBL has been in contact with NARA about the proper care and disposition of its paper records and is following all appropriate Federal standards.

> **Recommendation 2.6.b.** Investigate appropriate ways of making these data available digitally in the future, considering options such as digitizing the data through the BBL (perhaps in a cost-sharing program with interested users), or scanning the records as images so that they can be distributed to interested third parties to capture digitally.
>
> - The BBL received funding during 2009 to convert hard-copy band encounter records to digital files. This project was completed in September 2010, with approximately 4 million images created of these records. This project addresses both recommendations below. The BANDIT files submitting banding data to the BBL are currently

archived on Patuxent Wildlife Research Center (PWRC) computers. At this time (2013), only the paper banding schedules have not been digitized.

Objective 3.1:   Develop a Web-based, user-friendly system to provide full and open access to all banding data and information, except where such information may be of a sensitive nature (for example, exact locations of endangered species), along with appro¬priate guidelines for use of the data.

Recommendation 3.1.a. Develop a Web-based, user-friendly interface to allow for public retrieval of bird-banding data. All data, including recent data, should be available, with the exception that locations for biologically or commercially sensitive species should be limited to province or state. The database should be updated at regular intervals (once or a few times per year) but not con¬tinuously, so that the download is dated. Use methods such as a password-based login, with an e-mail-based verification, to gather information on who is downloading data.

- The BBL is working with the USGS CDI program to provide public access to U.S. banding data through the BISON Web site that was recently launched by USGS. Banding datasets will be made available during 2013 as data files are transformed into the appropriate format that can be accommodated by BISON. Individual banding records will be made available through this publicly available Web site, which also provides access to data for other taxa of animals and plants.

Recommendation 3.1.b. Develop a system to notify banders when their data are accessed so they have the ability to contact the person who downloaded the data.

- At this time (2013), the BBL has not taken action on this recommendation.

Recommendation 3.1.c. In consultation with banders and users of banding data, review and revise the current policy for use of band¬ing data, and require all data users to agree to this policy. The BBL should also encourage the adoption of this policy by ornithological societies and scientific journals as part of their scientific code of ethics.

- This recommendation does not reflect the fact that the BBL data are in the public domain and the BBL cannot legally restrict use of these data. The BBL and the Canadian Bird Banding Office have revised their data-release policies that provide voluntary guidance on the use of banding data, but all data maintained by the BBL are openly available for public use.

Objective 3.2:   Encourage development, adoption, and sharing of best practices related to project design, data collection, and data analysis for banding projects.

Recommendation 3.2.a. Maintain an up-to-date Web site with resource information (including links to other Web sites) on best practices for data collection and data analysis. Encourage researchers to provide information for such a Web page. Ensure that users downloading data are aware of these approaches and methods.

- This information is already available on existing Web resources and the banding community can use existing search-engine technology to identify and access these sites. There is no need for the BBL to duplicate existing efforts with little or no value added.

Recommendation 3.2.b. Provide a technical assistance function within the BBL to advise banders and researchers on best practices in project design, field data collection, and data analysis when requested.

- The BBL is in regular communication with the banding community to provide guidance on banding project design and data collection. Questions on data analyses are typically directed toward USGS PWRC statisticians, who have considerable expertise in this area.

Objective 3.3:   Encourage development of tools to make better use of banding data.

Recommendation 3.3.a. Work with partners to develop Web-based visualization tools that could be hosted on the BBL Web site to allow better use of banding data (for example, interactive Web-based mapping of band recovery data).

- The Smithsonian Institution is working collaboratively with the BBL to develop Web-based tools to summarize the movement of birds within the context of full life-cycle bird conservation. This project was initiated during fiscal year (FY) 2012. Some preliminary products may be available during FY 2013, but the full set of visualization tools may not be available until FY 2014 or later. The BBL is also working toward developing Web-based summaries of banding and band encounter data. The BBL hopes to start releasing some of these summaries during FY 2013, with continued releases as new summaries become available.

Objective 4.1:   Without significantly increasing the number of master permits, base the decision on whether or not to issue master or subpermits on evidence that the applicant has the skills and knowl¬edge to capture and handle birds of the requested species safely, to collect appropriate data (including age and sex) for those species, and to submit data timely and accurately to the BBL. **HIGH PRIORITY**

Recommendation 4.1.a. Ensure, through the permitting process, that applicants know how to safely handle birds, maintain birds in humane and healthful conditions, and collect data accurately.

- The BBL permitting procedures have been consistent with this recommendation during recent decades.

Recommendation 4.1.b. Use a variety of tools to evaluate the qualifi¬cations of the bander, including the following: (1) Recommendations of people who have worked with the bander; (2) Information on experience handling birds and numbers of birds handled; (3) Evidence of bander training; (4) Information provided by the applicant; (5) Online testing; and (6) Demonstrated proficiency at identifying the birds to be banded.

- Most of these "tools" are already in use to evaluate the applicant's qualifications. Development of online testing applications requires addressing a variety of complex administrative issues. Creating such a testing application is not anticipated in the short term.

Recommendation 4.1.c. Develop an online, self-administered test to ensure that banders applying for permits are aware of and under¬stand relevant regulations, animal welfare concerns, the banders' Code of Ethics, methods for coding and recording data, and other matters that do not require physically handling a bird.

- Developing online testing applications also requires creating appropriate training materials that can be reviewed before taking any test. The North American Banding Council (NABC) has assumed responsibility for developing training materials for the banding community and there is no need for the BBL to duplicate these efforts. The BBL cannot create a comprehensive online test until the NABC has developed these materials.

Recommendation 4.1.d. Use the permit renewal process to ensure that banders continue to be aware of current banding standards and practices, perhaps through updated Web-based testing, or completion of a questionnaire or checklist.

- The BBL has not taken action on this recommendation. Testing as a part of the permit renewal process would require changes to the Federal regulations that apply to bird banding permits, and such changes are not anticipated in the foreseeable future.

Recommendation 4.1.e. Require brief summaries of proposed band¬ing projects, but do not use these to decide whether or not to grant a permit.

- Banding project proposals have always been required of applicants and are typically used to determine the specific authorizations that need to be provided to the permittee.

Objective 4.2:   Streamline the permit application process to reduce costs and increase efficiency.

Recommendation 4.2.a. Develop a streamlined, online application system, including online submission of information on qualifications and letters of recommendation.

- The BBL created a streamlined form for the permit renewal process during FY 2011, a form that has been well received by the banding community. The BBL intends to develop a fully electronic application system. Because of funding and staffing limitations, work on developing an electronic permitting system will not begin until FY 2014 or FY 2015 at the earliest.

Recommendation 4.2.b. Issue permits for 3 years, and require all banders to actively renew their permits. As a prerequisite for renewal, demand up-to-date submission of all required banding data (for example, schedules).

- The BBL currently issues permits for 3 years and permit renewal is dependent on the bander's resolving all of the "up for banding" requests from the BBL to ensure that banding data are submitted for all banded birds that have been reported by the public.

Recommendation 4.2.c. Establish, if feasible, a link with the Law Enforcement Management Information System (LEMIS) to determine if an applicant has been found guilty of a violation of a Federal wildlife law and use this information as a factor in determining whether or not to issue a permit.

- Federal computer security guidelines will not allow the BBL to develop a direct link to LEMIS at this time (2013).

Objective 4.3:   Update regulations, policies, and guidance using best practices (including providing opportunity for public notice and comment) and clearly communicate the regulations, policies, and guidance to the community in writing.

Recommendation 4.3.a. Identify regulatory gaps (for example, use of radio and satellite transmitters, PIT tags, and issuing of subpermits) and revise regulations as needed. Regulations should allow the BBL to issue banding permits authorizing the taking of blood, feather, and cloacal samples.

- The BBL is currently in the process of revising relevant portions of the Code of Federal Regulations (CFR) that relate to bird banding.

Recommendation 4.3.b. Review and revise the North American Banding Manual to ensure that it clearly includes information on all policies, guidance, and regulations relevant to banding.

- The concept of a paper "North American Banding Manual" has become obsolete in this electronic era. The BBL Web site is evolving to provide the same information in an electronic format that can be easily updated as new information becomes available. A new BBL Web site was released during FY 2011 and is being revised and updated to meet the functions that were formerly served by the banding manual.

Objective 4.4:   Ensure consistency in written regulations, policies, and practices regarding revocation and suspension decisions.

Recommendation 4.4.a. Develop and implement policies for revocation and suspension of permits that reflect the current regulations and that protect the proprietary interests of banders, while ensuring that banders follow best practices.

- These policies are established in the portions of the CFR that apply to all permits related to the enforcement of the Migratory Bird Treaty Act, and have been followed in the few instances where banding permits have been proposed for suspension or revocation.

Recommendation 4.4.b. If feasible, use available information on convictions of violations of wildlife laws to inform revocation and suspension decisions.

- This remains a standard practice of the BBL as defined in the appropriate sections of the CFR that apply to all migratory bird permits.

Objective 5.1:   Work with partners to achieve shared goals and leverage available resources.

Recommendation 5.1.a. Involve partners in the creation of products and tools to meet the needs of the BBL and the partners and to deliver BBL messages.

- The BBL considers all constructive comments and suggestions that it receives from the banding community and others with an interest in its operations. For example, banders have provided a number of useful suggestions that were incorporated in improved versions of the BANDIT software. The Flyways receive annual updates on BBL activities and provide their comments on all aspects of the BBL program.

Recommendation 5.1.b. Maintain active interactions with banding schemes and organizations elsewhere in the world, such as EURING, AFRING, and the IOC standing committee on bird ring¬ing, and develop schemes in Latin America and the Caribbean to exchange and share experiences, expertise, and products.

- The BBL continues to interact with various international banding schemes/organizations to the extent possible under current budgets. Much of this interaction occurs through electronic communication.

Recommendation 5.1.c. Work with partners to identify key materials that promote ethics and bird welfare and proper capture, handling, and banding techniques for distribution by BBL. Use MTABs, the BBL Web site, permitting processes, workshops, and other com-munication tools.

- The BBL remains involved with the activities of the NABC and bird banding associations in ongoing efforts to address these issues.

Recommendation 5.1.d. Seek opportunities to augment BBL staff and resources through partnerships that further BBL's mission.

- The collaborative effort with USFWS to develop a data-management system for recapture data is a recent example of using partnerships to further the mission of the lab, as is the collaborative project with The Smithsonian Institution to develop data-visualization tools.

Recommendation 5.1.e. Where appropriate, use formal agreements, reviewed and updated from time to time, to document intra- and intergovernmental partnerships and to define clear roles and responsibilities.

- A new agreement between the USGS and the Canadian Wildlife Service regarding the joint operation of the BBL and the BBO was signed in January 2013. This agreements defines the roles and responsibilities of both banding offices with regards to the operation of the North American Bird Banding Program.

Objective 5.2:   Develop and implement a process that involves partners in advising the BBL.

Recommendation 5.2.a. Maintain and strengthen relationships with key Federal partners (for example, FWS).

- A representative from the USFWS Migratory Birds Management Division regularly attends meetings of the BBL management team to further communication between the two offices. BBL staff members attend annual meetings of the various Flyway Councils to further communication with important state agencies. These are just two examples of attempts to strengthen relationships with other government agencies.

Recommendation 5.2.b. Maintain a FAC composed similarly to but not necessarily the same as the current one, to monitor and advise the BBL on implementation of the recommendations of this report, and to maintain and enhance communication with and relationships between the BBL and its partners, stakeholders, and the broader bird-banding community.

- **USGS decided not to establish a formal Federal Advisory Committee at this time (2013).**

Recommendation 5.2.c. Establish and maintain an open-door policy for partners and stakeholders. Consult to the extent possible with affected partners and stakeholders while making major operational decisions.

- The BBL has always maintained an open-door policy for stakeholders, but has also had to balance the often conflicting demands of the entire banding community. It will strive to improve communication as much as possible given current staffing shortages.

Recommendation 5.2.d. Provide for BBL presence at key partner and stakeholder meetings.

- BBL staff members attend meetings of the various bird banding associations, flyway councils, NABC, and other stakeholders to the extent possible under current budgets.

Objective 5.3:   Encourage development of banding programs in Latin America and the Caribbean.
HIGH PRIORITY

Recommendation 5.3.a. Play a central role in building capacity for bird-banding programs elsewhere in the Western Hemisphere. The BBL should be flexible in helping to develop Latin American and Caribbean banding schemes that are appropriate for the partners and feasible for the BBL, considering options ranging from inde¬pendent schemes that exchange data, to expanding the North American Bird Banding Program to include additional countries with agreements similar to that between Canada and the U.S.

- The BBL remains active in the development of the Western Hemisphere Bird Banding Network to better coordinate banding activities among the various banding programs in this hemisphere.

Recommendation 5.3.b. Allow the use of U.S. Federal bands on resident as well as migratory birds for projects within the American Ornithologists' Union (AOU) checklist area, in consultation with the affected countries, subject to the same terms and conditions as are currently applied to projects banding migratory birds in these countries with U.S. bands. Specifically, the bander must qualify for and possess a permit in the U.S. or Canada, and must obtain appro¬priate permits to capture and handle birds in the country where banding will take place. The BBL must modify its database to be able to receive, process, and store data on these resident birds (but without investing heavily in data-vetting procedures).

- USGS guidelines require the BBL to have formal international agreements with countries to allow the use of U.S. bird bands in those countries. Creating these agreements requires considerable time and effort, but will be attempted as staffing allows and specific needs are identified.

Objective 6.1:   Ensure that all components of the program are delivered in the most efficient and cost-effective manner.

Recommendation 6.1.a. Continue to identify ways to improve the efficiency and effectiveness of BBL operations by looking at oppor¬tunities to outsource noncore functions.

- The BBL remains committed to identifying new approaches that will improve the efficiency and effectiveness of its operations, but "outsourcing" is frequently a more expensive option and should be carefully studied before implementation.

Recommendation 6.1.b. Work towards automation of BBL data-handling tasks to the highest extent possible, including passing responsibility for many tasks, such as data checking and data entry, to users. Specific areas for improvements are suggested elsewhere in the document. Priority for implementation should be determined based on an assessment of current staff time requirements and on areas where maximum gains in efficiency can be obtained.

- The new data-management system for the BBL provides innumerable examples of how automation has been successfully implemented into BBL operations. The BBL continues to identify and implement new approaches that automate data-quality procedures and other aspects of the lab's operations.

Objective 6.2: Maintain or enhance the financial foundation of the BBL to ensure that it can continue to meet its mandate.

Recommendation 6.2.a. Develop a business plan for the BBL that considers all costs and benefits of the program, while recognizing the primary mandate of the Department of Interior for the conserva¬tion of migratory birds.

- At this time (2013), the BBL has not taken action on this recommendation.

Objective 6.3: Ensure that the workforce at the BBL continues to meet the needs of an evolving organization.

Recommendation 6.3.a. Develop a staffing plan that recognizes the changing workforce needs of the BBL over time, as increased auto¬mation reduces the need for clerical staff but increases the need for more highly trained staff, such as computer programmers to main¬tain and develop systems, and biologists to develop standards and procedures and to serve as liaison between banders, data analysts, and conservation practitioners.

- A staffing plan exists for the BBL that reflects this recommendation. Staffing changes will have to occur opportunis-tically through retirements of existing staff members and are limited by current budgetary restraints.

Appendix 2. Scientific Publications Supported by Bird Banding Efforts (2000–13)

2013

Boomer, G. S., Zimmerman, G. S., Zimpfer, N. L., and others, 2013, Band reporting probabilities for mallards recovered in the United States and Canada, p. 1059–1066.

Conklin, Jesse R., Battley, Phil F., and Potter, Murray A., 2013, Absolute Consistency: Individual versus Population Variation in Annual-Cycle Schedules of a Long-Distance Migrant Bird: PLOS ONE, v. 8, no. 1, article e54535.

Ishihara, Shingo, Bitner, Jessica J., Farley, Greg H., and others, 2013, Vancomycin-Resistant Gram-Positive Cocci Isolated from the Saliva of Wild Songbirds: Current Microbiology, v. 66, no. 4, p. 337–343.

Streby, Henry M., and Andersen, David E., 2013, Movements, cover-type selection, and survival of fledgling Ovenbirds in managed deciduous and mixed coniferous-deciduous forests: Forest Ecology and Management, v. 287, p. 9–16.

Streby, Henry M., Peterson, Sean M., Scholtens, Brian, and others, 2013, The Ovenbird (*Seiurus aurocapilla*) as a Model for Testing Food-Value Theory: American Midland Naturalist, v. 169, no. 1, p. 214–220.

2012

Adams, Josh, Macleod, Catriona, Suryan, Robert M., and others, 2012, Summer-time use of west coast US National Marine Sanctuaries by migrating sooty shearwaters (*Puffinus griseus*): Biological Conservation, v. 156, no. Sp. Iss. SI, p. 105–116.

Baeta, R., Belisle, M., and Garant, D., 2012, Agricultural intensification exacerbates female-biased primary brood sex-ratio in tree swallows: Landscape Ecology, v. 27, no. 10, p. 1395–1405.

Bai, M. L., and Schmidt, D., 2012, Differential migration by age and sex in central European Ospreys *Pandion haliaetus*: Journal of Ornithology, v. 153, no. 1, p. 75–84.

Bakian, Amanda V., Sullivan, Kimberly A., and Paxton, Eben H., 2012, Elucidating spatially explicit behavioral landscapes in the Willow Flycatcher: Ecological Modelling, v. 232, p. 119–132.

Baubock, L., Miller-Rushing, A. J., Primack, R. B., and others, 2012, Climate change does not affect protandry in seven passerines in North America: Wilson Journal of Ornithology, v. 124, no. 2, p. 208–216.

Beason, J. P., Gunn, C., Potter, K. M., and others, 2012, The northern black swift: migration path and wintering area revealed: Wilson Journal of Ornithology, v. 124, no. 1, p. 1–8.

Beckett, S. R., and Proudfoot, G. A., 2012, Sex-specific migration trends of northern saw-whet owls in Eastern North America: Journal of Raptor Research, v. 46, no. 1, p. 98–108.

Behney, Adam C., Grisham, Blake A., Boal, Clint W., and others, 2012, Sexual selection and mating chronology of lesser prairie-chickens: Wilson Journal of Ornithology, v. 124, no. 1, p. 96–105.

Benson, T. J., Ward, M. P., Lampman, R. L., and others, 2012, Implications of Spatial Patterns of Roosting and Movements of American Robins for West Nile Virus Transmission: Vector-Borne and Zoonotic Diseases, v. 12, no. 10, p. 877–885.

Bildstein, K. L., and Peterjohn, B. G., 2012, The future of banding in raptor science: Journal of Raptor Research, v. 46, no. 1, p. 3–11.

Bildstein, Keith L., 2012, The role of banding in raptor conservation: Proceedings of a special session at the 2010 RRF annual meeting, Fort Collins, Colorado: Journal of Raptor Research, v. 46, no. 1, p. 1–147.

Booms, Travis L., 2012, Banded Alaskan gyrfalcon discovered in Arabian falconry: Journal of Raptor Research, v. 46, no. 2, p. 226–227.

Borkhataria, Rena R., Frederick, Peter C., Keller, Rebecca A., and others, 2012, Temporal variation in local wetland hydrology influences postdispersal survival of juvenile wood storks (*Mycteria americana*): Auk, v. 129, no. 3, p. 517–528.

Boves, Than J., and Buehler, David A., 2012, Breeding Biology, Behavior, and Ecology of *Setophaga cerulea* in the Cumberland Mountains, Tennessee: Southeastern Naturalist, v. 11, no. 2, p. 319–330.

Bowling, Andrea C., Martin, Julien, and Kitchens, Wiley M., 2012, The effect of changes in habitat conditions on the movement of juvenile Snail Kites *Rostrhamus sociabilis*: Ibis, v. 154, no. 3, p. 554–565.

Braun, Clait E., Taylor, William P., Ebbert, Steve E., and others, 2012, Protocols for Successful Translocation of Ptarmigan, *in* Watson, Richard T., Cade, T. J., Fuller, Mark, and others, eds., Gyrfalcons and Ptarmigan in a Changing World: Proceedings of a Conference Held February 2011, Boise, Idaho. Volume ii: Boise, Peregrine Fund, p. 339–348.

Burger, J., Niles, L. J., Porter, R. R., and others, 2012, Migration and over-wintering of red knots (*Calidris canutus rufa*) along the Atlantic Coast of the United States: Condor, v. 114, no. 2, p. 302–313.

Burger, Joanna, Niles, Lawrence J., Porter, Ronald R., and others, 2012, Using geolocator data to reveal incubation periods and breeding biology in red knots *Calidris canutus rufa*: Wader Study Group Bulletin, v. 119, no. 1, p. 26–36.

Bystrak, D., Nakash, E., and Lutmerding, J. A., 2012, Summary of raptor banding records at the bird banding lab: Journal of Raptor Research, v. 46, no. 1, p. 12–16.

Cade, T. J., and Nielsen,Ó,K., 2011, Surveys for Gyrfalcons in the Scoresbysund region of northeast Greenland in 1999, *in* Watson, R.T., Cade, T.J., Fuller, M., Hunt, G., and Potapov, E., eds., Gyrfalcons and ptarmigan in a changing world, v. 2, p. 73–80.

Caswell, Jason H., Alisauskas, Ray T., and Leafloor, James O., 2012, Effect of neckband color on survival and recovery rates of Ross's geese: Journal of Wildlife Management, v. 76, no. 7, p. 1456–1461.

Chamberlain, Michael J., Grisham, Blake A., Norris, Jennifer L., and others, 2012, Effects of Variable Spring Harvest Regimes on Annual Survival and Recovery Rates of Male Wild Turkeys in Southeast Louisiana: Journal of Wildlife Management, v. 76, no. 5, p. 907–910.

Collier, Bret A., Kremer, Shelly R., Mason, Corey D., and others, 2012, Survival, fidelity, and recovery rates of white-winged doves in Texas: Journal of Wildlife Management, v. 76, no. 6, p. 1129–1134.

Conroy, M. J., Stodola, K. W., and Cooper, R. J., 2012, Effective use of data from monitoring programs and field studies for conservation decision making: predictions, designs and models working together: Journal of Ornithology, v. 152, p. S325–S338.

Converse, Sarah J., Royle, J. Andrew, and Urbanek, Richard P., 2012, Bayesian analysis of multi-state data with individual covariates for estimating genetic effects on demography: Journal of Ornithology , v. 152, p. S561–S572.

Cornell, Heather N., Marzluff, John M., and Pecoraro, Shannon, 2012, Social learning spreads knowledge about dangerous humans among American crows: Proceedings of the Royal Society Biological Sciences Series B, v. 279, no. 1728, p. 499–508.

Courtot, Karen N., Roby, Daniel D., Adkins, Jessica Y., and others, 2012, Colony connectivity of Pacific Coast double-crested cormorants based on post-breeding dispersal from the region's largest colony: Journal of Wildlife Management, v. 76, no. 7, p. 1462–1471.

Custer, Christine M., Custer, Thomas W., and Hines, James E., 2012, Adult tree swallow survival on the polychlorinated biphenyl-contaminated Hudson River, New York, USA, between 2006 and 2010: Environmental Toxicology and Chemistry, v. 31 , no. 8, p. 1788–1792.

Daniel, Nidun, and Cunningham, Gregory, 2012, Stress hormone in White-throated sparrows (*Zonotrichia albicollis*) is not influenced by the cleanliness of a cotton bag: Integrative and Comparative Biology, v. 52, suppl. 1, p. E234.

De Ruyck, Christopher C., Duncan, James, and Koper, Nicola, 2012, Northern saw-whet owl (*aegolius acadicus*) migratory behavior, demographics, and population trends in Manitoba: Journal of Raptor Research, v. 46, no. 1, p. 84–97.

Deguchi, Tomohiro, Yoshiyasu, Keiko, and Ozaki, Kiyoaki, 2012, Comparison of Barn Swallow migration and breeding based on banding records from the 1960s and 2000s: Japanese Journal of Ornithology, v. 61, no. 2, p. 273–282.

Delmore, K. E., Fox, J. W., and Irwin, D. E., 2012, Dramatic intraspecific differences in migratory routes, stopover sites and wintering areas, revealed using light-level geolocators: Proceedings of the Royal Society B-Biological Sciences, v. 279, no. 1747, p. 4582–4589.

Delmore, Kira E., Fox, James W., and Irwin, Darren E., 2012, Dramatic intraspecific differences in migratory routes, stopover sites and wintering areas, revealed using light-level geolocators: Proceedings of the Royal Society Biological Sciences Series B, v. 279, no. 1747, p. 4582–4589.

Dickson, D. Lynne, 2012, Seasonal movement of king eiders breeding in Western Arctic Canada and Northern Alaska: Canadian Wildlife Service Technical Report Series, v. 520, 94 p.

Diefenbach, Duane R., Casalena, Mary Jo, Schiavone, Michael V., and others, 2012, Variation in spring harvest rates of male wild turkeys in New York, Ohio, and Pennsylvania: Journal of Wildlife Management, v. 76, no. 3, p. 514–522.

Duerr, Adam E., Miller, Tricia A., Lanzone, Michael, and others, 2012, Testing an Emerging Paradigm in Migration Ecology Shows Surprising Differences in Efficiency between Flight Modes: PLOS ONE, v. 7, no. 4, article e35548.

Dwyer, James F., Fraser, James D., and Morrison, Joan L., 2012, Within-year survival of nonbreeding crested caracaras: Condor, v. 114, no. 2, p. 295–301.

Evans, David L., Niemi, Gerald J., and Etterson, Matthew A., 2012, Autumn raptor banding at Hawk Ridge, Duluth, Minnesota U.S.A., 1972–2009: an overview: Journal of Raptor Research, v. 46, no. 1, p. 36–49.

Ewert, David N., Hall, Kimberly R., Wunderle, Joseph M. Jr, and others, 2012, Duration and rate of spring migration of Kirtland's warblers: Wilson Journal of Ornithology, v. 124, no. 1, p. 9–14.

Fedy, Bradley C., Aldridge, Cameron L., Doherty, Kevin E., and others, 2012, Interseasonal Movements of Greater Sage-Grouse, Migratory Behavior, and an Assessment of the Core Regions Concept in Wyoming: Journal of Wildlife Management, v. 76, no. 5, p. 1062–1071.

Finnegan, Sue, 2012, Atlantic Flyway review: region 1 (Northeast)—Fall 2011 report: North American Bird Bander, v. 37, no. 3, p. 110–116.

Fraser, Kevin C., Stutchbury, Bridget J. M., Silverio, Cassandra, and others, 2012, Continent-wide tracking to determine migratory connectivity and tropical habitat associations of a declining aerial insectivore: Proceedings of the Royal Society Biological Sciences Series B, v. 279, no. 1749, p. 4901–4906.

Frye, Graham G., 2012, Autumn migration ecology of the northern saw-whet owl (*Aegolius acadicus*) in Northern Montana: Journal of Raptor Research, v. 46, no. 2, p. 177–183.

Gaukler, Shannon M., Homan, H. Jeffrey, Linz, George M., and others, 2012, Using radio-telemetry to assess the risk European starlings pose in pathogen transmission among feedlots: Human-Wildlife Interactions, v. 6, no. 1, p. 30–37.

Gil-Weir, Karine C., Grant, William E., Slack, R. Douglas, and others, 2012, Demography and population trends of Whooping Cranes: Journal of Field Ornithology, v. 83, no. 1, p. 1–10.

Goodman, R. E., Lebuhn, G., Seavy, N. E., and others, 2012, Avian body size changes and climate change: warming or increasing variability?: Global Change Biology, v. 18, no. 1, p. 63–73.

Goodrich, Laurie J., Farmer, Christopher J., Barber, David R., and others, 2012, What banding tells us about the movement ecology of raptors: Journal of Raptor Research, v. 46, no. 1, p. 27–35.

Gordon, Shira D., and Uetz, George W., 2012, Environmental interference: impact of acoustic noise on seismic communication and mating success: Behavioral Ecology, v. 23, no. 4, p. 707–714.

Gunnarsson, G., Latorre-Margalef, N., Hobson, K. A., and others, 2012, Disease Dynamics and Bird Migration-Linking Mallards Anas platyrhynchos and Subtype Diversity of the Influenza A Virus in Time and Space: PLOS ONE, v. 7, no. 4, article e35679.

Harms, Craig A., and Harms, Ronald V., 2012, Venous blood gas and lactate values of mourning doves (*Zenaida macroura*), boat-tailed grackles (*Quiscalus major*), and house sparrows (*Passer domesticus*) after capture by mist net, banding, and venipuncture: Journal of Zoo and Wildlife Medicine, v. 43, no. 1, p. 77–84.

Hauber, Mark E., Strausberger, Bill M., Feldheim, Kevin A., and others, 2012, Indirect estimates of breeding and natal philopatry in an obligate avian brood parasite: Journal of Ornithology, v. 153, no. 2, p. 467–475.

Hipfner, J. Mark, Morrison, Kyle W., and Kouwenberg, Amy-Lee, 2012, Biology of black oystercatchers breeding on Triangle Island, British Columbia, 2003–2011: Northwestern Naturalist, v. 93, no. 2, p. 145–153.

Hobson, K. A., Van Wilgenburg, S. L., Wassenaar, L. I., and others, 2012, Linking Hydrogen (delta H-2) Isotopes in Feathers and Precipitation: Sources of Variance and Consequences for Assignment to Isoscapes: PLOS ONE, v. 7, no. 4, article e35137.

Horton, Kyle G., and Morris, Sara R., 2012, Estimating mass change of migrant songbirds during stopover: comparison of three different methods: Journal of Field Ornithology, v. 83, no. 4, p. 412–419.

Hutcheson, Cathie, 2012, Report of banding and re-encounters of ruby-throated hummingbirds from 2000–2011: North American Bird Bander, v. 37, no. 2, p. 84–86.

Iglay, Raymond B., Demarais, Steve, Wigley, T. Bentley, and others, 2012, Bird community dynamics and vegetation relationships among stand establishment practices in intensively managed pine stands: Forest Ecology and Management, v. 283, p. 1–9.

James, J. Dale, Thompson, Jonathan E., and Ballard, Bart M., 2012, Evidence of Double Brooding by Black-bellied Whistling-Ducks: Wilson Journal of Ornithology, v. 124, no. 1, p. 183–185.

Johnson, James A., Matsuoka, Steven M., Tessler, David F., and others, 2012, Identifying migratory pathways used by rusty blackbirds breeding in Southcentral Alaska: Wilson Journal of Ornithology, v. 124, no. 4, p. 698–703.

Johnson, Oscar W., Fielding, Lauren, Fisher, Joshua P., and others, 2012, New insight concerning transoceanic migratory pathways of Pacific Golden-Plovers (*Pluvialis fulva*): the Japan stopover and other linkages as revealed by geolocators: Wader Study Group Bulletin, v. 119 , no. 1, p. 1–8.

Katzner, Todd, Winton, Julia D., Mcmorris, F. Arthur, and others, 2012, Dispersal, band encounters, and causes of death in a reintroduced and rapidly growing population of peregrine falcons: Journal of Raptor Research, v. 46, no. 1, p. 75–83.

Katzner, Todd E., Brandes, David, Miller, Tricia, and others, 2012, Topography drives migratory flight altitude of golden eagles: implications for on-shore wind energy development: Journal of Applied Ecology, v. 49, no. 5, p. 1178–1186.

Kilgo, John C., and Vukovich, Mark, 2012, Factors affecting breeding season survival of red-headed woodpeckers in South Carolina: Journal of Wildlife Management, v. 76, no. 2, p. 328–335.

Kleen, Vernon M., 2012, Margery Adams Bird Banding Station—Spring 2012 report. Adams Wildlife Sanctuary, Springfield, IL: North American Bird Bander, v. 37, no. 2, p. 86–88.

Klimstra, Jon D., and Padding, Paul I., 2012, Harvest Distribution and Derivation of Atlantic Flyway Canada Geese: Journal of Fish and Wildlife Management, v. 3, no. 1, p. 43–55.

Knutie, Sarah A., and Pereyra, Maria E., 2012, A comparison of winter stress responses in cardueline finches: Auk, v. 129, no. 3, p. 479–490.

Kreakie, Betty J., Fan, Ying, and Keitt, Timothy H., 2012, Enhanced Migratory Waterfowl Distribution Modeling by Inclusion of Depth to Water Table Data: PLOS ONE, v. 7, no. 1, article e30142.

Kreakie, Betty J., and Keitt, Timothy H., 2012, Integration of distance, direction and habitat into a predictive migratory movement model for blue-winged teal (*Anas discors*): Ecological Modelling , v. 224, no. 1, p. 25–32.

Krementz, David G., Asante, Kwasi, and Naylor, Luke W., 2012, Autumn Migration of Mississippi Flyway Mallards as Determined by Satellite Telemetry: Journal of Fish and Wildlife Management, v. 3, no. 2, p. 238–251.

Krull, C. R., Ranjard, L., Landers, T. J., and others, 2012, Analyses of sex and individual differences in vocalizations of Australasian gannets using a dynamic time warping algorithm: Journal of the Acoustical Society of America, v. 132, no. 2, p. 1189–1198.

Lanzone, Michael J., Miller, Tricia A., Turk, Philip, and others, 2012, Flight responses by a migratory soaring raptor to changing meteorological conditions: Biology Letters, v. 8, no. 5, p. 710–713.

Latta, Steven C., De La Cueva, Horacio, and Harper, Alan B., 2012, Abundance and site fidelity of migratory birds wintering in riparian habitat of Baja California: Western Birds, v. 43, no. 2, p. 90–101.

Latta, Steven C., Howell, Christine A., Dettling, Mark D., and others, 2012, Use of Data on Avian Demographics and Site Persistence during Overwintering to Assess Quality of Restored Riparian Habitat: Conservation Biology, v. 26, no. 3, p. 482–492.

Lesko, Mark J., and Smallwood, John A., 2012, Ectoparasites of American kestrels in Northwestern New Jersey and their relationship to nestling growth and survival: Journal of Raptor Research, v. 46, no. 3, p. 304–313.

Lok, Erika K., Esler, Daniel, Takekawa, John Y., and others, 2012, Spatiotemporal associations between Pacific herring spawn and surf scoter spring migration: evaluating a 'silver wave' hypothesis: Marine Ecology Progress Series, v. 457, p. 139–150.

Lutmerding, J. A., Rogosky, M., Peterjohn, B., and others, 2012, Summary of raptor encounter records at the bird banding lab: Journal of Raptor Research, v. 46, no. 1, p. 17–26.

Maccarone, Alan D., Brzorad, John N., and Stone, Heather M., 2012, A Telemetry-based Study of Snowy Egret (*Egretta thula*) Nest-activity Patterns, Food-provisioning Rates and Foraging Energetics: Waterbirds, v. 35, no. 3, p. 394–401.

Mallory, M. L., Allard, K. A., Braune, B. M., and others, 2012, New Longevity Record for Ivory Gulls (*Pagophila eburnea*) and Evidence of Natal Philopatry: Arctic, v. 65, no. 1, p. 98–101.

Marable, M. Kyle, Belant, Jerrold L., Godwin, David, and others, 2012, Effects of resource dispersion and site familiarity on movements of translocated wild turkeys on fragmented landscapes: Behavioural Processes, v. 91, no. 1, p. 119–124.

Mcintyre, C. L., 2012, Quantifying sources of mortality and wintering ranges of golden eagles from interior Alaska using banding and satellite tracking: Journal of Raptor Research, v. 46, no. 1, p. 129–134.

Mcintyre, Carol L., 2012, Quantifying sources of mortality and wintering ranges of golden eagles from interior Alaska using banding and satellite banding: Journal of Raptor Research, v. 46, no. 1, p. 129–134.

Mckibbin, Rene, and Bishop, Christine A., 2012, Size of Territories and Home Ranges of Male Western Yellow-breasted Chats (*Icteria virens auricollis*) in British Columbia: Canadian Field-Naturalist, v. 126, no. 2, p. 152–156.

Mitchell, Greg W., Newman, Amy E. M., Wikelski, Martin, and others, 2012, Timing of breeding carries over to influence migratory departure in a songbird: an automated radiotracking study: Journal of Animal Ecology, v. 81, no. 5, p. 1024–1033.

Montevecchi, William, Fifield, David, Burke, Chantelle, and others, 2012, Tracking long-distance migration to assess marine pollution impact: Biology Letters, v. 8, no. 2, p. 218–221.

Moore, Bret A., Baumhardt, Patrice, Doppler, Megan, and others, 2012, Oblique color vision in an open-habitat bird: spectral sensitivity, photoreceptor distribution and behavioral implications: Journal of Experimental Biology, v. 215, no. 19, p. 3442–3452.

Muzaffar, Sabir B., Hill, Nichola J., Takekawa, John Y., and others, 2012, Role of bird movements in the epidemiology of West Nile and avian influenza virus: Human-Wildlife Interactions, v. 6, no. 1 , p. 72–88.

Nemeth, Zoltan, and Moore, Frank R., 2012, Differential timing of spring passage of Ruby-throated Hummingbirds along the northern coast of the Gulf of Mexico: Journal of Field Ornithology, v. 83, no. 1, p. 26–31.

Niles, Lawrence J., Burger, Joanna, Porter, Ronald R., and others, 2012, Migration pathways, migration speeds and non-breeding areas used by northern hemisphere wintering Red Knots *Calidris canutus* of the subspecies *rufa*: Wader Study Group Bulletin, v. 119, no. 3, p. 195–203.

Ogden, Lesley J. Evans, Martin, Michaela, and Martin, Kathy, 2012, Mating and breeding success decline with elevation for the Pacific wren (*Troglodytes pacificus*) in coastal mountain forests: Wilson Journal of Ornithology, v. 124, no. 2, p. 270–276.

Ortego, Brent, 2012, IBBA annual report of birds banded, 2011: North American Bird Bander, v. 37, no. 3, p. 118–122.

Osenkowski, J. E., Paton, P. W. C., and Kraus, D., 2012, Using long-term constant-effort banding data to monitor population trends of migratory birds: a 33-year assessment of adjacent coastal stations: Condor, v. 114, no. 3, p. 470–481.

Padding, Paul I., and Royle, J. Andrew, 2012, Assessment of bias in US waterfowl harvest estimates: Wildlife Research, v. 39, no. 4, p. 336–342.

Pagel, Joel E., Sharpe, Peter B., Garcelon, David K., and others, 2012, Exposure of bald eagles to lead on the Northern Channel Islands, California: Journal of Raptor Research, v. 46, no. 2, p. 168–176.

Ramey, Andrew M., Ely, Craig R., Schmutz, Joel A., and others, 2012, Molecular Detection of Hematozoa Infections in Tundra Swans Relative to Migration Patterns and Ecological Conditions at Breeding Grounds: PLOS ONE, v. 7, no. 9, article: e45789.

Ramirez-Barajas, Pablo J., Islebe, Gerald A., and Calme, Sophie, 2012, Impact of Hurricane Dean (2007) on Game Species of the Selva Maya, Mexico: Biotropica, v. 44, no. 3, p. 402–411.

Redig, Patrick T., and Goyal, Sagar M., 2012, Serologic Evidence of Exposure of Raptors to Influenza A Virus: Avian Diseases, v. 56, no. 2, p. 411–413.

Redmond, Lucas J., and Murphy, Michael T., 2012, Using complementary approaches to estimate survival of juvenile and adult Eastern Kingbirds: Journal of Field Ornithology, v. 83, no. 3, p. 247–259.

Rigby, Elizabeth A., and Haukos, David A., 2012, Breeding Season Survival and Breeding Incidence of Female Mottled Ducks on the Upper Texas Gulf Coast: Waterbirds, v. 35, no. 2, p. 260–269.

Ruder, Mark G., Noel, Brandon L., Bednarz, James C., and others, 2012, Exertional Myopathy in Pileated Woodpeckers (*Dryocopus pileatus*) Subsequent to Capture: Journal of Wildlife Diseases, v. 48, no. 2, p. 514–516.

Ruiz-Gutierrez, Viviana, Doherty, Paul F. Jr., Santana C, Eduardo, and others, 2012, Survival of resident Neotropical birds: considerations for sampling and analysis based on 20 years of bird-banding efforts in Mexico: Auk, v. 129, no. 3, p. 500–509.

Sanders, Todd A., and Otis, David L., 2012, Mourning dove reporting probabilities for web-address versus toll-free bands: Journal of Wildlife Management, v. 76, no. 3, p. 480–488.

Santo, Trish, 2012, Band-tailed pigeon in Saskatoon, Sk: Blue Jay, v. 70, no. 1, p. 56.

Seavy, Nathaniel E., Humple, Diana L., Cormier, Renee L., and others, 2012, Establishing the Breeding Provenance of a Temperate-Wintering North American Passerine, the Golden-Crowned Sparrow, Using Light-Level Geolocation: PLOS ONE, v. 7, no. 4, article e34886.

Sechrist, Juddson D., Paxton, Eben H., Ahlers, Darrell D., and others, 2012, One year of migration data for a western yellow-billed cuckoo: Western Birds, v. 43, no. 1, p. 2–11.

Sgueo, Carrie, Wells, Marion E., Russell, David E., and others, 2012, Acclimatization of seasonal energetics in northern cardinals (*Cardinalis cardinalis*) through plasticity of metabolic rates and ceilings: Journal of Experimental Biology, v. 215, no. 14, p. 2418–2424.

Siegel, Rodney B., Bond, Monica L., Wilkerson, Robert L., and others, 2012, Lethal procyrnea infection in a black-backed woodpecker (*Picoides arcticus*) from California: Journal of Zoo and Wildlife Medicine, v. 43, no. 2, p. 421–424.

Small, Daniel M., Gimpel, Maren E., and Gill, Douglas E., 2012, Site Fidelity and Natal Philopatry in Dickcissels: Northeastern Naturalist, v. 19, no. 1, p. 123–129.

Spotswood, Erica N., Goodman, Kari Roesch, Carlisle, Jay, and others, 2012, How safe is mist netting? evaluating the risk of injury and mortality to birds: Methods in Ecology and Evolution, v. 3, no. 1, p. 29–38.

Stake, Mike M., 2012, Trends in vagrant capture rates at a coastal California banding station (1993–2010): Bird Populations, v. 11, p. 14–21.

Stanley, Calandra Q., Macpherson, Maggie, Fraser, Kevin C., and others, 2012, Repeat Tracking of Individual Songbirds Reveals Consistent Migration Timing but Flexibility in Route: PLOS ONE, v. 7, no. 7, article e40688.

Suomala, Rebecca W., Morris, Sara R., and Babbitt, Kimberly J., 2012, Comparison of migrant songbird stopover ecology on two islands in the Gulf of Maine: Wilson Journal of Ornithology, v. 124, no. 2, p. 217–229.

Swatantran, Anu, Dubayah, Ralph, Goetz, Scott, and others, 2012, Mapping Migratory Bird Prevalence Using Remote Sensing Data Fusion: PLOS ONE, v. 7, no. 1, article: e28922, 11 p.

Swem, Ted, and Matz, Angela, 2012, Observations of Gyrfalcons Along the Colville River, Alaska, 1981–2005, *in* Watson, Richard T., Cade, T. J., Fuller, Mark, and others, eds., Gyrfalcons and Ptarmigan in a Changing World: Proceedings of a Conference Held February 2011, Boise, Idaho. Volume I: Boise, Peregrine Fund, p. 229–235.

Taff, Conor C., Littrell, Katherine A., and Freeman-Gallant, Corey R., 2012, Female Song in the Common Yellowthroat: Wilson Journal of Ornithology, v. 124, no. 2, p. 370–374.

Templeton, Christopher N., Reed, Veronica A., Campbell, S. Elizabeth, and others, 2012, Spatial movements and social networks in juvenile male song sparrows: Behavioral Ecology, v. 23, no. 1, p. 141–152.

Traylor, Joshua J., Alisauskas, Ray T., Slattery, Stuart M., and others, 2012, Comparative survival and recovery of Ross's and lesser snow geese from Canada's Central Arctic: Journal of Wildlife Management, v. 76, no. 6, p. 1135–1144.

Varland, Daniel E., Buchanan, Joseph B., Fleming, Tracy L., and others, 2012, Peregrine falcons on coastal beaches of Washington: fifteen years of banding and surveys: Journal of Raptor Research, v. 46, no. 1, p. 57–74.

Vogt, David F., Hopey, Mark E., Mayfield, G. Rad, and others, 2012, Stopover Site Fidelity by Tennessee Warblers at a Southern Appalachian High-elevation Site: Wilson Journal of Ornithology, v. 124, no. 2, p. 366–370.

2011

Atlantic flyway review: Region 1 (Northeast), Fall 2010 Report, 2011, North American Bird Bander, v. 36, no. 3, p. 124–130.

Alisauskas, Ray, Rockwell, Robert F., Dufour, Kevin W., and others, 2011, Harvest, Survival, and Abundance of Midcontinent Lesser Snow Geese Relative to Population Reduction Efforts: Wildlife Monographs, v. 179, p. 1–42.

Alisauskas, Ray, and Zimmerman, Guthrie S., 2011, An Experimental Assessment of Shotgun Discharge on Aluminum Legband Retention: Journal of Wildlife Management, v. 75, no. 8, p. 1710–1715.

Amundson, Courtney L., and Arnold, Todd W., 2011, The role of predator removal, density-dependence, and environmental factors on mallard duckling survival in North Dakota: Journal of Wildlife Management, v. 75, no. 6, p. 1330–1339.

Anich, Nicholas M., Trick, Joel A., Grveles, Kim M., and others, 2011, Characteristics of a red pine plantation occupied by Kirtland's warblers in Wisconsin: Wilson Journal of Ornithology, v. 123, no. 2, p. 199–205.

Aubry, Yves, Desrochers, Andre, and Seutin, Gilles, 2011, Response of Bicknell's Thrush (*Catharus bicknelli*) to boreal silviculture and forest stand edges: a radio-tracking study: Canadian Journal of Zoology, v. 89, no. 6, p. 474–482.

Augustine, Jacqueline K., and Sandercock, Brett K., 2011, Demography of Female Greater Prairie-Chickens in Unfragmented Grasslands in Kansas: Avian Conservation and Ecology, v. 6, no. 1, article 2.

Avery, Michael L., Humphrey, John S., Daughtery, Trey S., and others, 2011, Vulture Flight Behavior and Implications for Aircraft Safety: Journal of Wildlife Management, v. 75, no. 7, p. 1581–1587.

Bartlett, Tom, 2011, Inland Bird Banding Association 2011 Annual Meeting, Weslaco, TX 2–4 Dec 2011: North American Bird Bander, v. 36, no. 4, p. 194–196.

Beckett, S. R., and Proudfoot, G. A., 2011, Large-scale movement and migration of northern saw-whet owls in Eastern North America: Wilson Journal of Ornithology, v. 123, no. 3, p. 521–535.

Berdeen, James B., Maxson, Stephen, and Rave, David P., 2011, Final report: Harvest characteristics of large Canada geese in Minnesota, 2002–2007: Minnesota Department of Natural Resources Summaries of Wildlife Research Findings, v. 2010, p. 43–87.

Bisson, I. A., Butler, L., Hayden, T. J., and others, 2011, Energetic response to human disturbance in an endangered songbird: Animal Conservation, v. 14, no. 5, p. 484–491.

Bloom, P. H., Scott, J. M., Papp, J. M., and others, 2011, Vagrant western red-shouldered hawks: origins, natal dispersal patterns, and survival: Condor, v. 113, no. 3, p. 538–546.

Blundell, Melissa A., and Kus, Barbara E., 2011, First Record of Interspecific Breeding of Least Bell's Vireo and White-eyed Vireo: Wilson Journal of Ornithology, v. 123, no. 3, p. 628–631.

Brewer, Larry W., Redmond, Christine A., Stafford, Jennifer M., and others, 2011, Marking Ruby-Throated Hummingbirds With Radio Frequency Identification Tags: Journal of Wildlife Management, v. 75, no. 7, p. 1664–1667.

Brindock, Kevin M., and Colwell, Mark A., 2011, Habitat Selection by Western Snowy Plovers During the Nonbreeding Season: Journal of Wildlife Management, v. 75, no. 4, p. 786–793.

Brooks, Elizabeth W., 2011, Atlantic Flyway Review: Region III (Western Ridge)—Fall 2010: North American Bird Bander, v. 36, no. 4, p. 185–193.

—, 2011, Atlantic Flyway Review: Spring 2010: North American Bird Bander, v. 36, no. 4, p. 173–185.

Browers, Howard, 2011, Western Bird Banding Association 2011 Annual Meeting Report: North American Bird Bander, v. 36, no. 4, p. 198–205.

Butler, Matthew J., Collier, Bret A., Holt, R. Douglas, and others, 2011, Retention of Butt-End Aluminum Leg Bands by Wild Turkeys: Journal of Wildlife Management, v. 75, no. 8, p. 1807–1811.

Carlson, James C., Clark, Larry, Antolin, Michael F., and others, 2011, Rock pigeon use of livestock facilities in northern Colorado: implications for improving farm bio-security: Human-Wildlife Interactions, v. 5, no. 1, p. 112–122.

Cline, Brittany B., and Haig, Susan M., 2011, Seasonal movement, residency, and migratory patterns of Wilson's snipe (*Gallinago delicata*): Auk, v. 128, no. 3, p. 543–555.

Colwell, Rita R., 2011, Leg injuries in banded female Anna's hummingbirds (*Calypte anna*) in Central California: North American Bird Bander, v. 36, no. 2, p. 57–64.

Conover, Michael R., 2011, Population growth and movements of Canada geese in New Haven County, Connecticut, during a 25-year period: Waterbirds, v. 34, no. 4, p. 414–421.

Culliney, Susan, and Gardali, Thomas, 2011, Patterns in movement, captures, and phenology of sharp-shinned hawks in Central Coastal California: Journal of Raptor Research, v. 45, no. 2, p. 160–167.

Danner, R. M., Greenberg, R., and Walters, J. R., 2011, Winter food limits the body condition, survival, and molt of a migratory sparrow: Integrative and Comparative Biology, v. 51, p. E180.

Demaso, Stephen J., Grant, William E., Hernandez, Fidel, and others, 2011, A Population Model to Simulate Northern Bobwhite Population Dynamics in Southern Texas: Journal of Wildlife Management, v. 75, no. 2, p. 319–332.

Demaso, Stephen J., Hernandez, Fidel, Brennan, Leonard A., and others, 2011, Application of the Simple Saddlepoint Approximation to Estimate Probability Distributions in Wildlife Research: Journal of Wildlife Management, v. 75, no. 3, p. 740–746.

Desucre Medrano, Atahualpa Eduardo, Cervantes Zamudio, Osvaldo, Ramirez Bastida, Patricia, and others, 2011, Notes on the breeding biology of the Snowy Plover (*Charadrius nivosus*) at Lake Texcoco, Mexico: Huitzil, v. 12, no. 2, p. 32–38.

Drummer, Thomas D., Corace, R. Gregory III, and Sjogren, Stephen J., 2011, Sharp-Tailed Grouse Lek Attendance and Fidelity in Upper Michigan: Journal of Wildlife Management, v. 75, no. 2, p. 311–318.

Dzialak, Matthew R., Olson, Chad V., Harju, Seth M., and others, 2011, Identifying and Prioritizing Greater Sage-Grouse Nesting and Brood-Rearing Habitat for Conservation in Human-Modified Landscapes: PLOS ONE, v. 6, no. 10, article e26273, 18 p.

Esler, Daniel, Ballachey, Brenda E., Trust, Kimberly A., and others, 2011, Cytochrome P4501A biomarker indication of the timeline of chronic exposure of Barrow's goldeneyes to residual Exxon Valdez oil: Marine Pollution Bulletin, v. 62, no. 3, p. 609–614.

Fast, Peter L. F., Fast, Marie, Mosbech, Anders, and others, 2011, Effects of Implanted Satellite Transmitters on Behavior and Survival of Female Common Eiders: Journal of Wildlife Management, v. 75, no. 7, p. 1553–1557.

Fesenmyer, Kurt A., and Knick, Steven T., 2011, Seasonal Movements and Environmental Triggers to Fall Migration of Sage Sparrows: Wilson Journal of Ornithology, v. 123, no. 4, p. 803–807.

Fisher, Ryan J., and Davis, Stephen K., 2011, Post-fledging dispersal, habitat use, and survival of Sprague's pipits: Are planted grasslands a good substitute for native?: Biological Conservation, v. 144, no. 1, p. 263–271.

Flowers, Thomas L., 2011, The Eurasian collared-dove in Meade County, Kansas: Kansas Ornithological Society Bulletin, v. 62, no. 3, p. 25–31.

Flowers, Thomas L., and Miller, Edwin J., 2011, Two new banding returns for cedar waxwings from Kansas: Kansas Ornithological Society Bulletin, v. 62, no. 4, p. 46–47.

Gaddis, Philip K., 2011, Molt and body condition of Myrtle and Audubon's warblers during migration-stopover in Portland, Oregon: Northwestern Naturalist, v. 92, no. 2, p. 107–115.

Gaston, Anthony J., and Descamps, Sebastien, 2011, Population Change in a Marine Bird Colony is Driven By Changes in Recruitment: Avian Conservation and Ecology, v. 6, no. 2, article 5.

Gow, Elizabeth A., Done, Tyler W., and Stutchbury, Bridget J. M., 2011, Radio-tags have no behavioral or physiological effects on a migratory songbird during breeding and molt: Journal of Field Ornithology, v. 82, no. 2, p. 193–201.

Guilford, Tim, Freeman, Robin, Boyle, Dave, and others, 2011, A Dispersive Migration in the Atlantic Puffin and Its Implications for Migratory Navigation: PLOS ONE, v. 6, no. 7, article e21336, 8 p.

Guthrie, Joshua D., Byrne, Michael E., Hardin, Jason B., and others, 2011, Evaluation of a global positioning system backpack transmitter for wild turkey research: Journal of Wildlife Management, v. 75, no. 3, p. 539–547.

Hallgrimsson, Gunnar Thor, Van Swelm, Norman Deans, Gunnarsson, Hallgrimur V., and others, 2011, First two records of european-banded lesser black-backed gulls Larus fuscus in america: Marine Ornithology, v. 39, no. 1, p. 137–139.

Hamilton, Christine D., Golightly, Richard T., and Takekawa, John Y., 2011, Relationships between breeding status, social-congregation attendance, and foraging distance of Xantus's murrelets: Condor, v. 113, no. 1, p. 140–149.

Harmata, A. R., 2011, Environmental contaminants in tissues of bald eagles sampled in Southwestern Montana, 2006–2008: Journal of Raptor Research, v. 45, no. 2, p. 119–135.

Hatch, Scott A., Gill, Verena A., and Mulcahy, Daniel M., 2011, Migration and wintering areas of glaucous-winged gulls from South-Central Alaska: Condor, v. 113, no. 2, p. 340–351.

—-, 2011, Migration and wintering sites of Pelagic Cormorants determined by satellite telemetry: Journal of Field Ornithology, v. 82, no. 3, p. 269–278.

Heckscher, Christopher M., Taylor, Syrena M., Fox, James W., and others, 2011, Veery (*Catharus fuscescens*) wintering locations, migratory connectivity, and a revision of its winter range using geolocator technology: Auk, v. 128, no. 3, p. 531–542.

Hedd, A., Montevecchi, W. A., Tranquilla, L. Mcfarlane, and others, 2011, Reducing uncertainty on the Grand Bank: tracking and vessel surveys indicate mortality risks for common murres in the North-West Atlantic: Animal Conservation, v. 14, no. 6, p. 630–641.

Herbert, Percy N., Carter, Harry R., and Golightly, Richard T., 2011, Extra-pair visitations to a marbled murrelet nest in northern California: Northwestern Naturalist, v. 92, no. 2, p. 95–100.

Hogan, D., Thompson, J. E., Esler, D., and others, 2011, Discovery of Important Postbreeding Sites for Barrow's Goldeneye in the Boreal Transition Zone of Alberta: Waterbirds, v. 34, no. 3, p. 261–268.

Holroyd, G. L., and Trefry, H. E., 2011, Tracking movements of Athene owls: the application of North American experiences to Europe: Animal Biodiversity and Conservation, v. 34, no. 2, p. 379–387.

Homann, Peter H., 2011, Year-round resident white-eyed vireos (*Vireo griseus*) in the Florida Panhandle: Florida Field Naturalist, v. 39, no. 4, p. 111–115.

Houston, C. Stuart, Mcloughlin, Philip D., Mandel, James T., and others, 2011, Breeding home ranges of migratory turkey vultures near their northern limit: Wilson Journal of Ornithology, v. 123, no. 3, p. 472–478.

Hu, J. H., Xie, F., Li, C., and others, 2011, Elevational Patterns of Species Richness, Range and Body Size for Spiny Frogs: PLOS ONE, v. 6, no. 5, article e19817.

Hudgens, Brian, Beaudry, Frederic, George, T. Luke, and others, 2011, Shifting threats faced by the San Clemente sage sparrow: Journal of Wildlife Management, v. 75, no. 6, p. 1350–1360.

Ibarra-Macias, Ana, Robinson, W. Douglas, and Gaines, Michael S., 2011, Experimental evaluation of bird movements in a fragmented Neotropical landscape: Biological Conservation, v. 144, no. 2, p. 703–712.

Jackson, Allyson K., Froneberger, Joshua P., and Cristol, Daniel A., 2011, Postfledging Survival of Eastern Bluebirds in an Urbanized Landscape: Journal of Wildlife Management, v. 75, no. 5, p. 1082–1093.

Johnson, Oscar W., Fielding, Lauren, Fox, James W., and others, 2011, Tracking the migrations of Pacific Golden-Plovers (*Pluvialis fulva*) between Hawaii and Alaska: New insight on flight performance, breeding ground destinations, and nesting from birds carrying light level geolocators: Wader Study Group Bulletin, v. 118, no. 1, p. 26–31.

Judd, Erica R., Butler, Christopher J., and Batchelder, Ned, 2011, Hybridization between black-chinned (*archilochus alexandri*) and ruby-throated (*a. Colubris*) hummingbirds in Oklahoma: Bulletin of the Oklahoma Ornithological Society, v. 44, no. 3–4, p. 1–7.

Kelley, Samuel W., Ransom, Dean, Jr., Butcher, Jerrod A., and others, 2011, Home range dynamics, habitat selection, and survival of Greater Roadrunners: Journal of Field Ornithology, v. 82, no. 2, p. 165–174.

Kerlin, Nick, 2011, Pine siskin banding recovery: State College of Seattle: Pennsylvania Birds, v. 25, no. 1, p. 30.

King, David I., Yamasaki, Mariko, Degraaf, Richard M., and others, 2011, Three decades of avian research on the Bartlett Experimental Forest, New Hampshire, USA: Forest Ecology and Management, v. 262, no. 1, Sp. Iss. SI, p. 3–11.

Kirchman, J. J., Ralston, J., and Gifford, N. A., 2011, Stable isotope analysis of fall migration stopover by six passerine species in an inland pitch pine-scrub oak barren: Wilson Journal of Ornithology, v. 123, no. 3, p. 548–556.

Kneib, Thomas, Knauer, Felix, and Kuechenhoff, Helmut, 2011, A general approach to the analysis of habitat selection: Environmental and Ecological Statistics, v. 18, no. 1, p. 1–25.

Kochert, Michael N., Fuller, Mark R., Schueck, Linda S., and others, 2011, Migration patterns, use of stopover areas, and austral summer movements of Swainson's hawks: Condor, v. 113, no. 1, p. 89–106.

Krapu, G. L., Brandt, D. A., Jones, K. L., and others, 2011, Geographic Distribution of the Mid-Continent Population of Sandhill Cranes and Related Management Applications: Wildlife Monographs, no. 175, p. 1–38.

Krementz, D. G., Asante, K., and Naylor, L. W., 2011, Spring Migration of Mallards from Arkansas as Determined by Satellite Telemetry: Journal of Fish and Wildlife Management, v. 2, no. 2, p. 156–168.

Kushlan, James A., 2011, Longevity of the Tricolored Heron (*Egretta tricolor*): Journal of Heron Biology and Conservation, v. 1, 3 p.

Lane, Vanessa R., Miller, Karl V., Castleberry, Steven B., and others, 2011, Bird community responses to a gradient of site preparation intensities in pine plantations in the Coastal Plain of North Carolina: Forest Ecology and Management, v. 262, no. 9, p. 1668–1678.

Lashelle, Dan, 2011, Banded white-faced ibis observed in Northeastern Kansas: Kansas Ornithological Society Bulletin, v. 62, no. 3, p. 32.

Leppold, Adrienne J., and Mulvihill, Robert S., 2011, The Boreal Landbird Component of Migrant Bird Communities in Eastern North America, Boreal Birds of North America: a Hemispheric View of Their Conservation Links and Significance: Studies in Avian Biology, p. 73–83.

Link, Paul T., Afton, Alan D., Cox, Robert R., Jr., and others, 2011, Daily Movements of Female Mallards Wintering in Southwestern Louisiana: Waterbirds, v. 34, no. 4, p. 422–428.

Link, Paul T., Afton, Alan D., Cox, Robert R. Jr, and others, 2011, Use of habitats by female mallards wintering in southwestern Louisiana: Waterbirds, v. 34, no. 4, p. 429–438.

Lohr, Michael, Collins, Bridget M., Castelli, Paul M., and others, 2011, Life on the Edge: Northern Bobwhite Ecology at the Northern Periphery of Their Range: Journal of Wildlife Management, v. 75, no. 1, p. 52–60.

Lok, Erika K., Esler, Daniel, Takekawa, John Y., and others, 2011, Stopover Habitats of Spring Migrating Surf Scoters in Southeast Alaska: Journal of Wildlife Management, v. 75, no. 1, p. 92–100.

Macintosh, T., Stutchbury, B. J. M., and Evans, M. L., 2011, Gap-crossing by Wood Thrushes (*Hylocichla mustelina*) in a fragmented landscape: Canadian Journal of Zoology, v. 89, no. 11, p. 1091–1097.

Mandel, James T., Bohrer, Gil, Winkler, David W., and others, 2011, Migration path annotation: cross-continental study of migration-flight response to environmental conditions: Ecological Applications, v. 21, no. 6, p. 2258–2268.

Manske, Mark, 2011, American kestrel nest box management program in northern New York State: Kingbird, v. 61, no. 1, p. 23–32.

Mattsson, Brady J., Latta, Steven C., Cooper, Robert J., and others, 2011, Latitudinal variation in reproductive strategies by the migratory Louisiana waterthrush: Condor, v. 113, no. 2, p. 412–418.

Mcknight, Aly, Irons, David B., Allyn, Andrew J., and others, 2011, Winter dispersal and activity patterns of post-breeding black-legged kittiwakes *Rissa tridactyla* from Prince William Sound, Alaska: Marine Ecology Progress Series, v. 442, p. 241–253.

Mills, Alexander M., Thurber, Bethany G., Mackenzie, Stuart A., and others, 2011, Passerines use nocturnal flights for landscape-scale movements during migration stopover: Condor, v. 113, no. 3, p. 597–607.

Mills, William E., Harrigal, Dean E., Owen, Sheldon F., and others, 2011, Capturing Clapper Rails Using Thermal Imaging Technology: Journal of Wildlife Management, v. 75, no. 5, p. 1218–1221.

Moorhead, Luke, Breuner, Creagh, and Blank, Lisa, 2011, Impacting Science Teacher Candidate Practices through Authentic Research Experience: Integrative and Comparative Biology, v. 51, no. Suppl. 1 , p. E95.

Morrissey, Christy A., and Elliott, John E., 2011, Toxic Trees: Arsenic Pesticides, Woodpeckers, and the Mountain Pine Beetle, *in* Elliott, John E., Bishop, Christine A., and Morrissey, Christy A., eds., Wildlife Ecotoxicology—Forensic Approaches [Emerging Topics in Ecotoxicology—Principles Approaches and Perspectives, Volume 3], p. 239–265.

Nicoletti, Frank J., 2011, Two Prairie falcons banded in Lakewood Township, St. Louis County: Loon, v. 83, no. 2, p. 89–91.

Ortego, Brent, 2011, IBBA Annual Report of birds banded, 2010: summary of bird banding reported from the IBBA region for 2010: North American Bird Bander, v. 36, no. 2, p. 91–96.

Oyler-Mccance, Sara J., Fike, Jennifer A., Talley-Farnham, Tiffany, and others, 2011, Characterization of ten microsatellite loci in the Broad-tailed Hummingbird (*Selasphorus platycercus*): Conservation Genetics Resources, v. 3, no. 2, p. 351–353.

Pearce, J. M., Reeves, A. B., Ramey, A. M., and others, 2011, Interspecific exchange of avian influenza virus genes in Alaska: the influence of trans-hemispheric migratory tendency and breeding ground sympatry: Molecular Ecology, v. 20, no. 5, p. 1015–1025.

Poole, Richard, and Brown, Christine, 2011, Autumn migration of thrushes (*Catharus*) at a banding site in central Florida: Florida Field Naturalist, v. 39, no. 1, p. 19–20.

Potter, Lisa M., Otis, David L., and Bogenschutz, Todd R., 2011, Nest Success of Northern Bobwhite on Managed and Unmanaged Landscapes in Southeast Iowa: Journal of Wildlife Management, v. 75, no. 1, p. 46–51.

Redmond, Lucas J., and Murphy, Michael T., 2011, Multistate mark-recapture analysis reveals no effect of blood sampling on survival and recapture of eastern kingbirds (*Tyrannus tyrannus*): Auk, v. 128, no. 3, p. 514–521.

Rogers, C. M., 2011, Use of Fecundity Measured Directly Throughout the Breeding Season to Test a Source-Sink Demographic Model: Conservation Biology, v. 25, no. 6, p. 1212–1219.

Roy, Charlotte, Herwig, Christine, Rave, David, and others, 2011, Movements, survival, and refuge use by ring-necked ducks after fledging in Minnesota: Minnesota Department of Natural Resources Summaries of Wildlife Research Findings, v. 2010, p. 8–19.

Ryder, Thomas B., Fox, James W., and Marra, Peter P., 2011, Estimating migratory connectivity of gray catbirds (*Dumetella carolinensis*) using geolocator and mark-recapture data: Auk, v. 128, no. 3, p. 448–453.

Savard, Jean-Pierre L., Cousineau, Melanie, and Drolet, Bruno. 2011, Exploratory analysis of correlates of the abundance of rusty blackbirds (*Euphagus carolinus*) during fall migration: Ecoscience, v. 18, no. 4, p. 402–408.

Savard, Jean-Pierre L., Lesage, Louis, Gilliland, Scott G., and others, 2011, Molting, Staging, and Wintering Locations of Common Eiders Breeding in the Gyrfalcon Archipelago, Ungava Bay: Arctic, v. 64, no. 2, p. 197–206.

Schmaljohann, Heiko, Becker, Philipp J. J., Karaardic, Hakan, and others, 2011, Nocturnal exploratory flights, departure time, and direction in a migratory songbird: Journal of Ornithology, v. 152, no. 2, p. 439–452.

Sedinger, James S., and Nicolai, Christopher A., 2011, Recent trends in first-year survival for black brant breeding in southwestern Alaska: Condor, v. 113, no. 3, p. 511–517.

Selman, Will, Hess, Thomas J. Jr, Linscombe, Jeb, and others, 2011, An extralimital record of a Louisiana-banded mottled duck recovered in South Dakota: Southeastern Naturalist, v. 10, no. 3, p. 570–574.

Silvergieter, Michael P., and Lank, David B., 2011, Patch Scale Nest-Site Selection by Marbled Murrelets (*Brachyramphus marmoratus*): Avian Conservation and Ecology, v. 6, no. 2, article 6.

Sittler, Benoit, Aebischer, Adrian, and Gilg, Olivier, 2011, Post-breeding migration of four Long-tailed Skuas (*Stercorarius longicaudus*) from North and East Greenland to West Africa: Journal of Ornithology, v. 152, no. 2, p. 375–381.

Smith, Susan B., and Paton, Peter W., 2011, Long-term shifts in autumn migration by songbirds at a coastal eastern North American stopover site: Wilson Journal of Ornithology, v. 123, no. 3, p. 557–566.

Snipes, Katie C., and Sanders, Felicia J., 2011, Recoveries of Black Skimmers (*Rynchops niger*) Banded in South Carolina: Chat (Raleigh), v. 75, no. 3, p. 81–87.

Sonne, Christian, Andersen, Steen, Mosbech, Anders, and others, 2011, Monitoring Temperature and Heart Rate during Surgical Field Implantation of PTT-100 Satellite Transmitters in Greenland Sea Birds: Veterinary Medicine International, v. 2011, p. 1–5.

Stake, Mike M., and Sorenson, Kelly, 2011, Trends in riparian songbirds banded at Big Sur, Central California Coast: Western Birds, v. 42, no. 2, p. 85–95.

Streby, H. M., Peterson, S. M., Mcallister, T. L., and others, 2011, Use of early-successional managed northern forest by mature-forest species during the post-fledging period: Condor, v. 113, no. 4, p. 817–824.

Stumpf, Joshua P., Denis, Nathalie, Hamer, Thomas E., and others, 2011, Flight height distribution and collision risk of the marbled Murrelet *brachyramphus marmoratus*: methodology and preliminary results: Marine Ornithology, v. 39, no. 1, p. 123–128.

Taylor, Audrey R., Lanctot, Richard B., Powell, Abby N., and others, 2011, Residence time and movements of postbreeding shorebirds on the Northern Coast of Alaska: Condor, v. 113, no. 4, p. 779–794.

Taylor, Philip D., Mackenzie, Stuart A., Thurber, Bethany G., and others, 2011, Landscape Movements of Migratory Birds and Bats Reveal an Expanded Scale of Stopover: PLOS ONE, v. 6, no. 11, article e27054.

Tingley, R., and Shine, R., 2011, Desiccation Risk Drives the Spatial Ecology of an Invasive Anuran (*Rhinella marina*) in the Australian Semi-Desert: PLOS ONE, v. 6, no. 10, article e25979.

Van Wilgenburg, S. L., and Hobson, K. A., 2011, Combining stable-isotope (delta D) and band recovery data to improve probabilistic assignment of migratory birds to origin: Ecological Applications, v. 21, no. 4, p. 1340–1351.

Vormwald, Lisa M., Morrison, Michael L., Mathewson, Heather A., and others, 2011, Survival and movements of fledgling willow and dusky flycatchers: Condor, v. 113, no. 4, p. 834–842.

Walters, Benjamin J., and Nol, Erica, 2011, Natal and Adult Dispersal of Red-eyed Vireos in a Large Southern Ontario Forest: Wilson Journal of Ornithology, v. 123, no. 3, p. 638–641.

Wille, M., Robertson, G. J., Whitney, H., and others, 2011, Reassortment of American and Eurasian genes in an influenza A virus isolated from a great black-backed gull (*Larus marinus*), a species demonstrated to move between these regions: Archives of Virology, v. 156, no. 1, p. 107–115.

Woolley, Colin, 2011, Fall 2011 bird banding at Wildcat Hills Nature Center: Nebraska Bird Review, v. 79, no. 4, p. 142.

Zydelis, Ramunas, Lewison, Rebecca L., Shaffer, Scott A., and others, 2011, Dynamic habitat models: using telemetry data to project fisheries bycatch: Proceedings of the Royal Society Biological Sciences Series B, v. 278, no. 1722, p. 3191–3200.

2010

Abstracts, 2010, Eastern Bird Banding Association Annual meeting minutes 10 Ap. 2010: North American Bird Bander, v. 35, no. 2, p. 78–83.

Adelman, James S., Cordoba-Cordoba, Sergio, Spoelstra, Kamiel, and others, 2010, Radiotelemetry reveals variation in fever and sickness behaviours with latitude in a free-living passerine: Functional Ecology, v. 24, no. 4, p. 813–823.

Amundson, Courtney L., and Arnold, Todd W., 2010, Effects of radiotransmitters and plasticine bands on mallard duckling survival: Journal of Field Ornithology, v. 81, no. 3, p. 310–316.

Arimitsu, M., Piatt, J., Romano, M., and others, 2010, Kittlitz's and Marbled Murrelets in Kenai Fjords National Park, South-Central Alaska: At-Sea Distribution, Abundance, and Foraging Habitat, 2006–08: U.S. Geological Survey Open-File Report 2010–1181, 68 p.

Ashley, P., Hobson, K. A., Van Wilgenburg, S. L., and others, 2010, Linking Canadian Harvested Juvenile American Black Ducks to Their Natal Areas Using Stable Isotope (delta D, delta 13C, and delta 15N) Methods: Avian Conservation and Ecology, v. 5, no. 2, article 7.

Bader, Troy J., and Bednarz, James C., 2010, Home Range, Habitat Use, and Nest Site Characteristics of Mississippi Kites in the White River National Wildlife Refuge, Arkansas: Wilson Journal of Ornithology, v. 122, no. 4, p. 706–715.

Baldwin, Heather Q., Jeske, Clinton W., Powell, Melissa A., and others, 2010, Home-Range Size and Site Tenacity of Overwintering Le Conte's Sparrows in a Fire Managed Prairie: Wilson Journal of Ornithology, v. 122, no. 1, p. 139–145.

Balkcom, Gregory D., 2010, Demographic parameters of rural and urban adult resident Canada geese in Georgia: Journal of Wildlife Management, v. 74, no. 1, p. 120–123.

Balkcom, Gregory D., Garrettson, Pamela R., and Padding, Paul I., 2010, Predicting Wood Duck Harvest Rates in Eastern North America: Journal of Wildlife Management, v. 74, no. 7, p. 1575–1579.

Bartlett, H. Thomas, 2010, 2009 Banding at Kelleys Island, Ohio: North American Bird Bander, v. 35, no. 1, p. 43–44.

Bartlett, H. Thomas, 2010, 2009 Banding at Springville Marsh State Nature Preserve, Ohio: North American Bird Bander, v. 35, no. 1, p. 41–43.

Black, Jeffrey M., Lee, Derek E., and Ward, David H., 2010, Foraging home ranges of Black Brant Branta *bernicla nigricans* during spring stopover at Humboldt Bay, California, USA: Wildfowl, v. 60, p. 85–94.

Bluso-Demers, Jill D., Ackerman, Joshua T., and Takekawa, John Y., 2010, Colony attendance patterns by mated Forster's Terns *Sterna forsteri* using an automated data-logging receiver system: Ardea, v. 98, no. 1, p. 59–65.

Bomberger Brown, Mary, and Jorgensen, Joel G., 2010, Observations of piping plovers (*Charadrius melodus*) color banded in Nebraska and re-sighted on the United States Gulf Coast: Nebraska Bird Review, v. 78, no. 1, p. 30–34.

Bowman, Jeff, Badzinski, Debbie S., and Brooks, Ronald J., 2010, The numerical response of breeding Northern Saw-whet Owls *Aegolius acadicus* suggests nomadism: Journal of Ornithology, v. 151, no. 2, p. 499–506.

Brooks, Elizabeth, and Sherony, Dominic, 2010, Some Note on the Fall Migration of Bicknell's and Gray-cheeked Thrushes in New York State and Eastern United States: Kingbird, v. 60, no. 1, p. 7–14.

Brooks, Elizabeth W., 2010, Atlantic Flyway review: spring 2009: North American Bird Bander, v. 35, no. 2, p. 84–98.

Butler, Christopher J., Pham, Lisa H., Stinedurf, Jill N., and others, 2010, Yellow Rails Wintering in Oklahoma: Wilson Journal of Ornithology, v. 122, no. 2, p. 385–387.

Calabuig, C. P., Green, A. J., Menegheti, J. O., and others, 2010, Phenology of Coscoroba Swan (*Coscoroba coscoroba*) in southern Brazil and their movements to Argentina: Ornitologia Neotropical, v. 21, no. 4, p. 555–566.

Calvert, Anna M., Woodcock, John, and Mccracken, Jon D., 2010, Contrasting Seasonal Survivorship of Two Migratory Songbirds Wintering in Threatened Mangrove Forests: Avian Conservation and Ecology, v. 5, no. 1, article 2.

Cimprich, David A., Strebe, Wayne G., and Comolli, Kristin A., 2010, Longevity of the black-capped vireo: Bulletin of the Texas Ornithological Society, v. 43, no. 1–2, p. 41–44.

Clarke, Travis C. R., Diamond, Antony W., and Chardine, John W., 2010, Origin of Canadian Razorbills (*Alca torda*) Wintering in the Outer Bay of Fundy Confirmed by Radio-Tracking: Waterbirds, v. 33, no. 4, p. 541–545.

Cohen, Jonathan B., Karpanty, Sarah M., and Fraser, James D., 2010, Habitat selection and behavior of red knots on the New Jersey Atlantic Coast during spring stopover: Condor, v. 112, no. 4, p. 655–662.

Collier, Travis C., Kirschel, Alexander N., and Taylor, Charles E., 2010, Acoustic localization of antbirds in a Mexican rainforest using a wireless sensor network: Journal of the Acoustical Society of America, v. 128, no. 1, p. 182–189.

Coulon, Aurelie, Fitzpatrick, John W., Bowman, Reed, and others, 2010, Effects of Habitat Fragmentation on Effective Dispersal of Florida Scrub-Jays: Conservation Biology, v. 24, no. 4, p. 1080–1088.

Coulson, Jennifer O., Taft, Stephen J., and Coulson, Thomas D., 2010, Gastrointestinal parasites of the swallow-tailed kite (*Elanoides forficatus*), including a report of lesions associated with the nematode *dispharynx* sp: Journal of Raptor Research, v. 44, no. 3, p. 208–214.

Davies, J. Chris, and Pollard, Bruce, 2010, Ontario Cooperative Banding Program 2009 banding results: Ontario Bird Banding, v. 41, p. 28–29.

Dieter, Charles D., Anderson, Bobby J., Gleason, Jeffrey S., and others, 2010, Late summer movements by giant Canada geese in relation to a September hunting season: Human-Wildlife Interactions, v. 4, no. 2, p. 232–246.

Dieter, Charles D., Gleason, Jeffrey S., Anderson, Bobby J., and others, 2010, Survival and harvest characteristics of giant Canada geese in eastern South Dakota, 2000–2004: Human-Wildlife Interactions , v. 4, no. 2, p. 213–231.

Diuk-Wasser, Maria A., Molaei, Goudarz, Simpson, Jennifer E., and others, 2010, Avian Communal Roosts as Amplification Foci for West Nile Virus in Urban Areas in Northeastern United States: American Journal of Tropical Medicine and Hygiene, v. 82, no. 2, p. 337–343.

Dorr, Brian S., Aderman, Tony, Butchko, Peter H., and others, 2010, Management effects on breeding and foraging numbers and movements of double-crested cormorants in the Les Cheneaux Islands, Lake Huron, Michigan: Journal of Great Lakes Research, v. 36, no. 2, p. 224–231.

Dugger, Bruce D., Finger, Richard, and Melvin, Stefani L., 2010, Nesting ecology of Mottled Ducks Anas fulvigula in interior Florida, USA: Wildfowl, v. 60, p. 95–105.

Dunn, Erica H., Brewer, A. David, Diamond, Antony W., and others, 2010, Canadian Atlas of Bird Banding. Volume 4: Shorebirds, 1921–1995, Canadian Atlas of Bird Banding. Volume 4: Shorebirds, 1921–1995. [IV. Series: Special Publication (Canadian Wildlife Service).]: Gatineau, Environment Canada, 104 p.

Farmer, C. J., Safi, K., Barber, D. R., and others, 2010, Efficacy of Migration Counts for Monitoring Continental Populations of Raptors: An Example using the Osprey (*Pandion haliaetus*): Auk, v. 127, no. 4, p. 863–870.

Finnegan, Sue, 2010, Atlantic Flyway review: region 1 (Northeast)—Fall 2009 report: North American Bird Bander, v. 35, no. 3, p. 147–154.

Flesch, Aaron D., Epps, Clinton W., Cain, James W., and others, 2010, Potential effects of the United States-Mexico border fence on wildlife: Conservation Biology, v. 24, no. 1, p. 171–181.

Flockhart, D. T. Tyler, 2010, Timing of events on the breeding grounds for five species of sympatric warblers: Journal of Field Ornithology, v. 81, no. 4, p. 373–382.

Flowers, Thomas L., 2010, Hybrid Vermivora warbler banded in Meade County, Kansas: Kansas Ornithological Society Bulletin, v. 61, no. 4, p. 29–31.

Franke, Alastair, Setterington, Mike, Court, Gordon, and others, 2010, Long-term trends of persistent organochlorine pollutants, occupancy and reproductive success in peregrine falcons (*Falco peregrinus tundrius*) breeding near rankin inlet, Nunavut, Canada: Arctic, v. 63, no. 4, p. 442–450.

Frey, Robert I., Stephens, Jaime L., and Alexander, John D., 2010, Klamath Bird Observatory banding in 2009: North American Bird Bander, v. 35, no. 1, p. 48–50.

Greenberg, Russell, Olsen, Brian J., and Etterson, Matthew A., 2010, Patterns of seasonal abundance and social segregation in inland and coastal plain swamp sparrows in a delaware tidal marsh: Condor, v. 112, no. 1, p. 159–167.

Gregoire, John A., 2010, Atlantic Flyway review: region II (North Central) fall 2009: North American Bird Bander, v. 35, no. 1, p. 32–40.

Groh, Terri, and Wernaart, Martin, 2010, Banding in Ontario: 2009: Ontario Bird Banding, v. 41, p. 1–19.

Handel, Colleen M., and Gill, Robert E. Jr, 2010, Wayward Youth: Trans-Beringian Movement and Differential Southward Migration by Juvenile Sharp-tailed Sandpipers: Arctic, v. 63, no. 3, p. 273–288.

Harrington, B. A., Koch, S., Niles, L. K., and others, 2010, Red Knots with Different Winter Destinations: Differential Use of an Autumn Stopover Area: Waterbirds, v. 33, no. 3, p. 357–363.

Hilton, Bill Jr., 2010, Broad-billed Hummingbird (*Cynanthus latirostris*): First South Carolina Banding and Photographic Record: Chat (Raleigh), v. 74, no. 2, p. 44–47.

Hinnebusch, Daniel M., Therrien, Jean-Francois, Valiquette, Marc-Andre, and others, 2010, Survival, site fidelity, and population trends of American kestrels wintering in Southwestern Florida: Wilson Journal of Ornithology, v. 122, no. 3, p. 475–483.

Houston, C. Stuart, 2010, Early Saskatchewan bird banders: Memoirs of the Nuttall Ornithological Club, v. 17, p. 319–354.

Hupp, Jerry W., Hodges, John I. Jr, Conant, Bruce P., and others, 2010, Winter distribution, movements, and annual survival of radiomarked vancouver Canada geese in southeast Alaska: Journal of Wildlife Management, v. 74, no. 2, p. 274–284.

Imlay, T., Crowley, J., Argue, A., and others, 2010, Survival, dispersal and early migration movements of captive-bred juvenile eastern loggerhead shrikes (*Lanius ludovicianus migrans*): Biological Conservation, v. 143, no. 11, p. 2578–2582.

Ingold, Danny J., Dooley, James L., and Cavender, Nicole, 2010, Nest-site Fidelity in Grassland Birds on Mowed Versus Unmowed Areas on a Reclaimed Surface Mine: Northeastern Naturalist, v. 17, no. 1, p. 125–134.

Jacob, Benjamin G., Burkett-Cadena, Nathan D., Luvall, Jeffrey C., and others, 2010, Developing GIS-based eastern equine encephalitis vector-host models in Tuskegee, Alabama: International Journal of Health Geographics, v. 9, no. 12, p. 1–16.

Johnson, M., Clarkson, P., Goldstein, M. I., and others, 2010, Seasonal movements, winter range use, and migratory connectivity of the black oystercatcher: Condor, v. 112, no. 4, p. 731–743.

King, D. Tommy, Blackwell, Bradley F., Dorr, Brian S., and others, 2010, Effects of aquaculture on migration and movement patterns of double-crested cormorants: Human-Wildlife Interactions, v. 4, no. 1, p. 77–86.

Kissling, Michelle L., Lewis, Stephen B., and Pendleton, Grey, 2010, Factors influencing the detectability of forest owls in Southeastern Alaska: Condor, v. 112, no. 3, p. 539–548.

Lamble, David R., 2010, 2009 Banding highlights for Dave Lamble and crew at or near Fergus, Ontario: Ontario Bird Banding, v. 41, p. 30.

Lorenz, T. J., and Sullivan, K. A., 2010, Comparison of survey methods for monitoring Clark's Nutcrackers and predicting dispersal of whitebark pine seeds: Journal of Field Ornithology, v. 81, no. 4, p. 430–441.

Mahoney, Peter J., Meyer, Kenneth D., Zimmerman, Gina M., and others, 2010, An Aquatic Bal-Chatri for Trapping Snail Kites (*Rostrhamus sociabilis*): Southeastern Naturalist, v. 9, no. 4, p. 721–730.

Marzluff, John M., Walls, Jeff, Cornell, Heather N., and others, 2010, Lasting recognition of threatening people by wild American crows: Animal Behaviour, v. 79 , no. 3, p. 699–707.

Meese, Robert J., and Simmons, Stephen B., 2010, Safe and effective methods for trapping and color banding tricolored blackbirds in the Central Valley of California: California Fish and Game, v. 96, no. 1, p. 23–35.

Mestre, Luiz Augusto Macedo, Roos, Andrei Langeloh, and Nunes, Maria Flavia, 2010, Analysis of birds banded abroad and recovered in Brazil from 1927 to 2006: Ornithologia, v. 4, no. 1, p. 15–35.

Miller, David A., and Otis, David L., 2010, Calibrating Recruitment Estimates for Mourning Doves From Harvest Age Ratios: Journal of Wildlife Management, v. 74, no. 5, p. 1070–1079.

Mitchell, Greg W., Taylor, Philip D., and Warkentin, Ian G., 2010, Assessing the function of broad-scale movements made by juvenile songbirds prior to migration: Condor, v. 112, no. 4, p. 644–654.

Mock, Douglas W., and Schwagmeyer, P. L., 2010, Not the nice sparrow: the 2007 Margaret Morse Nice Lecture: Wilson Journal of Ornithology, v. 122, no. 2, p. 207–216.

Morris, Gail, Conner, L. Mike, and Oli, Madan K., 2010, Use of supplemental northern bobwhite (*Colinus virginianus*) food by non-target species: Florida Field Naturalist, v. 38, no. 3, p. 99–105.

Nol, Erica, Williams, Simone, and Sandercock, Brett K., 2010, Natal philopatry and apparent survival of juvenile semipalmated plovers: Wilson Journal of Ornithology, v. 122, no. 1, p. 23–28.

O'neal, Benjamin J., Stafford, Joshua D., and Larkin, Ronald P., 2010, Waterfowl on weather radar: applying ground-truth to classify and quantify bird movements: Journal of Field Ornithology, v. 81, no. 1, p. 71–82.

Oppel, Steffen, and Powell, Abby N., 2010, Age-specific survival estimates of king eiders derived from satellite telemetry : Condor, v. 112, no. 2, p. 323–330.

Ortego, Brent, 2010, Capture rates of shorebirds at managed and riverine freshwater wetlands near the Central Texas Coast: Bulletin of the Texas Ornithological Society, v. 43, no. 1–2, p. 25–29.

—, 2010, IBBA Annual report of birds banded, 2009: North American Bird Bander, v. 35, no. 2, p. 112–119.

Osborne, Carrie E., Swift, Bryan L., and Baldassarre, Guy A., 2010, Fate of captive-reared and released mallards on eastern Long Island, New York: Human-Wildlife Interactions, v. 4, no. 2, p. 266–274.

Overton, Cory T., Casazza, Michael L., and Coates, Peter S., 2010, Scale-dependent associations of band-tailed pigeon counts at mineral sites: Northwestern Naturalist, v. 91, no. 3, p. 299–308.

Potvin, Annette J., and Bishop, Christine A., 2010, An endangered population and roadside mortality: three western Yellow-breasted Chat fatalities in the south Okanagan valley, British Columbia: British Columbia Birds, v. 20, p. 45–48.

Powell, Luke L., Hodgman, Thomas P., and Glanz, William E., 2010, Home ranges of rusty blackbirds breeding in wetlands: how much would buffers from timber harvest protect habitat?: Condor, v. 112, no. 4, p. 834–840.

Prescott, David R.C., Engley, Lance C., and Sturgess, Dan, 2010, Implementation of the Alberta Piping Plover Recovery Plan, 2005–2010: final program report: Alberta Species at Risk Report, v. 129, 27 p.

Priestley, Lisa Takats, Priestley, Chuck, Collister, Douglas M., and others, 2010, Encounters of northern saw-whet owls (*Aegolius acadicus*) from banding stations in Alberta and Saskatchewan, Canada: Journal of Raptor Research, v. 44, no. 4, p. 300–310.

Reynolds, Michelle H., Hatfield, Jeff S., Crampton, Lisa H., and others, 2010, Circadian habitat use, home range and behaviour of Laysan Teal Anas laysanensis: Wildfowl, v. 60, p. 106–123.

Rice, Mindy B., Haukos, David A., Dubovsky, James A., and others, 2010, Continental Survival and Recovery Rates of Northern Pintails Using Band-Recovery Data: Journal of Wildlife Management, v. 74, no. 4, p. 778–787.

Robbins, Chandler S., 2010, Atlantic Flyway review: Region IV Piedmont-Coastal Plain, Fall 2009: North American Bird Bander, v. 35, no. 2, p. 99–109.

Robert, M., Vaillancourt, M. A., and Drapeau, P., 2010, Characteristics of nest cavities of Barrow's Goldeneyes in eastern Canada: Journal of Field Ornithology, v. 81, no. 3, p. 287–293.

Robinson, W. Douglas, Hau, Michaela, Klasing, Kirk C., and others, 2010, Diversification of life histories in new world birds: Auk, v. 127, no. 2, p. 253–262.

Roche, Erin A., Arnold, Todd W., and Cuthbert, Francesca J., 2010, Apparent nest abandonment as evidence of breeding-season mortality in great lakes piping plovers (*Charadrius melodus*): Auk, v. 127, no. 2, p. 402–410.

Roche, Erin A., Arnold, Todd W., Stucker, Jennifer H., and others, 2010, Colored plastic and metal leg bands do not affect survival of piping plover chicks: Journal of Field Ornithology, v. 81, no. 3, p. 317–324.

Roy, Charlotte, Sousa, Christine, Rave, David, and others, 2010, Movements, survival, and refuge use by ring-necked ducks after fledging in Minnesota: Minnesota Department of Natural Resources Summaries of Wildlife Research Findings, v. 2009, p. 79–88.

Rush, Scott A., Mordecai, Rua, Woodrey, Mark S., and others, 2010, Prey and Habitat Influences the Movement of Clapper Rails in Northern Gulf Coast Estuaries: Waterbirds, v. 33, no. 3, p. 389–396.

Sakai, Walter H., 2010, Western regional news. WBBA's annual banding report for 2009: North American Bird Bander, v. 35, no. 3, p. 161–171.

Santamaria, Carlos A., Kelley, Samuel, Schulz, Gerral G., and others, 2010, Polymerase Chain Reaction-Based Sex Identification in the Greater Roadrunner: Journal of Wildlife Management, v. 74, no. 6, p. 1395–1399.

Saracco, James F., Royle, J. Andrew, Desante, David F., and others, 2010, Modeling spatial variation in avian survival and residency probabilities: Ecology (Washington D.C.), v. 91, no. 7, p. 1885–1891.

Sedinger, James S., White, Gary C., Espinosa, Shawn, and others, 2010, Assessing compensatory versus additive harvest mortality: an example using greater sage-grouse: Journal of Wildlife Management, v. 74, no. 2, p. 326–332.

Seewagen, Chad L., Slayton, Eric J., and Guglielmo, Christopher G., 2010, Passerine migrant stopover duration and spatial behaviour at an urban stopover site: Acta Oecologica, v. 36, no. 5, p. 484–492.

Shoji, Akiko M., and Gaston, Anthony J., 2010, Comparing Methods for Monitoring Nest Attendance in Ancient Murrelets: Waterbirds, v. 33, no. 2, p. 260–263.

Smith, Bradley S., 2010, Patterns of nonbreeding snowy plover (*Charadrius alexandrinus*), piping plover (*C. melodus*), and red knot (*Calidris canutus*) distribution in Northwest Florida: Florida Field Naturalist, v. 38, no. 2, p. 43–54.

Smith, Brian, 2010, Banded white-rumped sandpiper in Brown county: Loon, v. 82, no. 1, p. 46.

Soehren, Eric C., 2010, Summary of the Wehle MAPS Banding Station in Bullock County, Alabama (2006–2010): North American Bird Bander, v. 35, no. 3, p. 140–142.

Stoskopf, Michael K., Mulcahy, Daniel M., and Esler, Daniel, 2010, Evaluation of a Portable Automated Serum Chemistry Analyzer for Field Assessment of Harlequin Ducks, *Histrionicus histrionicus*: Veterinary Medicine International, v. 2010, p. 1–5.

Streby, Henry M., and Andersen, David E., 2010, When is Success not Success? When it's Songbird Nesting Success: Integrative and Comparative Biology, v. 50, no. Suppl. 1, p. E170.

Stucker, Jennifer H., Cuthbert, Francesca J., Winn, Brad, and others, 2010, Distribution of Non-Breeding Great Lakes Piping Plovers (*Charadrius melodus*) along Atlantic and Gulf of Mexico Coastlines: Ten Years of Band Sightings: Waterbirds, v. 33, no. 1, p. 22–32.

Takekawa, J. Y., Prosser, D. J., Newman, S. H., and others, 2010, Victims and vectors: highly pathogenic avian influenza H5N1 and the ecology of wild birds: Avian Biology Research, v. 3, no. 2, p. 51–73.

Templeton, Christopher N., Akcay, Caglar, Campbell, S. Elizabeth, and others, 2010, Juvenile sparrows preferentially eavesdrop on adult song interactions: Proceedings of the Royal Society Biological Sciences Series B, v. 277, no. 1680, p. 447–453.

Tremblay, Junior A., Ibarzabal, Jacques, and Savard, Jean-Pierre L., 2010, Foraging ecology of black-backed woodpeckers (*Picoides arcticus*) in unburned eastern boreal forest stands: Canadian Journal of Forest Research, v. 40, no. 5, p. 991–999.

Tucker, James W. Jr, Schrott, Gregory R., Delany, Michael F., and others, 2010, Metapopulation structure, population trends, and status of Florida grasshopper sparrows: Journal of Field Ornithology, v. 81, no. 3, p. 267–277.

Underwood, Emma C., Viers, Joshua H., Quinn, James F., and others, 2010, Using Topography to Meet Wildlife and Fuels Treatment Objectives in Fire-Suppressed Landscapes: Environmental Management, v. 46, no. 5, p. 809–819.

Van Buskirk, Josh, Mulvihill, Robert S., and Leberman, Robert C., 2010, Declining body sizes in North American birds associated with climate change: Oikos, v. 119, no. 6, p. 1047–1055.

Wick, Jill M., and Wang, Yong, 2010, Habitat use of two songbird species in pine-hardwood forests treated with prescribed burning and thinning: first year results: U.S. Forest Service General Technical Report SRS-121, p. 501–504.

Womack, Ellie, 2010, History of hummingbird banding in the United States: North American Bird Bander, v. 35, no. 1, p. 15–21.

Wood, Douglas R., and Tucker, Jona A., 2010, Spring migration banding at Tishomingo National Wildlife Refuge, Johnston county, Oklahoma, 2004–2007: Bulletin of the Oklahoma Ornithological Society, v. 43, no. 1, p. 1–6.

Yates, Michael A., Fuller, Mark R., Henny, Charles J., and others, 2010, Wintering area DDE source to migratory white-faced ibis revealed by satellite telemetry and prey sampling: Ecotoxicology, v. 19, no. 1, p. 153–162.

Young, L. C., 2010, Inferring colonization history and dispersal patterns of a long-lived seabird by combining genetic and empirical data: Journal of Zoology (London), v. 281, no. 4, p. 232–240.

Zimmerman, G. S., Link, W. A., Conroy, M. J., and others, 2010, Estimating migratory game-bird productivity by integrating age ratio and banding data: Wildlife Research, v. 37, no. 7, p. 612–622.

Zimpfer, Nathan, and Popko, Richard, 2010, Western Canada Cooperative Waterfowl Banding Program Willow Lake, Northwest Territories report 2009: North American Bird Bander, v. 35, no. 1, p. 50.

2009

2008 WBBA annual summary of birds banded, 2009, North American Bird Bander, v. 34, no. 3, p. 145–155.

Atlantic Flyway Review: Region III (Western Ridge)—Fall 2008, 2009, North American Bird Bander, v. 34, no. 4, p. 187–195.

Aaltonen, Kristen, Bryant, Andrew A., Hostetler, Jeffrey A., and others, 2009, Reintroducing endangered Vancouver Island marmots: Survival and cause-specific mortality rates of captive-born versus wild-born individuals: Biological Conservation, v. 142, no. 10, p. 2181–2190.

Abstracts, 2009, EBBA's 85th Annual Meeting, 27–29 March 2009: North American Bird Bander, v. 34, no. 2, p. 74–77.

Anich, Nicholas M., Benson, Thomas J., and Bednarz, James C., 2009, Effect of radio transmitters on return rates of Swainson's warblers: Journal of Field Ornithology, v. 80, no. 2, p. 206–211.

Anonymous, 2009, Inland Bird Banding Association 2009 Annual Meeting, St. Louis, Missouri: North American Bird Bander, v. 34, no. 3, p. 128–134.

—-, 2009, Western Bird Banding Association 2009 Annual Meeting: North American Bird Bander, v. 34, no. 3, p. 135–145.

Bassett, Fred, and Cubie, Doreen, 2009, Wintering hummingbirds in Alabama and Florida: species diversity, sex and age ratios, and site fidelity: Journal of Field Ornithology, v. 80, no. 2, p. 154–162.

Benedict, Lauryn, 2009, Long-term occupancy of home ranges and short-term changes in use of habitat by California towhees (*Pipilo crissalis*): Southwestern Naturalist, v. 54, no. 3, p. 324–330.

Bisson, Isabelle-Anne, Butler, Luke K., Hayden, Tim J., and others, 2009, No energetic cost of anthropogenic disturbance in a songbird: Proceedings of the Royal Society Biological Sciences Series B, v. 276, no. 1658, p. 961–969.

Blomberg, Erik J., Tefft, Brian C., Endrulat, Erik G., and others, 2009, Predicting landscape-scale habitat distribution for ruffed grouse *Bonasa umbellus* using presence-only data: Wildlife Biology, v. 15, no. 4, p. 380–394.

Bond, Monica L., Lee, Derek E., Siegel, Rodney B., and others, 2009, Habitat Use and Selection by California Spotted Owls in a Postfire Landscape: Journal of Wildlife Management, v. 73, no. 7, p. 1116–1124.

Breininger, David R., Nichols, James D., Carter, Geoffrey M., and others, 2009, Habitat-specific breeder survival of Florida Scrub-Jays: inferences from multistate models: Ecology (Washington D C), v. 90, no. 11, p. 3180–3189.

Brittain, Ross A., Meretsky, Vicky J., Gwinn, Jess A., and others, 2009, Northern saw-whet owl (*Aegolius acadicus*) autumn migration magnitude and demographics in south-central Indiana: Journal of Raptor Research, v. 43, no. 3, p. 199–209.

Carfagno, Gerardo L., and Weatherhead, Patrick J., 2009, Ratsnake response to bottomland flooding: implications for avian nest predation: Acta Herpetologica, v. 4, no. 2, p. 191–194.

Casazza, M.L., Overton, C.T., Farinha, M.A., Torregrosa, Alicia, Fleskes, J.P., Miller, M.R., Sedinger, J.S., and Kolada, Eric, 2009, Ecology of greater sage-grouse in the Bi-State Planning Area Final Report, September 2007: U.S. Geological Survey Open-File Report 2009-1113, 50 p.

Cimprich, David A., 2009, Effect of count duration on abundance estimates of black-capped vireos: Journal of Field Ornithology, v. 80, no. 1, p. 94–100.

Cimprich, David A., Sexton, Charles W., Mcdowell, P. Kelly, and others, 2009, Long-distance dispersal records for the black-capped vireo: Bulletin of the Texas Ornithological Society, v. 42, no. 1–2, p. 44–47.

Cohen, J. B., Karpanty, S. M., Fraser, J. D., and others, 2009, Residence Probability and Population Size of Red Knots During Spring Stopover in the Mid-Atlantic Region of the United States: Journal of Wildlife Management, v. 73, no. 6, p. 939–945.

Collins, Bridget M., Williams, Christopher K., and Castelli, Paul M., 2009, Reproduction and microhabitat selection in a sharply declining northern bobwhite population: Wilson Journal of Ornithology, v. 121, no. 4, p. 688–695.

Cooper, Sheldon J., 2009, Bird banding records for Heckrodt Wetland Reserve, Menasha, Wisconsin: Passenger Pigeon, v. 71, no. 1, p. 33–36.

Craves, Julie A., 2009, A fifteen-year study of fall stopover patterns of Catharus thrushes at an inland, urban site: Wilson Journal of Ornithology, v. 121, no. 1, p. 112–118.

Dalley, Kate L., Taylor, Philip D., and Shutler, Dave, 2009, Success of migratory songbirds breeding in harvested boreal forests of northwestern Newfoundland: Condor, v. 111, no. 2, p. 314–325.

Davis, S. K., 2009, Renesting intervals and duration of the incubation and nestling periods of Sprague's Pipits: Journal of Field Ornithology, v. 80, no. 3, p. 265–269.

Davis, S. K., and Fisher, R. J., 2009, Post-fledging Movements of Sprague's Pipit: Wilson Journal of Ornithology, v. 121, no. 1, p. 198–202.

Diefenbach, Duane R., Casalena, Mary Jo, Schiavone, Michael V., and others, 2009, Loss of butt-end leg bands on male wild turkeys: Journal of Wildlife Management, v. 73, no. 6, p. 996–999.

Dieter, C. D., Murano, R. J., and Galster, D., 2009, Capture and mortality rates of ducks in selected trap types: Journal of Wildlife Management, v. 73, no. 7, p. 1223–1228.

Dieter, Charles D., and Anderson, Bobby J., 2009, Molt migration by giant Canada geese in eastern South Dakota: Human-Wildlife Conflicts, v. 3, no. 2, p. 260–270.

—, 2009, Reproductive Success and Brood Movements of Giant Canada Geese in Eastern South Dakota: American Midland Naturalist, v. 162, no. 2, p. 373–381.

Duncan, James R., Swengel, Scott R., and Swengel, Ann B., 2009, Correlations of Northern Saw-whet Owl *Aegolius acadicus* calling indices from surveys in southern Wisconsin, USA, with owl and small mammal surveys in Manitoba, Canada, 1986–2006: Ardea, v. 97, no. 4, Sp. Iss. SI, p. 489–496.

Dwyer, James F., and Mannan, R. William, 2009, Return rates of aluminum versus plastic leg bands from electrocuted Harris's hawks (*Parabuteo unicinctus*): Journal of Raptor Research, v. 43, no. 2, p. 152–154.

Elliott, Kyle Hamish, and Gaston, Anthony J., 2009, Accuracy of Depth Recorders: Waterbirds, v. 32, no. 1, p. 183–191.

Emslie, Steven D., Weske, John S., Browne, Micou M., and others, 2009, Population Trends in Royal and Sandwich Terns Along the Mid-Atlantic Seaboard, USA, 1975–2005: Waterbirds, v. 32, no. 1, p. 54–63.

Fajardo, Natalia, Strong, Allan M., Perlut, Noah G., and others, 2009, Natal and breeding dispersal of bobolinks (*Dolichonyx oryzivorus*) and savannah sparrows (*Passerculus sandwichensis*) in an agricultural landscape: Auk, v. 126, no. 2, p. 310–318.

Finnegan, Sue, 2009, Atlantic Flyway review: region 1 (northeast)—Fall 2008 report: North American Bird Bander, v. 34, no. 2, p. 77–83.

Fisher, Harold, 2009, Summary of northern saw-whet owl banding—2008: Blue Jay, v. 67, no. 1, p. 34–36.

Flint, Paul L., Ozaki, Kiyoaki, Pearce, John M., and others, 2009, Breeding-season sympatry facilitates genetic exchange among allopatric wintering populations of northern pintails in Japan and California: Condor, v. 111, no. 4, p. 591–598.

Gill, Robert E., Jr. , Tibbitts, T. Lee, Douglas, David C., and others, 2009, Extreme endurance flights by landbirds crossing the Pacific Ocean: ecological corridor rather than barrier?: Proceedings of the Royal Society Biological Sciences Series B, v. 276, no. 1656, p. 447–458.

Goddard, Alicia D., and Dawson, Russell D., 2009, Factors influencing the survival of neonate sharp-tailed grouse *Tympanuchus phasianellus*: Wildlife Biology, v. 15, no. 1, p. 60–67.

Gonzalez-Solis, Jacob, Felicisimo, Angel, Fox, James W., and others, 2009, Influence of sea surface winds on shearwater migration detours: Marine Ecology Progress Series, v. 391, p. 221–230.

Griffin, Amanda D., Durbian, Francis E., Easterla, David A., and others, 2009, Spatial ecology of breeding least bitterns in northwest Missouri: Wilson Journal of Ornithology, v. 121, no. 3, p. 521–527.

Hilton, Bill Jr., 2009, Confirming fall migration routes for South Carolina ruby-throated hummingbirds, *Archilochus colubris*: North American Bird Bander, v. 34, no. 2, p. 41–45.

Hobson, Keith A., Wunder, Michael B., Van Wilgenburg, Steven L., and others, 2009, A method for investigating population declines of migratory birds using stable isotopes: origins of harvested lesser scaup in North America: PLOS ONE, v. 4, no. 11, article e7915, 10 p.

Holt, R. Douglas, Burger, L. Wes Jr, Dinsmore, Stephen J., and others, 2009, Estimating duration of short-term acute effects of capture handling and radiomarking : Journal of Wildlife Management, v. 73, no. 6, p. 989–995.

Hull, Joshua M., Ernest, Holly B., Harley, Jill A., and others, 2009, Differential migration between discrete populations of juvenile red-tailed hawks (*Buteo jamaicensis*): Auk, v. 126, no. 2, p. 389–396.

Humberg, Lee. A., Devault, Travis L., and Rhodes, Olin E. Jr, 2009, Survival and cause-specific mortality of wild turkeys in northern Indiana: American Midland Naturalist, v. 161, no. 2, p. 313–322.

Humphries, Elizabeth M., Peters, Jeffrey L., Jonsson, Jon E., and others, 2009, Genetic differentiation between sympatric and allopatric wintering populations of snow geese: Wilson Journal of Ornithology, v. 121, no. 4, p. 730–738.

Ingold, Danny J., Dooley, James L., and Cavender, Nicole, 2009, Return rates of breeding Henslow's sparrows on mowed versus unmowed areas on a reclaimed surface mine: Wilson Journal of Ornithology, v. 121, no. 1, p. 194–197.

Jamison, Brent E., and Alleger, Max R., 2009, Status of Missouri greater prairie-chicken populations and preliminary observations from ongoing translocations and telemetry: Grouse News, v. 38, p. 15–24.

Jimenez Perez, Luis C., De La Cueva, Horacio, Molina-Peralta, Fernando, and others, 2009, Birds of Estero de Punta Banda, Baja California, Mexico: Acta Zoologica Mexicana Nueva Serie, v. 25, no. 3, p. 589–608.

Johnson, Brian, and Usyk, Lena M., 2009, Unusual recovery and longevity record of a banded Le Conte's sparrow: North American Bird Bander, v. 34, no. 2, p. 46–49.

Johnson, Matthew, Conklin, Jesse R., Johnson, Branden L., and others, 2009, Behavior and reproductive success of rock sandpipers breeding on the Yukon-Kuskokwim River Delta, Alaska: Wilson Journal of Ornithology, v. 121, no. 2, p. 328–337.

Kenow, Kevin P., Adams, David, Schoch, Nina, and others, 2009, Migration Patterns and Wintering Range of Common Loons Breeding in the Northeastern United States: Waterbirds, v. 32, no. 2, p. 234–247.

Kleen, Vernon, Coogan, Steve, Edmonds, Thad, and others, 2009, Fall 2009 report from Margery Adams Bird Banding Station (MABBS)—394–0893 Springfield, IL: North American Bird Bander, v. 34, no. 4, p. 198–199.

Legagneux, Pierre, Blaize, Christine, Latraube, Franck, and others, 2009, Variation in home-range size and movements of wintering dabbling ducks: Journal of Ornithology, v. 150, no. 1, p. 183–193.

Lehnen, Sarah E., and Rodewald, Amanda D., 2009, Dispersal, interpatch movements, and survival in a shrubland breeding bird community: Journal of Field Ornithology, v. 80, no. 3, p. 242–252.

—-, 2009, Investigating area-sensitivity in shrubland birds: responses to patch size in a forested landscape: Forest Ecology and Management, v. 257, no. 11, p. 2308–2316.

Lyons, Eddie K., Collier, Bret A., Silvy, Nova J., and others, 2009, Breeding and non-breeding survival of lesser prairie-chickens *Tympanuchus pallidicinctus* in Texas, USA: Wildlife Biology, v. 15, no. 1, p. 89–96.

Martin, Kate H., Lindberg, Mark S., Schmutz, Joel A., and others, 2009, Lesser scaup breeding probability and female survival on the Yukon Flats, Alaska: Journal of Wildlife Management, v. 73, no. 6, p. 914–923.

Martin, Michaela, Camfield, Alaine F., and Martin, Kathy, 2009, Demography of an alpine population of savannah sparrows: Journal of Field Ornithology, v. 80, no. 3, p. 253–264.

Mcintyre, Carol L., Douglas, David C., and Adams, Layne G., 2009, Movements of juvenile gyrfalcons from western and interior Alaska following departure from their natal areas: Journal of Raptor Research, v. 43, no. 2, p. 99–109.

Meese, Robert J., 2009, An efficient and effective method for sealing Darvic color bands: North American Bird Bander, v. 34, no. 4, p. 175–178.

Mestre, Luis A. M., and Bierregaard, Richard O., 2009, The role of Amazonian rivers for wintering ospreys (*Pandion haliaetus*): clues from North American band recoveries in Brazil between 1937 and 2006: Studies on Neotropical Fauna and Environment, v. 44, no. 3, p. 141–147.

Mitchell, Greg W., Warkentin, Ian G., and Taylor, Philip D., 2009, Movement of juvenile songbirds in harvested boreal forest: assessing residency time and landscape connectivity: Avian Conservation and Ecology, v. 4, no. 1, article 5.

Molina, Kathy C., Garrett, Kimball L., and Larson, Keith W., 2009, The winter distribution of the western gull-billed tern (*Gelochelidon nilotica vanrossemi*): Western Birds, v. 40, no. 1, p. 2–20.

Morrison, Kyle W., Hipfner, J. Mark, Gjerdrum, Carina, and others, 2009, Wing length and mass at fledging predict local juvenile survival and age at first return in tufted puffins: Condor, v. 111, no. 3, p. 433–441.

Mosbech, Anders, Merkel, Flemming, Boertmann, David, and others, 2009, Thick-billed murre studies in Disko Bay (Ritenbenk), West Greenland: Neri Technical Report, v. 749, p. 1–59.

Olson, David, Warren, Jeff, and Reed, Tom, 2009, Satellite-tracking the seasonal locations of Trumpeter Swans Cygnus buccinator from Red Rock Lakes National Wildlife Refuge, Montana, USA: Wildfowl, v. 59, p. 3–16.

Oppel, S., Dickson, D. L., and Powell, A. N., 2009, International importance of the eastern Chukchi Sea as a staging area for migrating king eiders: Polar Biology, v. 32, no. 5, p. 775–783.

Oppel, Steffen, and Powell, Abby N., 2009, Does winter region affect spring arrival time and body mass of king eiders in northern Alaska?: Polar Biology, v. 32, no. 8, p. 1203–1209.

Ortega, Joseph C., and Ortega, Catherine P., 2009, Sex ratios and survival probabilities of brown-headed cowbirds (*Molothrus ater*) in southwest Colorado: Auk, v. 126, no. 2, p. 268–277.

Ortego, Brent, 2009, IBBA Annual Report of birds banded, 2008: summary of banding reported from the IBBA region for 2008: North American Bird Bander, v. 34, no. 2, p. 84–90.

Ortego, Brent, Gregory, Chris, Mabie, David, and others, 2009, Texas bald eagles: Bulletin of the Texas Ornithological Society, v. 42, no. 1–2, Sp. Iss. SI, p. 1–17.

Parish, Christopher N., Hunt, W. Grainger, Feltes, Edward, and others, 2009, Lead Exposure Among a Reintroduced Population of California Condors in Northern Arizona and Southern Utah, *in* Watson, Richard T., Fuller, Mark, Pokras, Mark, and others, eds., Ingestion of Lead From Spent Ammunition: Implications for Wildlife and Humans. Proceedings of the Conference, 12–15 May 2008, Boise State University, Idaho: Boise, Peregrine Fund, p. 259–264.

Pearce, John M., and Petersen, Margaret R., 2009, Post-fledging Movements of Juvenile Common Mergansers (*Mergus merganser*) in Alaska as Inferred by Satellite Telemetry: Waterbirds, v. 32, no. 1, p. 133–137.

Pearce, John M., Zwiefelhofer, Denny, and Mayanski, Nate, 2009, Mechanisms of population heterogeneity among molting common mergansers on Kodiak Island, Alaska: implications for genetic assessments of migratory connectivity: Condor, v. 111, no. 2, p. 283–293.

Powell, Abby N., and Backensto, Stacia, 2009, Common ravens (*Corvus corax*) nesting on Alaska's North Slope oil fields: Ocs Study Report Mms, v. 2009–007, p. 1–36.

Pyle, Peter, Leitner, Wade A., Lozano-Angulo, Lydia, and others, 2009, Temporal, spatial, and annual variation in the occurrence of molt-migrant passerines in the Mexican monsoon region: Condor, v. 111, no. 4, p. 583–590.

Rae, Lauren F., Mitchell, Greg W., Mauck, Robert A., and others, 2009, Radio transmitters do not affect the body condition of savannah sparrows during the fall premigratory period: Journal of Field Ornithology, v. 80, no. 4, p. 419–426.

Refsnider, Ronald L., Trick, Joel A., and Goyette, Jennifer L., 2009, 2008 capture and banding of Kirtland's warblers (*Dendroica kirtlandii*) in Wisconsin: Passenger Pigeon, v. 71, no. 2, p. 115–122.

Reilly, J. R., and Reilly, R. J., 2009, Bet-hedging and the orientation of juvenile passerines in fall migration: Journal of Animal Ecology, v. 78, no. 5, p. 990–1001.

Robinson, Aaron C., Larsen, Randy T., Flinders, Jerran T., and others, 2009, Chukar seasonal survival and probable causes of mortality: Journal of Wildlife Management, v. 73, no. 1, p. 89–97.

Ropert-Coudert, Y., Kato, A., Poulin, N., and others, 2009, Leg-attached data loggers do not modify the diving performances of a foot-propelled seabird: Journal of Zoology (London), v. 279, no. 3, p. 294–297.

Roy, Charlotte, Sousa, Christine, Rave, David, and others, 2009, Movements, survival, and refuge use by ring-necked ducks after fledging in Minnesota: Minnesota Department of Natural Resources Summaries of Wildlife Research Findings, v. 2008, p. 162–168.

Santolo, Gary M., and Yamamoto, Julie T., 2009, Nest box and site use by, and selenium concentrations in, American kestrels at Kesterson Reservoir, Central California: Journal of Raptor Research, v. 43, no. 4, p. 315–324.

Schmutz, J. A., Trust, K. A., and Matz, A. C., 2009, Red-throated loons (*Gavia stellata*) breeding in Alaska, USA, are exposed to PCBs while on their Asian wintering grounds: Environmental Pollution, v. 157, no. 8–9, p. 2386–2393.

Seamans, Thomas W., Clemons, Scott E., and Gosser, Allen L., 2009, Observations of neck-collared Canada geese near John F. Kennedy International Airport, New York : Human-Wildlife Conflicts, v. 3, no. 2 , p. 242–250.

Seston, Rita Marie, Zwiernik, Matthew John, Fredricks, Timothy Brian, and others, 2009, Utilizing the great blue heron (*Ardea herodias*) in ecological risk assessments of bioaccumulative contaminants : Environmental Monitoring and Assessment, v. 157, no. 1–4, p. 199–210.

Small, Michael F., Baccus, John T., and Roberson, Jay A., 2009, Intra-annual variation in white-winged dove density in the Texas Hill Country: Bulletin of the Texas Ornithological Society, v. 42, no. 1–2, p. 56–61.

Somershoe, Scott G., Cohrs, D., and Cohrs, Doris A., 2009, Stopover-site fidelity at a near-coastal banding site in Georgia: Southeastern Naturalist, v. 8, no. 3, p. 537–546.

Sperry, Jinelle H., and Weatherhead, Patrick J., 2009, Sex differences in behavior associated with sex-biased mortality in an oviparous snake species: Oikos, v. 118, no. 4, p. 627–633.

St-Louis, Veronique, Pidgeon, Anna M., Clayton, Murray K., and others, 2009, Satellite image texture and a vegetation index predict avian biodiversity in the Chihuahuan Desert of New Mexico: Ecography, v. 32, no. 3, p. 468–480.

Streby, Henry M., Peterson, Sean M., and Kapfer, Paul M., 2009, Fledging success is a poor indicator of the effects of bird blow flies on ovenbird survival: Condor, v. 111, no. 1, p. 193–197.

Stutchbury, Bridget J. M., Hill, James R., Kramer, Patrick M., and others, 2009, Sex and age-specific annual survival in a neotropical migratory songbird, the purple martin (*Progne subis*): Auk, v. 126, no. 2, p. 278–287.

Stutchbury, Bridget J. M., Tarof, Scott A., Done, Tyler, and others, 2009, Tracking long-distance songbird migration by using geolocators: Science (Washington D.C.), v. 323, no. 5916, p. 896.

Tittler, Rebecca, Villard, Marc-Andre, and Fahrig, Lenore, 2009, How far do songbirds disperse?: Ecography, v. 32, no. 6, p. 1051–1061.

Townsend, Andrea K., Clark, Anne B., Mcgowan, Kevin J., and others, 2009, Disease-mediated inbreeding depression in a large, open population of cooperative crows: Proceedings of the Royal Society Biological Sciences Series B, v. 276, no. 1664, p. 2057–2064.

Van Buskirk, Josh, Mulvihill, Robert S., and Leberman, Robert C., 2009, Variable shifts in spring and autumn migration phenology in North American songbirds associated with climate change: Global Change Biology, v. 15, no. 3, p. 760–771.

Vukovich, Mark, and Kilgo, John C., 2009, Effects of radio transmitters on the behavior of red-headed Woodpeckers: Journal of Field Ornithology, v. 80, no. 3, p. 308–313.

—, 2009, Notes on Breeding Sharp-shinned Hawks and Cooper's Hawks in Barnwell County, South Carolina: Southeastern Naturalist, v. 8, no. 3 , p. 547–552.

Wood, Petra Bohall, 2009, Recovery distances of nestling bald eagles banded in Florida and implications for natal dispersal and philopatry: Journal of Raptor Research, v. 43, no. 2, p. 127–133.

Worland, Mike, Martin, Karl J., and Gregg, Larry, 2009, Spruce grouse distribution and habitat relationships in Wisconsin: Passenger Pigeon, v. 71, no. 1, p. 5–18.

Zimmerman, Guthrie S., Kendall, William L., Moser, Timothy J., and others, 2009, Temporal patterns of apparent leg band retention in North American geese: Journal of Wildlife Management, v. 73, no. 1, p. 82–88.

Zimmerman, Guthrie S., Moser, Timothy J., Kendall, William L., and others, 2009, Factors influencing reporting and harvest probabilities in North American geese: Journal of Wildlife Management, v. 73, no. 5, p. 710–719.

[Symposium "Celebrating 100 years of bird banding in North America" held on September 26, 2002 at the Third North American Ornithological Conference, New Orleans, Louisiana.], 2008, Memoirs of the Nuttall Ornithological Club, v. 15, 280 p.

2008

WBBA Annual Report of birds banded, 2007, 2008, North American Bird Bander, v. 33, no. 3, p. 154–164.

Abstracts, 2008, Abstracts from papers given at EBBA's Annual Meeting 11–12 April 2008: North American Bird Bander, v. 33, no. 2, p. 80–85.

Ackerman, Joshua T., Eagles-Smith, Collin A., Takekawa, John Y., and others, 2008, Survival of postfledging Forster's terns in relation to mercury exposure in San Francisco Bay: Ecotoxicology, v. 17, no. 8, p. 789–801.

Ackerman, Joshua T., Takekawa, John Y., Eagles-Smith, Collin A., and others, 2008, Mercury contamination and effects on survival of American avocet and black-necked stilt chicks in San Francisco Bay: Ecotoxicology, v. 17, no. 2, p. 103–116.

Adams, Josh, and Takekawa, John Y., 2008, At-sea distribution of radio-marked ashy storm-petrels *Oceanodroma homochroa* captured on the California Channel Islands: Marine Ornithology, v. 36, no. 1, p. 9–17.

Andres, Brad A., 2008, Contributions of bird banding to international waterbird conservation: Memoirs of the Nuttall Ornithological Club, v. 15, p. 221–229.

Bailey, Jordan Perkins, and Servello, Frederick A., 2008, Chick survival, fledgling residency and evaluation of methods for estimating fledging success in least terns: Waterbirds, v. 31, no. 4, p. 571–579.

Barnes, Keith P., and Belthoff, James R., 2008, Probability of detection of flammulated owls using nocturnal broadcast surveys: Journal of Field Ornithology, v. 79, no. 3, p. 321–328.

Benedict, Lauryn, 2008, Unusually high levels of extrapair paternity in a duetting songbird with long-term pair bonds: Behavioral Ecology and Sociobiology, v. 62, no. 6, p. 983–988.

Blohm, Robert J., 2008, The role of bird banding in management of migratory bird hunting: Memoirs of the Nuttall Ornithological Club, v. 15, p. 163–179.

Bluso-Demers, Jill, Colwell, Mark A., Takekawa, John Y., and others, 2008, Space use by Forster's terns breeding in South San Francisco Bay: Waterbirds, v. 31, no. 3, p. 357–364.

Bond, Jeanine, and Esler, Daniel, 2008, Bill entanglement in subcutaneously-anchored radio transmitters on harlequin ducks : Wilson Journal of Ornithology, v. 120, no. 3, p. 599–602.

Bondo, Kristin J., Gilson, Lauren N., and Bowman, Reed, 2008, Anvil use by the red-cockaded woodpecker: Wilson Journal of Ornithology, v. 120, no. 1, p. 217–221.

Borkhataria, Rena R., Frederick, Peter C., Hylton, Rebecca, and others, 2008, A preliminary model of Wood Stork population dynamics in the southeastern United States: Waterbirds, v. 31, no. Sp. Iss. 1, p. 42–49.

Casazza, Michael L., Overton, Cory T., Takekawa, John Y., and others, 2008, Breeding behavior and dispersal of radio-marked California clapper rails: Western Birds, v. 39, no. 2, p. 101–106.

Chubbs, Tony E., Trimper, Perry G., Humphries, Gary W., and others, 2008, Tracking Seasonal Movements of Adult Male Harlequin Ducks from Central Labrador Using Satellite Telemetry: Waterbirds, v. 31, no. Sp. Iss. 2, p. 173–182.

Davies, J. Chris, 2008, Ontario cooperative duck banding program 2007 banding results: Ontario Bird Banding, v. 39, p. 41–42.

Davis, A. K., 2008, Factors influencing fidelity of House Finches to a feeding station: Wilson Journal of Ornithology, v. 120, no. 2, p. 371–377.

Davis, Andrew K., Diggs, Nora E., Cooper, Robert J., and others, 2008, Hematological stress indices reveal no effect of radio-transmitters on wintering Hermit Thrushes: Journal of Field Ornithology, v. 79, no. 3, p. 293–297.

Delaney, David K., Pater, Larry L., Carlile, Lawrence D., and others, 2008, Red-cockaded woodpecker (Picoides borealis) response to nest depredation by an eastern rat snake (*Elaphe alleghaniensis*): Southeastern Naturalist, v. 7, no. 4, p. 753–759.

Demers, Scott A., Colwell, Mark A., Takekawa, John Y., and others, 2008, Breeding Stage Influences Space Use of Female American Avocets in San Francisco Bay, California: Waterbirds, v. 31, no. 3, p. 365–371.

Detwiler, Don L., Romano, W. Brad, and Master, Terry L., 2008, Foraging success, habitat selection, and reproductive activities of black crown night herons (*Nycticorax nycticorax*) at Pennsylvania's largest mixed species heronry: Journal of the Pennsylvania Academy of Science, v. 81, no. Sp. Iss. SI, p. 114.

Devine, Buzz, 2008, A banded red knot: Connecticut Warbler, v. 28, no. 3, p. 115–116.

Devlin, Catherine M., Diamond, Antony W., Kress, Stephen W., and others, 2008, Breeding dispersal and survival of Arctic terns (*Sterna paradisaea*) nesting in the Gulf of Maine: Auk, v. 125, no. 4, p. 850–858.

Dietsch, Thomas V., 2008, A relationship between avian foraging behavior and infestation by trombiculid larvae (Acari) in Chiapas, Mexico: Biotropica, v. 40, no. 2, p. 196–202.

Dombroski, Peter, Robinson, Georgina, Fuesner, Megan, and others, 2008, Determining secondary dispersal of red oak (*Quercus rubra*) by small mammals using radio telemetry: Journal of the Pennsylvania Academy of Science, v. 81, no. Sp. Iss. SI, p. 114.

Evans-Ogden, Lesley J., Bittman, Shabtai, and Lank, David B., 2008, A review of agricultural land use by shorebirds with special reference to habitat conservation in the Fraser River Delta, British Columbia: Canadian Journal of Plant Science, v. 88, no. 1, p. 71–83.

Fearon, Peter, and Grundy, Kevin, 2008, Ausable Bird Observatory 2007 annual report: Ontario Bird Banding, v. 39, p. 28–32.

Fedy, B. C., Martin, K., Ritland, C., and others, 2008, Genetic and ecological data provide incongruent interpretations of population structure and dispersal in naturally subdivided populations of white-tailed ptarmigan (*Lagopus leucura*): Molecular Ecology, v. 17, no. 8, p. 1905–1917.

Finnegan, Sue, 2008, Atlantic Flyway review: Region 1 (Northeast)—Fall 2007 report: North American Bird Bander, v. 33, no. 2, p. 86–93.

Foote, A. D., and Nystuen, J. A., 2008, Variation in call pitch among killer whale ecotypes: Journal of the Acoustical Society of America, v. 123, no. 3, p. 1747–1752.

Francis, Charles M., 2008, The role of the North American bird-banding scheme in bird population monitoring: Memoirs of the Nuttall Ornithological Club, v. 15, p. 93–118.

Ghilain, A., and Belisle, M., 2008, Breeding success of tree swallows along a gradient of agricultural intensification: Ecological Applications, v. 18, no. 5, p. 1140–1154.

Godley, Brendan J., and Wilson, Rory P., 2008, Tracking vertebrates for conservation: Introduction: Endangered Species Research, v. 4, no. 1–2, p. 1–2.

Green, Adam W., and Krementz, David G., 2008, Mallard harvest distributions in the Mississippi and Central Flyways: Journal of Wildlife Management, v. 72, no. 6, p. 1328–1334.

Groh, Terri, and Wernaart, Martin, 2008, Banding in Ontario: 2007: Ontario Bird Banding, v. 39, 18 p.

Hamel, Nathalie J., Parrish, Julia K., and Laake, Jeff, 2008, Linking colonies to fisheries: Spatio-temporal overlap between common murres (Uria aalge) from Tatoosh Island and coastal gillnet fisheries in the Pacific Northwest, USA: Biological Conservation, v. 141, no. 12, p. 3101–3115.

Haseltine, Susan D., Schmidt, Paul R., Bales, Bradley D., and others, 2008, Report of the Federal Advisory Committee on the Bird Banding Laboratory: U.S. Geological Survey Circular 1320, 19 p.

Hebert, Percy N., and Golightly, Richard T., 2008, At-sea distribution and movements of nesting and non-nesting marbled murrelets *Brachyramphus marmoratus* in Northern California: Marine Ornithology, v. 36, no. 2, p. 99–105.

Herring, Garth, Gawlik, Dale E., and Beerens, James M., 2008, Evaluating two new methods for capturing large wetland birds: Journal of Field Ornithology, v. 79, no. 1, p. 102–110.

Hines, James E., and Brook, Rodney W., 2008, Changes in annual survival estimates for Black Brant from the Western Canadian Arctic, 1962–2001: Waterbirds, v. 31, no. 2, p. 220–230.

Houston, C. Stuart, Klimkiewicz, M. Kathleen, and Robbins, Chandler S., 2008, History of "computerization" of bird-banding records: North American Bird Bander, v. 33, no. 2, p. 53–65.

Hupp, Jerry W., Schmutz, Joel A., and Ely, Craig R., 2008, The annual migration cycle of emperor geese in western Alaska: Arctic, v. 61, no. 1, p. 23–34.

Jackson, Jerome A., 2008, The early history of bird banding in North America: Memoirs of the Nuttall Ornithological Club, v. 15, 30 p.

Johnson, Matthew, and Walters, Jeffrey R., 2008, Effects of mate and site fidelity on nest survival of western sandpipers (*Calidris mauri*): Auk, v. 125, no. 1, p. 76–86.

Keenan, Patrick C., and Benkman, Craig W., 2008, Call imitation and call modification in red crossbills: Condor, v. 110, no. 1, p. 93–101.

Kirk, David Anthony, Bellerby, Gordon, Brook, Rodney W., and others, 2008, Assessing seasonal variation in counts and movements of Bonaparte's gulls *Larus philadelphia* on the Niagara River, Ontario: Waterbirds, v. 31, no. 2, p. 193–202.

Kirk, Molly, Esler, Daniel, Iverson, Samuel A., and others, 2008, Movements of wintering surf scoters: predator responses to different prey landscapes: Oecologia (Berlin), v. 155, no. 4, p. 859–867.

Koenig, Walter D., and Walters, Eric L., 2008, A tale of two worlds: molecular ecology and population structure of the threatened Florida scrub-jay: Molecular Ecology, v. 17, no. 7, p. 1632–1633.

Kostecke, Richard M., and Cimprich, David A., 2008, Adult and juvenile survival of black-capped vireos within a large breeding population in Texas: Condor, v. 110, no. 2, p. 251–259.

Larsen, Randy T., Bentley, Daniel F., and Flinders, Jerran T., 2008, Implications of woodrats and other scavengers for avian telemetry studies: Journal of Wildlife Management, v. 72, no. 5, p. 1152–1155.

Lavers, Jennifer L., and Jones, Ian L., 2008, Assessing the type and frequency of band resighting errors for razorbill Alca torda with implications for other wildlife studies: Marine Ornithology, v. 36, no. 1, p. 19–23.

Lehman, Chad P., Flake, Lester D., Rumble, Mark A., and others, 2008, Merriam's turkey poult survival in the Black Hills, South Dakota: Intermountain Journal of Sciences, v. 14, no. 4, p. 78–88.

Leonard, Tina D., Taylor, Philip D., and Warkentin, Ian G., 2008, Landscape structure and spatial scale affect space use by songbirds in naturally patchy and harvested boreal forests: Condor, v. 110, no. 3, p. 467–481.

Lewis, Tyler L., and Flint, Paul L., 2008, Modified method for external attachment of transmitters to birds using two subcutaneous anchors: Journal of Field Ornithology, v. 79, no. 3, p. 336–341.

Lok, Erika K., Kirk, Molly, Esler, Daniel, and others, 2008, Movements of pre-migratory surf and white-winged scoters in response to Pacific herring spawn: Waterbirds, v. 31, no. 3, p. 385–393.

Lynn, Janet C., Rosenstock, Steven S., and Chambers, Carol L., 2008, Avian use of desert wildlife water developments as determined by remote videography: Western North American Naturalist, v. 68, no. 1, p. 107–112.

Mcdonald, M. Victoria, Jackson, Jerome A., and Davis, William E. Jr., 2008, History of the role of bird banding in avian behavioral research: Memoirs of the Nuttall Ornithological Club, v. 15, p. 245–264.

Mcintyre, Carol L., Douglas, David C., and Collopy, Michael W., 2008, Movements of Golden Eagles (*Aquila chrysaetos*) from interior Alaska during their first year of independence: Auk, v. 125, no. 1, p. 214–224.

Mckibbin, Rene, and Bishop, Christine A., 2008, Observations on the longevity and fecundity of the western yellow-breasted chat in the south Okanagan valley, British Columbia, Canada: British Columbia Birds, v. 18, p. 26–27.

Mclean, Robert G., and Guptill, Stephen C., 2008, Use of bird-banding information to investigate disease, safety, and economic issues of birds and their interactions with humans: Memoirs of the Nuttall Ornithological Club, v. 15, p. 231–244.

Menu, Stephane, 2008, Bruce Peninsula Bird Observatory annual report 2007: Ontario Bird Banding, v. 39, p. 25–27.

Miller-Rushing, Abraham J., Primack, Richard B., and Stymeist, Robert, 2008, Interpreting variation in bird migration times as observed by volunteers: Auk, v. 125, no. 3, p. 565–573.

Mitro, Matthew G., Evers, David C., Meyer, Michael W., and others, 2008, Common loon survival rates and mercury in New England and Wisconsin: Journal of Wildlife Management, v. 72, no. 3, p. 665–673.

Mojica, Elizabeth K., Meyers, J. Michael, Millsap, Brian A., and others, 2008, Migration of Florida sub-adult Bald Eagles: Wilson Journal of Ornithology, v. 120, no. 2, p. 304–310.

Morris, Sara R., Dale, Brenda, and Gustafson, Mary, 2008, Roles and contributions of banding organizations to the North American banding program: Memoirs of the Nuttall Ornithological Club, v. 15, p. 31–64.

Nelson, M., Jones, S., Edwards, C., and others, 2008, Characterization of Escherichia coli populations from gulls, landfill trash, and wastewater using ribotyping: Diseases of Aquatic Organisms, v. 81, no. 1, p. 53–63.

Nesbitt, Stephen A., 2008, Bird banding and the restoration of extirpated and declining populations: Memoirs of the Nuttall Ornithological Club, v. 15, p. 119–131.

Nichols, James D., and Tautin, John, 2008, North American bird banding and quantitative population ecology: Memoirs of the Nuttall Ornithological Club, v. 15, p. 133–161.

Noel, Brandon L., and Chandler, C. Ray, 2008, Spatial distribution and site fidelity of non-breeding piping plovers on the Georgia Coast: Waterbirds, v. 31, no. 2, p. 241–251.

O'brien, Valerie A., Moore, Amy T., Huyvaert, Kathryn P., and others, 2008, No evidence for spring re-introduction of an arbovirus by cliff swallows: Wilson Journal of Ornithology, v. 120, no. 4, p. 910–913.

Oppel, S., Powell, A. N., and Dickson, D. L., 2008, Timing and distance of King Eider migration and winter movements: Condor, v. 110, no. 2, p. 296–305.

Oppel, Steffen, and Powell, Abby N., 2008, Assigning king eiders to wintering regions in the Bering Sea using stable isotopes of feathers and claws: Marine Ecology Progress Series, v. 373, p. 149–156.

Ortego, Brent, 2008, IBBA annual report of birds banded, 2007: North American Bird Bander, v. 33, no. 2, p. 93–99.

Paxton, Kristina L., Van Riper, Charles III, and O'brien, Chris, 2008, Movement patterns and stopover ecology of Wilson's warblers during spring migration on the lower Colorado River in southwestern Arizona: Condor, v. 110, no. 4, p. 672–681.

Pearce, J. M., Blums, P., and Lindberg, M. S., 2008, Site fidelity is an inconsistent determinant of population structure in the hooded merganser (*Lophodytes cucullatus*): Evidence from genetic, mark-recapture, and comparative data: Auk, v. 125, no. 3, p. 711–722.

Perlut, Noah G., 2008, Female bobolink molts into male-like plumage and loses fertility: Journal of Field Ornithology, v. 79, no. 2, p. 198–201.

Pugesek, Bruce H., and Diem, Kenneth L., 2008, Timing and location of mortality of fledgling, subadult, and adult California gulls: Wilson Journal of Ornithology, v. 120, no. 1, p. 159–166.

Renner, Heather M., and Mccaffery, Brian J., 2008, Demography of eastern yellow wagtails at Cape Romanzof, Alaska: Wilson Journal of Ornithology, v. 120, no. 1, p. 85–91.

Reynolds, Richard T., Gpkham, Russell T., and Boyce, Douglas A. Jr, 2008, Northern goshawk habitat: An intersection of science, management, and conservation: Journal of Wildlife Management, v. 72, no. 4, p. 1047–1055.

Robert, M., Mittelhauser, G. H., Jobin, B., and others, 2008, New Insights on Harlequin Duck Population Structure in Eastern North America as Revealed by Satellite Telemetry: Waterbirds, v. 31, p. 159–172.

Roche, Erin A., Cuthbert, Francesca J., and Arnold, Todd W., 2008, Relative fitness of wild and captive-reared piping plovers: does egg salvage contribute to recovery of the endangered Great Lakes population?: Biological Conservation, v. 141, no. 12, p. 3079–3088.

Rodewald, Amanda D., and Shustach, Daniel P., 2008, Urban flight: understanding individual and populational-level responses of Nearctic-Neotropical migratory birds to urbanization: Journal of Animal Ecology, v. 77, no. 1, p. 83–91.

Roy, Charlotte, Rave, David, Brininger, Wayne, and others, 2008, Movements, survival, and refuge use by locally produced post-fledging ring-necked ducks in Minnesota: Minnesota Department of Natural Resources Summaries of Wildlife Research Findings, v. 2007, p. 480–485.

Safine, D. E., and Lindberg, M. S., 2008, Nest habitat selection of White-winged Scoters on Yukon Flats, Alaska: Wilson Journal of Ornithology, v. 120, no. 3, p. 582–593.

Sandercock, Brett K., Jensen, William E., Williams, Christopher K., and others, 2008, Demographic sensitivity of population change in northern bobwhite: Journal of Wildlife Management, v. 72, no. 4, p. 970–982.

Saracco, J. F., Desante, D. F., and Kaschube, D. R., 2008, Assessing Landbird Monitoring Programs and Demographic Causes of Population Trends: Journal of Wildlife Management, v. 72, no. 8, p. 1665–1673.

Sargent, Robert R., and Sargent, Martha B., 2008, The significance of banding in the study of wintering rufous hummingbirds: Pennsylvania Birds, v. 21, no. 4, p. 164–165.

Schlossberg, Scott, Hoover, Jeffrey P., Blood, Courtney, and others, 2008, Contributions of banding to understanding habitat use by birds: Memoirs of the Nuttall Ornithological Club, v. 15, p. 209–220.

Schmidt, Kenneth A., Rush, Scott A., and Ostfeld, Richard S., 2008, Wood thrush nest success and post-fledging survival across a temporal pulse of small mammal abundance in an oak forest: Journal of Animal Ecology, v. 77, no. 4, p. 830–837.

Schmutz, Josef K., Flockhart, D. T. Tyler, Houston, C. Stuart, and others, 2008, Demography of ferruginous hawks breeding in western Canada: Journal of Wildlife Management, v. 72, no. 6, p. 1352–1360.

Sedinger, J., Chelgren, N. D., Ward, D., and others, 2008, Fidelity and breeding probability related to population density and individual quality in black brent geese Branta bernicla nigricans: Journal of Animal Ecology, v. 77, no. 4, p. 702–712.

Siegel, Rodney B., Wilkerson, Robert L., and Desante, David F., 2008, Extirpation of the Willow Flycatcher from Yosemite National Park: Western Birds, v. 39, no. 1, p. 8–21.

Small, Michael F., Baccus, John T., and Schwertner, T. Wayne, 2008, Survivorship of radio-transmittered [transmitted] urban white-winged doves on the Edwards Plateau, Texas: Texas Journal of Science, v. 60, no. 1, p. 45–56.

Smith, James, 2008, Haldimand Bird Observatory overview and 2007 annual report: Ontario Bird Banding, v. 39, p. 19–24.

Sprague, Ashley J., Hamilton, Diana J., and Diamond, Antony W., 2008, Site Safety and Food Affect Movements of Semipalmated Sandpipers (Calidris pusilla) Migrating Through the Upper Bay of Fundy: Avian Conservation and Ecology, v. 3, no. 2, article 4.

—, 2008, Site safety and food affect movements of semipalmated sandpipers (Calidris pusilla) migrating through the upper Bay of Fund: Avian Conservation and Ecology, v. 3, no. 2, article 4.

Stiles, Donald J., 2008, An Alberta banded tree swallow recovered in east Texas: Blue Jay, v. 66, no. 1, p. 52.

Stromberg, Mark R., Koenig, Walter D., Walters, Eric L., and others, 2008, Estimate of Trichomonas gallinae-induced mortality in band-tailed pigeons, Upper Carmel Valley, California, winter 2006–2007: Wilson Journal of Ornithology, v. 120, no. 3, p. 603–606.

Tautin, John, 2008, A history of the Bird Banding Laboratory: 1920–2002: Memoirs of the Nuttall Ornithological Club, v. 15, p. 65–91.

Trejo, Edgar, Mcneil, Raymond, Morales, Luis Gonzalo, and others, 2008, Daily movements, home range and habitat use by radio-tracked crested bobwhites (Colinus cristatus) in a Venezuelan savanna: Interciencia, v. 33, no. 3, p. 207–212.

Varland, Daniel E., Powell, Larkin A., Kenney, Mary Kay, and others, 2008, Peregrine falcon survival and resighting frequencies on the Washington coast, 1995–2003: Journal of Raptor Research, v. 42, no. 3, p. 161–171.

Wheelwright, Nathaniel T., Swett, Meredith B., Levin, Iris I., and others, 2008, The influence of different tutor types on song learning in a natural bird population: Animal Behaviour, v. 75, no. 4, p. 1479–1493.

White, Jennifer D., and Faaborg, John, 2008, Post-fledging movement and spatial habitat-use patterns of juvenile Swainson's Thrushes: Wilson Journal of Ornithology, v. 120, no. 1, p. 62–73.

Willson, Mary F., and Hocker, Katherine M., 2008, American dippers wintering near Juneau, Alaska: Northwestern Naturalist, v. 89, no. 1, p. 24–32.

2007

2006 Annual Banding Report, 2007, North American Bird Bander, v. 32, no. 3, p. 135–144.

Aborn, David A., 2007, Abundance, density, and diversity of neotropical migrants at the Lula Lake Land Trust, GA: Southeastern Naturalist, v. 6, no. 2, p. 293–304.

Ackerman, J. T., Eagles-Smith, C. A., Takekawa, J. Y., and others, 2007, Mercury concentrations and space use of pre-breeding American avocets and black-necked stilts in San Francisco Bay: Science of the Total Environment, v. 384, no. 1–3, p. 452–466.

Amirault-Langlais, Diane L., Thomas, Peter W., and Mcknight, Julie, 2007, Oiled piping plovers (*Charadrius melodus melodus*) in eastern Canada: Waterbirds , v. 30, no. 2, p. 271–274.

Anderson, Scott K., Roby, Daniel D., Lyons, Donald E., and others, 2007, Relationship of Caspian tern foraging ecology to nesting success in the Columbia River estuary, Oregon, USA: Estuarine Coastal and Shelf Science, v. 73, no. 3–4, p. 447–456.

Awkerman, Jill A., Westbrock, Mark A., Huyvaert, Kathryn P., and others, 2007, Female-biased sex ratio arises after parental care in the sexually dimorphic waved albatross (*Phoebastria irrorata*): Auk, v. 124, no. 4, p. 1336–1346.

Barbosa Filho, Roberto C., Lacerda, Raquel C., Roos, Andrei L., and others, 2007, Report of the National Banding System (1973–1985): Ornithologia, v. 2, no. 2, p. 88–118.

Barbosa Filho, Roberto C., Roos, Andrei L., Alves Lacerda, Raquel C., and others, 2007, Report of the Brazilian National Banding System (1986–1995): Ornithologia, v. 2, no. 2, p. 119–169.

Bedrosian, Bryan, and Craighead, Derek, 2007, Band wear in common ravens: North American Bird Bander, v. 32, no. 4, p. 149–152.

—-, 2007, Evaluation of techniques for attaching transmitters to common raven nestlings: Northwestern Naturalist, v. 88, no. 1, 6 p.

Blanchette, P., Bourgeois, J. C., and St-Onge, S., 2007, Ruffed grouse winter habitat use in mixed softwood-hardwood forests, Quebec, Canada: Journal of Wildlife Management, v. 71, no. 6, p. 1758–1764.

Boal, C. W., and Estabrook, T. S., 2007, Occurrence and condition of migrating Swainson's thrushes in the British Virgin Islands: Wilson Journal of Ornithology, v. 119, no. 4, p. 716–720.

Burger, Alan E., and Page, Richard E., 2007, The need for biological realism in habitat modeling: a reinterpretation of Zharikov et al. (2006): Landscape Ecology, v. 22, no. 9, p. 1273–1281.

Businga, Nancy K., Langenberg, Julie, and Carlson, Lavinda, 2007, Successful treatment of capture myopathy in three wild greater sandhill cranes (*Grus canadensis tabida*): Journal of Avian Medicine and Surgery, v. 21, no. 4, p. 294–298.

Butler, Christopher J., Ledbetter, Dick, Batchelder, Ned, and others, 2007, Black-chinned hummingbirds breed in Grady County: Bulletin of the Oklahoma Ornithological Society, v. 40, no. 3–4, p. 13–16.

Collins, Charles T., 2007, Band wear in elegant terns: North American Bird Bander, v. 32, no. 1, p. 4–10.

Collins, Charles T., Garrett, Kimball L., and Schew, William A., 2007, Survival and band wear in black skimmers: North American Bird Bander, v. 32, no. 4, p. 159–161.

Conover, Michael R., and Dolbeer, Richard A., 2007, Use of decoy traps to protect blueberries from juvenile European starlings: Human-Wildlife Conflicts, v. 1, no. 2, p. 265–270.

Costa, L. G., and Giordano, G., 2007, Developmental neurotoxicity of polybrominated diphenyl ether (PBDE) flame retardants: Neurotoxicology, v. 28, no. 6, p. 1047–1067.

Cox, James A., and Jones, Clark D., 2007, Home range and survival characteristics of male Bachman's sparrows in an old-growth forest managed with breeding season burns: Journal of Field Ornithology, v. 78, no. 3, p. 263–269.

Custer, Christine M., Custer, Thomas W., Hines, James E., and others, 2007, Adult tree swallow (*Tachycineta bicolor*) survival on the polychlorinated biphenyl-contaminated Housatonic River, Massachusetts, USA: Environmental Toxicology and Chemistry, v. 26, no. 5, p. 1056–1065.

Davies, J. Chris, 2007, Cooperative banding program: Ontario banding results for 2006: Ontario Bird Banding, v. 38, p. 30–31.

De Ita, Adan Oliveras, and De Silva, Hector Gomez, 2007, Territoriality and survivorship of the Sierra Madre sparrow in La Cima, Mexico: Biodiversity and Conservation, v. 16, no. 4, p. 1055–1061.

Dunk, Jeffrey R., Vigallon, Stacey M., Narahashi, Taro, and others, 2007, Potential impacts of off highway vehicles on juvenile northern goshawks: Ecological Society of America Annual Meeting Abstracts.

Elliott, John E., Morrissey, Christy A., Henny, Charles J., and others, 2007, Satellite telemetry and prey sampling reveal contaminant sources to pacific northwest Ospreys: Ecological Applications, v. 17, no. 4, p. 1223–1233.

Fearon, Peter, and Brewer, David, 2007, Ausauble Bird Observatory Annual Report: Ontario Bird Banding, v. 38, p. 22–29.

Finlay, J. Cam, 2007, Nine years of banding and recapture of hummingbirds in southern British Columbia: British Columbia Birds, v. 15, p. 9–23.

Finnegan, Sue, 2007, Atlantic flyway review: region 1 (northeast)—Fall 2006 report: North American Bird Bander, v. 32, no. 2, p. 92–97.

Flockhart, D. T. Tyler, and Wiebe, Karen L., 2007, The role of weather and migration in assortative pairing within the northern flicker (*Colaptes auratus*) hybrid zone: Evolutionary Ecology Research, v. 9, no. 6, p. 887–903.

Gould, Patrick, and Elwonger, David, 2007, Movement of banded black-capped chickadees along Trout Creek: Colorado Birds, v. 41, no. 2, p. 91–94.

Groh, Terri, and Wernaart, Martin, 2007, Banding in Ontario: 2006: Ontario Bird Banding, v. 38, 18 p.

Guzy, Michael J., and Ribic, Christine A., 2007, Post-breeding season habitat use and movements of eastern Meadowlarks in southwestern Wisconsin: Wilson Journal of Ornithology, v. 119, no. 2, p. 198–204.

Hagen, Christian A., Pitman, James C., Robel, Robert J., and others, 2007, Niche partitioning by lesser prairie-chicken *Tympanuchus pallidicinctus* and ring-necked pheasant *Phasianus colchicus* in southwestern Kansas: Wildlife Biology, v. 13, p. 34–41.

Hagen, Christian A., Pitman, James C., Sandercock, Brett K., and others, 2007, Age-specific survival and probable causes of mortality in female lesser prairie-chickens: Journal of Wildlife Management, v. 71, no. 2, p. 518–525.

Hall, Galon I., Wallace, Mark C., Ballard, Warren B., and others, 2007, Rio Grande wild turkey habitat selection in the southern great plains: Journal of Wildlife Management, v. 71, no. 8, p. 2583–2591.

Haramis, G. Michael, and Kearns, Gregory D., 2007, Soras in tidal marsh: Banding and telemetry studies on the Patuxent River, Maryland: Waterbirds, v. 30, no. Sp. Iss. 1, p. 105–121.

Harman, Lindsay M., and Barclay, John H., 2007, A Summary of California Burrowing Owl Banding Records, *in* Barclay, John H., Hunting, Kevin W., Lincer, Jeffrey L., and others, eds., Proceedings of the California Burrowing Owl Symposium, November 2003. [Bird Populations Monographs No 1.]: Point Reyes Station, California, The Institute for Bird Populations and Albion Environmental, Inc., p. 123–131.

Hayes, Matthew A., 2007, Observation of an extra-pair copulation by sandhill cranes: Wilson Journal of Ornithology, v. 119, no. 1, p. 113–116.

Hayes, Matthew A., Lacy, Anne E., Barzen, Jeb, and others, 2007, An unusual journey of non-migratory Whooping Cranes: Southeastern Naturalist, v. 6, no. 3, p. 551–558.

Hobson, K. A., Van Wilgenburg, S., Wassenaar, L. I., and others, 2007, Estimating origins of three species of neotropical migrant songbirds at a gulf coast stopover site: Combining stable isotope and GIS tools: Condor, v. 109, no. 2, p. 256–267.

Holevinski, Robin A., Curtis, Paul D., and Malecki, Richard A., 2007, Hazing of Canada geese is unlikely to reduce nuisance populations in urban and suburban communities: Human-Wildlife Conflicts, v. 1, no. 2, p. 257–264.

Hoover, Jeffrey P., and Hauber, Mark E., 2007, Individual patterns of habitat and nest-site use by hosts promote transgenerational transmission of avian brood parasitism status: Journal of Animal Ecology, v. 76, no. 6, p. 1208–1214.

Hosner, Peter A., and Winkler, David W., 2007, Dispersal distances of Tree Swallows estimated from continent-wide and limited-area data: Journal of Field Ornithology, v. 78, no. 3, p. 290–297.

Houston, C. Stuart, 2007, Starlings banded on wintering grounds and recovered in Saskatchewan: Blue Jay, v. 65, no. 1, p. 34–36.

Houston, C. Stuart, Mcloughlin, D., and Ludwig, James Pinson, 2007, Caspian tern banded at dore lake, sk: Third oldest at 28 years, 7 months: Blue Jay, v. 65, no. 3, p. 140–142.

Houston, C. Stuart, and Scott, Frank, 2007, Osprey banding program near loon lake, sk, 1975–2002: Blue Jay, v. 65, no. 3, p. 133–137.

Irwin, Larry L., Clark, Laurie A., Rock, Dennis C., and others, 2007, Modeling foraging habitat of California spotted owls: Journal of Wildlife Management, v. 71, no. 4, p. 1183–1191.

Jones, Stephanie L., Dieni, J. Scott, Green, Michael T., and others, 2007, Annual return rates of breeding grassland songbirds: Wilson Journal of Ornithology, v. 119, no. 1, p. 89–94.

Kirkpatrick, Chris, Conway, Courtney J., Hughes, Katie M., and others, 2007, Probability of detecting band-tailed pigeons during call-broadcast versus auditory surveys: Journal of Wildlife Management, v. 71, no. 1, p. 231–237.

Knoche, Michael J., Powell, Abby N., Quakenbush, Lori T., and others, 2007, Further evidence for site fidelity to wing molt locations by king eiders: integrating stable isotope analyses and satellite telemetry: Waterbirds, v. 30, no. 1, p. 52–57.

Lavers, J. L., Jones, I. L., and Diamond, A. W., 2007, Natal and breeding dispersal of Razorbills (*Alca torda*) in eastern North America: Waterbirds, v. 30, no. 4, p. 588–594.

Lehman, R. N., Kennedy, P. L., and Savidge, J. A., 2007, The state of the art in raptor electrocution research: A global review: Biological Conservation, v. 136, no. 2, p. 159–174.

Ligi, Spring, and Omland, Kevin, 2007, Contrasting breeding strategies of two sympatric orioles: first documentation of double brooding by orchard orioles: Journal of Field Ornithology, v. 78, no. 3, p. 298–302.

Macmynowski, D. P., Root, T. L., Ballard, G., and others, 2007, Changes in spring arrival of Nearctic-Neotropical migrants attributed to multiscalar climate: Global Change Biology, v. 13, no. 11, p. 2239–2251.

Mager, John N., and Walcott, Charles, 2007, Structural and contextual characteristics of territorial "yodels" given by male common loons (*Gavia immer*) in northern Wisconsin: Passenger Pigeon, v. 69, no. 3, p. 327–337.

Mannan, R. William, Mannan, R. Nicholas, Schmidt, Cecilia A., and others, 2007, Influence of natal experience on nest-site selection by urban-nesting Cooper's hawks: Journal of Wildlife Management, v. 71, no. 1, p. 64–68.

Mcdonough, Colleen M., Lockhart, J. Mitchell, and Loughry, W., 2007, Population dynamics of nine-banded armadillos: insights from a removal experiment: Southeastern Naturalist, v. 6, no. 3 , p. 381–392.

Mestre, Luiz A. M., 2007, Band recovery analysis of Sterna hirundo in North America (1928–2005) and Brazil (1983–2005): Ornithologia, v. 2, no. 2 , p. 81–87.

—, 2007, Recoveries in Brazil of peregrine falcons (*Falco peregrinus*) banded in North America between 1967 and 2001: Ornithologia, v. 2, no. 2, p. 72–80.

Michopoulos, Vasiliki, Maney, Donna L., Morehouse, Caroline B., and others, 2007, A genotyping assay to determine plumage morph in the white-throated sparrow (*Zonotrichia albicollis*): Auk, v. 124, no. 4, p. 1330–1335.

Mong, T. W., and Sandercock, B. K., 2007, Optimizing radio retention and minimizing radio impacts in a field study of upland sandpipers: Journal of Wildlife Management, v. 71, no. 3, p. 971–980.

Morrison, R. I. G., 2007, Body transformations, condition, and survival in red knots *Calidris canutus* travelling to breed at Alert, Ellesmere Island, Canada: Ardea, v. 94, no. 3, p. 607–618.

Mrykalo, Robert J., Grigione, Melissa M., and Sarno, Ronald J., 2007, Home range and dispersal of juvenile Florida burrowing owls: Wilson Journal of Ornithology, v. 119, no. 2, p. 275–279.

Myatt, Nick A., and Krementz, David G., 2007, American woodcock fall migration using central region band-recovery and wing-collection survey data: Journal of Wildlife Management, v. 71, no. 2, p. 336–344.

Myatt, Nick A., and Krementz, David G., 2007, Fall migration and habitat use of American woodcock in the central United States: Journal of Wildlife Management, v. 71, no. 4, p. 1197–1205.

Newbury, Roberta K., and Nelson, Thomas A., 2007, Habitat selection and movements of raccoons on a grassland reserve managed for imperiled birds: Journal of Mammalogy, v. 88, no. 4, p. 1082–1089.

Ortego, Brent, 2007, IBBA annual report of birds banded, 2006. Summary of banding reported from the IBBA region for 2006 with USFWS/CWS BANDS: North American Bird Bander, v. 32, no. 2, p. 97–103.

Palmer, William E., and Wellendorf, Shane D., 2007, Effect of radiotransmitters on northern bobwhite annual survival: Journal of Wildlife Management, v. 71, no. 4, p. 1281–1287.

Parks, S. E., Clark, C. W., and Tyack, P. L., 2007, Short- and long-term changes in right whale calling behavior: The potential effects of noise on acoustic communication: Journal of the Acoustical Society of America, v. 122, no. 6, p. 3725–3731.

Paton, Peter, 2007, Banding birds at Kingston Wildlife Research Station: the 39-year legacy of Douglas Kraus: Rhode Island Naturalist, v. 14, no. 1, p. 14–15.

Perkins, Deborah E., Smith, Paul A., and Gilchrist, H. Grant, 2007, The breeding ecology of ruddy turnstones (*Arenaria interpres*) in the eastern Canadian Arctic: Polar Record, v. 43, no. 225, p. 135–142.

Poole, Richard, and Brown, Christine, 2007, Survival after banding: North American Bird Bander, v. 32, no. 2, p. 78–80.

Post, William, and Shea, Norm, 2007, Recovery of a banded northern goshawk Accipiter gentilis in South Carolina: first documentation of its occurrence in the state: Chat (Raleigh), v. 71, no. 2, p. 30–33.

Probst, John R., Donner, Deahn M., and Bozek, Michael A., 2007, Continuous, age-related plumage variation in male Kirtland's warblers: Journal of Field Ornithology, v. 78, no. 1, p. 100–108.

Rimmer, Christopher C., Faccio, Steven D., and Mcfarland, Kent P., 2007, Ecology and demography of Bicknell's thrush on East Mountain and Mount Mansfield, Vermont: evaluating potential impacts of wind turbine construction. Year 3 progress report: VINS Technical Report 07–01, 18 p.

Robbins, Chandler S., 2007, Atlantic flyway review: region IV Piedmont—coastal plain, Fall 2006: North American Bird Bander, v. 32, no. 3, p. 127–133.

Rock, Jennifer C., Leonard, Marty L., and Boyne, Andrew W., 2007, Do co-nesting Arctic and Common Terns partition foraging habitat and chick diets?: Waterbirds, v. 30, no. 4, p. 579–587.

—, 2007, Foraging Habitat and Chick Diets of Roseate Tern, *Sterna dougallii*, Breeding on Country Island, Nova Scotia: Avian Conservation and Ecology, v. 2, no. 1, article 4.

Sallaberry, Michel, and Mann N., Mahina, 2007, Sanderlings (*Calidris alba*) banded in Canada recovered in Chile: Ornitologia Neotropical, v. 18, no. 4, p. 623–626.

Saumure, Raymond A., Herman, Thomas B., and Titman, Rodger D., 2007, Effects of haying and agricultural practices on a declining species: The North American wood turtle, Glyptemys insculpta: Biological Conservation, v. 135, no. 4, p. 565–575.

Sedinger, James S., Nicolai, Christopher A., Lensink, Calvin J., and others, 2007, Black brant harvest, density dependence, and survival: A record of population dynamics: Journal of Wildlife Management, v. 71, no. 2, p. 496–506.

Sheaffer, S. E., Malecki, R. A., Swift, B. L., and others, 2007, Management Implications of Molt Migration by the Atlantic Flyway Resident Population of Canada Geese, Branta canadensis: Canadian Field-Naturalist, v. 121, no. 3, p. 313–320.

Shealer, David A., 2007, Population dynamics of black terns breeding in southeastern Wisconsin, 1999–2007: Passenger Pigeon, v. 69, no. 4, p. 471–479.

Shihadeh, Karen, 2007, Big Sur bird banding and condor tracking: Ecological Society of America Annual Meeting Abstracts.

Small, Michael F., Taylor, Emariana S., Baccus, John T., and others, 2007, Nesting home range and movements of an urban white-winged dove population: Wilson Journal of Ornithology, v. 119, no. 3, p. 467–471.

Smith, James A., 2007, Rock Point Bird Banding Station 2006 Annual Report: Ontario Bird Banding, v. 38, p. 19–22.

Spear, Larry B., and Ainley, David G., 2007, Storm-petrels of the eastern Pacific Ocean: species assembly and diversity along marine habitat gradients: Ornithological Monographs, v. 62, 77 p.

Spiegel, O., and Nathan, R., 2007, Incorporating dispersal distance into the disperser effectiveness framework: frugivorous birds provide complementary dispersal to plants in a patchy environment: Ecology Letters, v. 10, no. 8, p. 718–728.

Stenzel, L. E., Page, G. W., Warriner, J. C., and others, 2007, Survival and natal dispersal of juvenile Snowy Plovers (*Charadrius alexandrinus*) in central coastal California: Auk, v. 124, no. 3, p. 1023–1036.

Swanson, David, 2007, II. Gray catbird banding recovery: South Dakota Bird Notes, v. 59, no. 2, p. 47.

Szymanski, Michael L., Afton, Alan D., and Hobson, Keith A., 2007, Use of stable isotope methodology to determine natal origins of mallards at a fine scale Midwest within the upper Midwest: Journal of Wildlife Management, v. 71, no. 4, p. 1317–1324.

Terhune, Theron M., Sisson, D. Clay, Grand, James B., and others, 2007, Factors influencing survival of radiotagged and banded northern bobwhites in Georgia: Journal of Wildlife Management, v. 71, no. 4, p. 1288–1297.

Thorup, K., Bisson, I. A., Bowlin, M. S., and others, 2007, Evidence for a navigational map stretching across the continental US in a migratory songbird: Proceedings of the National Academy of Sciences of the United States of America, v. 104, no. 46, p. 18115–18119.

Tietz, James R., and Johnson, Matthew D., 2007, Stopover ecology and habitat selection of juvenile Swainson's Thrushes during fall migration along the northern California coast: Condor, v. 109, no. 4, p. 795–807.

Todd, L. Danielle, Poulin, Ray G., Brigham, R. Mark, and others, 2007, Pre-migratory movements by juvenile burrowing owls in a patchy landscape: Avian Conservation and Ecology, v. 2, no. 2 , article 4.

Townsend, Darrell E. Ditchkoff Stephan S., and Fuhlendorf, Samuel D., 2007, Transmitter height influences error of ground-based radio-telemetry: Wildlife Biology, v. 13, no. 1, p. 98–101.

Vander Haegen, W. M., 2007, Fragmention by agriculture influences reproductive success of birds in a shrubsteppe landscape: Ecological Applications, v. 17, no. 3, p. 934–947.

Wescoat Dias, Nathan, 2007, Status, distribution and phenology of band-rumped storm-petrel in waters off South Carolina: Chat (Raleigh), v. 71, no. 1, p. 6–9.

Whidden, S. Erin, Williams, Cory T., Breton, Andre R., and others, 2007, Effects of transmitters on the reproductive success of tufted puffins: Journal of Field Ornithology, v. 78, no. 2, p. 206–212.

Willey, David W., and Van Riper, Charles, III, 2007, Home range characteristics of Mexican spotted owls in the canyonlands of Utah: Journal of Raptor Research, v. 41, no. 1, p. 10–15.

Williams, Tony D., Warnock, Nils, Takekawa, John Y., and others, 2007, Flyway-scale variation in plasma triglyceride levels as an index of refueling rate in spring-migrating western sandpipers (*Calidris mauri*): Auk, v. 124, no. 3, p. 886–897.

Woodcock, John, and Woodcock, Maureen, 2007, [Species diversity, fidelity to migration site and ecology of terrestrial migratory birds in the mangroves of Costa Rica.]: Zeledonia, v. 11, no. 1, 13 p.

Zharikov, Yuri, Lank, David B., and Cooke, Fred, 2007, Influence of landscape pattern on breeding distribution and success in a threatened Alcid, the marbled murrelet: model transferability and management implications: Journal of Applied Ecology, v. 44, no. 4, p. 748–759.

2006

WBBA annual report of birds banded, 2005, 2006, North American Bird Bander, v. 31, no. 3, p. 141–152.

Alisauskas, R. T., Drake, K. L., Slattery, S. M., and others, 2006, Neckbands, harvest, and survival of Ross's geese from Canada's Central Arctic: Journal of Wildlife Management, v. 70, no. 1, p. 89–100.

Amirault, Diane L., Mcknight, Julie, Shaffer, Francois, and others, 2006, Novel anodized aluminum bands cause leg injuries in piping plovers: Journal of Field Ornithology, v. 77, no. 1, p. 18–20.

Anthony, Robert G., Forsman, Eric D., Franklin, Alan B., and others, 2006, Status and trends in demography of northern spotted owls, 1985–2003: Wildlife Monographs, v. 163, 48 p.

Apanius, Victor, and Nisbet, Ian C. T., 2006, Serum immunoglobulin G levels are positively related to reproductive performance in a long-lived seabird, the common tern (*Sterna hirundo*): Oecologia (Berlin), v. 147, no. 1, p. 12–23.

Backlund, Doug, 2006, Northern saw-whet owl banding in central South Dakota 2002–2005: South Dakota Bird Notes, v. 58, no. 4, p. 65–67.

Baker, Lauren M., Peery, M. Zachariah, Burkett, Esther E., and others, 2006, Nesting habitat characteristics of the marbled murrelet in central California redwood forests: Journal of Wildlife Management, v. 70, no. 4, p. 939–946.

Barnard, Charlie, 2006, Notes on behavior, status and distribution: a banded glaucous gull: Connecticut Warbler, v. 26, no. 2, p. 62–63.

Berdeen, James B., and Otis, David L., 2006, Effects of subcutaneous transmitter implants on mourning doves: Wildlife Society Bulletin, v. 34, no. 1, p. 93–103.

Betts, Matthew G., Zitske, B. P., Hadley, A. S., and others, 2006, Migrant forest songbirds undertake breeding dispersal following timber harvest: Northeastern Naturalist, v. 13, no. 4, p. 531–536.

Binford, Laurence C., 2006, Birds of the Keweenaw Peninsula, Michigan: Miscellaneous Publications Museum of Zoology University of Michigan, no. 195, 297 p.

Blakesley, Jennifer A., Anderson, David R., and Noon, Barry R., 2006, Breeding dispersal in the California spotted owl: Condor, v. 108, no. 1, p. 71–81.

Boulet, Marylene, Gibbs, H. Lisle, and Hobson, Keith A., 2006, Integrated analysis of genetic, stable isotope, and banding data reveal migratory connectivity and flyways in the northern yellow warbler (*Dendroica petechia*; aestiva group): Ornithological Monographs, v. 61, p. 29–78.

Brady, Ryan, 2006, Great gray owls in northern Ashland and Bayfield counties, summer 2005: Passenger Pigeon, v. 68, no. 1, p. 19–34.

Breininger, David R., Toland, Brian, Oddy, Donna M., and others, 2006, Landcover characterizations and Florida scrub-jay (*Aphelocoma coerulescens*) population dynamics: Biological Conservation, v. 128, no. 2, p. 169–181.

Breton, Andre, Diamond, Antony W., and Kress, Stephen W., 2006, Surface wear of incoloy and darvic bands on Atlantic puffin adults and chicks: Journal of Field Ornithology, v. 77, no. 2, p. 111–119.

Breton, Andre R., Diamond, Antony W., and Kress, Stephen W., 2006, Encounter, survival, and movement probabilities from an Atlantic puffin (*Fratercula arctica*) metapopulation: Ecological Monographs, v. 76, no. 1, p. 133–149.

Brooks, Elizabeth W., 2006, Atlantic Flyway review: spring 2005: North American Bird Bander, v. 31, no. 1, p. 32–45.

Bulluck, Lesley P., and Buehler, David A., 2006, Avian use of early successional habitats: are regenerating forests, utility right-of-ways and reclaimed surface mines the same?: Forest Ecology and Management, v. 236, no. 1, p. 76–84.

Caldwell, Sarah S., and Mills, Alexander M., 2006, Comparative spring migration arrival dates in the two morphs of white-throated sparrow: Wilson Journal of Ornithology, v. 118, no. 3, p. 326–332.

Campbell, Susan, 2006, First black-chinned hummingbird (*Archilochus alexandri*) banded in North Carolina: Chat (Raleigh), v. 70, no. 1, p. 17–18.

Carfagno, Gerardo L., Heske, Edward J., and Weatherhead, Patrick J., 2006, Does mammalian prey abundance explain forest-edge use by snakes?: Ecoscience, v. 13, no. 3, p. 293–297.

Champoux, L., Masse, D. C., Evers, D., and others, 2006, Assessment of mercury exposure and potential effects on common loons (*Gavia immer*) in Quebec: Hydrobiologia, v. 567, p. 263–274.

Chassot, Olivier, Monge Arias, Guisselle, Mcreynolds, Mark S., and others, 2006, [Preliminary list of bibliographical references on parrots of Mesoamerica.]: Mesoamericana, v. 10, no. 2, p. 106–125.

Cink, Calvin L., 2006, Recoveries of eastern phoebes banded as nestlings in northeastern Kansas: Kansas Ornithological Society Bulletin, v. 57, no. 1, p. 12–20.

Collins, Charles T., 2006, Banding studies of Caspian terns in southern California: North American Bird Bander, v. 31, no. 1, p. 10–17.

—, 2006, Banding studies of elegant terns in southern California: North American Bird Bander, v. 31, no. 1, p. 17–22.

Cone, D. K., Marcogliese, D. J., Barse, A. M., and others, 2006, The myxozoan fauna of *Fundulus diaphanus* (Cyprinodontidae) from freshwater localities in eastern North America: Prevalence, community structure, and geographic distribution: Journal of Parasitology, v. 92, no. 1, p. 52–57.

Cotter, Richard C., and Hines, James E., 2006, Distribution and abundance of breeding and moulting brant on Banks Island, Northwest Territories, 1992–1994: Canadian Wildlife Service Occasional Paper, v. 112, p. 18–26.

Davidar, Priya, and Morton, Eugene S., 2006, Are multiple infections more severe for purple martins (*Progne subis*) than single infections?: Auk, v. 123, no. 1, p. 141–147.

Davies, J. Chris, 2006, Ontario cooperative banding program 2005: Ontario Bird Banding, v. 37, p. 46–47.

Dunn, Erica H., Hobson, Keith A., Wassenaar, Len I., and others, 2006, Identification of Summer Origins of Songbirds Migrating through Southern Canada in Autumn: Avian Conservation and Ecology, v. 1, no. 2, article 4.

Farmer, Gail C., Mccarty, Kyle, Robertson, Sue, and others, 2006, Suspected predation by accipiters on radio-tracked American kestrels (*Falco sparverius*) in Eastern Pennsylvania, USA: Journal of Raptor Research, v. 40, no. 4, p. 294–297.

Finnegan, Sue, 2006, Atlantic Flyway review: region I (Northeast)—Fall 2005 report: North American Bird Bander, v. 31, no. 2, p. 79–84.

Flint, Paul L., Grand, J. Barry, Fondell, Thomas F., and others, 2006, Population dynamics of greater scaup breeding on the Yukon-Kuskokwim Delta, Alaska: Wildlife Monographs, v. 162, 22 p.

Gill, Douglas E., Blank, Peter, Parks, Jared, and others, 2006, Plants and breeding bird response on a managed Conservation Reserve Program grassland in Maryland: Wildlife Society Bulletin, v. 34, no. 4, p. 944–956.

Gregoire, John A., 2006, Atlantic Flyway review: Region II (North Central) Fall 2005: North American Bird Bander, v. 31, no. 1, p. 46–53.

Groh, Terri, and Wernaart, Martin, 2006, Banding in Ontario: 2005: Ontario Bird Banding, v. 37, 17 p.

Hagen, Christian A., Sandercock, Brett K., Pitman, James C., and others, 2006, Radiotelemetry survival estimates of lesser prairie-chickens in Kansas: are there transmitter biases?: Wildlife Society Bulletin, v. 34, no. 4, p. 1064–1069.

Hall, Galon I., Butler, Matthew J., Wallace, Mark C., and others, 2006, Rio Grande wild turkey home ranges in the southern Great Plains: Proceedings of the Annual Conference Southeastern Association of Fish and Wildlife Agencies, v. 60, p. 36–42.

Hayes, Matthew A., and Barzen, Jeb, 2006, Dynamics of breeding and non-breeding sandhill cranes in South-central Wisconsin: Passenger Pigeon, v. 68, no. 4, p. 345–352.

Holevinski, R. A., Malecki, R. A., and Curtis, P. D., 2006, Can hunting of translocated nuisance Canada geese reduce local conflicts?: Wildlife Society Bulletin, v. 34, no. 3, p. 845–849.

Houston, C. Stuart, and Houston, Mary I., 2006, Bohemian waxwing banding results in North America, 1923–2003: North American Bird Bander, v. 31, no. 4, p. 161–168.

—, 2006, Ring-billed gulls banded in Saskatchewan, 1936–1989: Blue Jay, v. 64, no. 3, p. 131–148.

Hupp, Jerry W., Pearce, John M., Mulcahy, Daniel M., and others, 2006, Effects of abdominally implanted radiotransmitters with percutaneous antennas on migration, reproduction, and survival of Canada geese: Journal of Wildlife Management, v. 70, no. 3, p. 812–822.

Hylton, Rebecca A., Frederick, Peter C., De La Fuente, Teresa E., and others, 2006, Effects of nestling health on postfledging survival of wood storks: Condor, v. 108, no. 1, p. 97–106.

Hyrenbach, K. D., Keiper, C., Allen, S. G. , and others, 2006, Use of marine sanctuaries by far-ranging predators: commuting flights to the California Current System by breeding Hawaiian albatrosses: Fisheries Oceanography, v. 15, no. 2, p. 95–103.

Iverson, Samuel A., and Esler, Daniel, 2006, Site fidelity and the demographic implications of winter movements by a migratory bird, the harlequin duck *Histrionicus histrionicus*: Journal of Avian Biology, v. 37, no. 3, p. 219–228.

Jenkins, J. Mark, and Jackman, Ronald E., 2006, Lifetime reproductive success of bald eagles in northern California: Condor, v. 108, no. 3, p. 730–735.

King, D. I., Degraaf, R. M., Smith, M. L., and others, 2006, Habitat selection and habitat-specific survival of fledgling ovenbirds (*Seiurus aurocapilla*): Journal of Zoology (London), v. 269, no. 4, p. 414–421.

Lake, Bryce C., Walker, Johann, and Lindberg, Mark S., 2006, Survival of ducks banded in the boreal forest of Alaska: Journal of Wildlife Management, v. 70, no. 2, p. 443–449.

Lane, William H., 2006, Owls in Tofte: a summary report of Fall 2005 banding efforts in Tofte, Minnesota: Loon, v. 78, no. 4, p. 188–189.

Lariviere, Serge, Walton, Lyle R., and Messier, Francois, 2006, Summer movements and impact of individual Striped Skunks, Mephitis mephitis, on duck nests in Saskatchewan: Canadian Field-Naturalist, v. 120, no. 3, p. 342–346.

Liu, Wan-Chun, and Kroodsma, Donald E., 2006, Song learning by chipping sparrows: when, where, and from whom: Condor, v. 108, no. 3, p. 509–517.

Loughman, Kay, 2006, Western station reports: North American Bird Bander, v. 31, no. 2, p. 97–99.

Macgregor-Fors, Ian, 2006, Short note about the distribution of banded quail, an endemic species from Mexico: Huitzil, v. 7, no. 2, p. 30–31.

Martin, Julien, Nichols, James D., Kitchens, Wiley M., and others, 2006, Multiscale patterns of movement in fragmented landscapes and consequences on demography of the snail kite in Florida: Journal of Animal Ecology, v. 75, no. 2, p. 527–539.

Master, Terry, and Detwiler, Don, 2006, Foraging success and habitat use by a population of great egrets (*Egretta alba*) on the Susquehanna River: Journal of the Pennsylvania Academy of Science, v. 79, p. 116.

Mattsson, Brady J., Meyers, J. Michael, and Cooper, Robert J., 2006, Detrimental impacts of radiotransmitters on juvenile Louisiana waterthrushes: Journal of Field Ornithology, v. 77, no. 2, p. 173–177.

Mcintyre, Carol L., and Collopy, Michael W., 2006, Postfledging dependence period of migratory golden eagles (*Aquila chrysaetos*) in Denali National Park and preserve, Alaska: Auk, v. 123, no. 3, p. 877–884.

Mcintyre, Carol L., Collopy, Michael W., and Lindberg, Mark S., 2006, Survival probability and mortality of migratory juvenile golden eagles from interior Alaska: Journal of Wildlife Management, v. 70, no. 3, p. 717–722.

Mead, Alfred J., 2006, Recovering bird bands: the joy of discovery: Oriole, v. 70–71, no. 1–4, p. 21–22.

Morris, Sara R., Larracuente, Amanda M., Covino, Kristen M., and others, 2006, Utility of open population models: limitations posed by parameter estimability in the study of migratory stopover: Wilson Journal of Ornithology, v. 118, no. 4, p. 513–526.

Morrison, R. I. G., 2006, Body transformations, condition, and survival in Red Knots Calidris canutus travelling to breed at Alert, Ellesmere Island, Canada: Ardea, v. 94, no. 3, p. 607–618.

Morse, Julie A., Powell, Abby N., and Tetreau, Michael D., 2006, Productivity of black oystercatchers: effects of recreational disturbance in a national park: Condor, v. 108, no. 3, p. 623–633.

Mosbech, Anders, Dano, Rikke S., Merkel, Flemming, and others, 2006, Use of Satellite Telemetry to Locate Key Habitats for King Eiders Somateria Spectabilis in West Greenland, *in* Boere, G.C., Galbraith, C.A., and Stroud, D.A., eds., Waterbirds Around the World: a Global Overview of the Conservation, Management and Research of the World's Waterbird Flyways. International Conference on Waterbirds Held in Edinburgh in April 2004: Edinburgh, The Stationery Office, p. 769–776.

Mosbech, Anders, Gilchrist, Grant, Merkel, Flemming, and others, 2006, Year-round movements of Northern Common Eiders Somateria mollissima borealis breeding in Arctic Canada and West Greenland followed by satellite telemetry: Ardea, v. 94, no. 3, Sp. Iss. SI, p. 651–665.

Nack, Robert R., and Andersen, David E., 2006, Brood movements of Eastern Prairie Population Canada geese: Potential influence of light goose abundance: Journal of Wildlife Management, v. 70, no. 2, p. 435–442.

Newton, Ian, 2006, Advances in the study of irruptive migration: Ardea, v. 94, no. 3, p. 433–460.

O'leary, Betty, 2006, A leg banding success: Journal of Wildlife Rehabilitation, v. 28, no. 1, p. 33.

Olsen, Ben T., Hannon, Susan J., and Court, Gordon S., 2006, Short-term Response of Breeding Barred Owls to Forestry in a Boreal Mixedwood Forest Landscape: Avian Conservation and Ecology, v. 1, no. 3, article 1.

Ortego, Brent, 2006, IBBA Annual Report of birds banded, 2005: North American Bird Bander, v. 31, no. 2, p. 91–96.

Overton, Cory T., Schmitz, Richard A., and Casazza, Michael L., 2006, Linking landscape characteristics to mineral site use by band-tailed pigeons in western Oregon: coarse-filter conservation with fine-filter tuning: Natural Areas Journal, v. 26, no. 1, p. 38–46.

Pandolfino, Edward R., Kwolek, Jeremy, and Kreitinger, Kim, 2006, Expansion of the breeding range of the Hooded Merganser within California: Western Birds, v. 37, no. 4, p. 228–236.

Pascoe, Carl A., 2006, 2005 HBMO passerine and hummingbird banding report: Ontario Bird Banding, v. 37, p. 37–45.

Pearce, John M., and Talbot, Sandra L., 2006, Demography, genetics, and the value of mixed messages: Condor, v. 108, no. 2, p. 474–479.

Phillips, L. M., Oppel, S., and Powell, A. N., 2006, Movements of the King Eider during the non-breeding period revealed by satellite telemetry: Journal of Ornithology, v. 147, no. 5, Suppl. 1, p. 118–119.

Phillips, Laura M., and Powell, Abby N., 2006, Evidence for wing molt and breeding site fidelity in king eiders: Waterbirds, v. 29, no. 2, p. 148–153.

Phillips, Laura M., Powell, Abby N., and Rexstad, Eric A., 2006, Large-scale movements and habitat characteristics of king eiders throughout the nonbreeding period: Condor, v. 108, no. 4, p. 887–900.

Pollock, Mark G., and Paxton, Eben H., 2006, Floating mist nets: a technique for capturing birds in flooded habitat: Journal of Field Ornithology, v. 77, no. 3, p. 335–338.

Post, William, 2006, A South Carolina winter banding recovery of a broad-winged hawk (*Buteo platypterus*), and a review of the species' regional winter status: Chat (Raleigh), v. 70, no. 4, p. 117–120.

Poulin, Ray G., Todd, L. Danielle, Wellicome, Troy I., and others, 2006, Assessing the feasibility of release techniques for captive-bred burrowing owls: Journal of Raptor Research, v. 40, no. 2, p. 142–150.

Pranty, Bill, 2006, Field observations: Spring Report: March-May 2006: Florida Field Naturalist, v. 34, no. 4, p. 124–135.

Proudfoot, Glenn A., Teel, Pete D., and Mohr, Rachel M., 2006, Ferruginous pygmy-owl (*Glaucidium brasilianum*) and eastern screech-owl (*Megascopes* [Megascops] *asio*): new hosts for *Philornis mimicola* (Diptera: Muscidae) and Ornithodoros concanensis (Acari: Argasidae): Journal of Wildlife Diseases, v. 42, no. 4, p. 873–876.

Rimmer, Christoper C., Faccio, Steven D., Mcfarland, Kent P., and others, 2006, Ecology and demography of Bicknell's thrush on East Mountain, East Haven, Vermont: evaluating potential impacts of wind turbine construction. Year 2 progress report: VINS Technical Report, v. 06–01, 32 p.

Robbins, Chandler S., 2006, Atlantic Flyway review: region IV, Piedmont-coastal plain, fall 2005: North American Bird Bander, v. 31, no. 2, p. 85–90.

Robert, M., Drolet, B., and Savard, J. P. L., 2006, Effects of backpack radio-transmitters on female Barrow's Goldeneyes: Waterbirds, v. 29, no. 1, p. 115–120.

Robinson, James A., Gudmundsson, G., and Clausen, P., 2006, Flyways of the East Canadian High Arctic Light-Bellied Brent Goose Branta Bernicla Hrota: Results of a Satellite Telemetry Study, *in* Boere, G.C., Galbraith, C.A., and Stroud, D.A., eds., Waterbirds Around the World: a Global Overview of the Conservation, Management and Research of the World's Waterbird Flyways. International Conference on Waterbirds Held in Edinburgh in April 2004: Edinburgh, The Stationery Office, p. 519.

Rosier, Jeff R., Ronan, Noelle A., and Rosenberg, Daniel K., 2006, Post-breeding dispersal of burrowing owls in an extensive California grassland: American Midland Naturalist, v. 155, no. 1, p. 162–167.

Roth, T. C., Lima, S. L., and Vetter, W. E., 2006, Determinants of predation risk in small wintering birds: the hawk's perspective: Behavioral Ecology and Sociobiology, v. 60, no. 2, p. 195–204.

Rousseau, Amelie, 2006, Monitoring fall migration on the sunshine coast of British Columbia: British Columbia Birds, v. 14, p. 12–20.

Schaefer, Richard R., and Fagan, Jesse F., 2006, Commensal foraging by a fan-tailed warbler (*Euthlypis lachrymosa*) with a nine-banded armadillo (*Dasypus novemcinctus*) in southwestern Mexico: Southwestern Naturalist, v. 51, no. 4, p. 560–562.

Shields, Roger D., and Flake, Lester D., 2006, Survival and reproduction of translocated Eastern Wild Turkeys in a sparsely wooded landscape in northeastern South Dakota: Western North American Naturalist, v. 66, no. 3, p. 298–309.

Shipley, Kathryn L., and Scott, David P., 2006, Survival and nesting habitat use by sichuan and ring-necked pheasants released in Ohio: Ohio Journal of Science, v. 106, no. 3, p. 78–85.

Sonsthagen, Sarah A., Rodriguez, Ronald L., and White, Clayton M., 2006, Satellite telemetry of Northern Goshawks breeding in Utah—I. Annual movements: Studies in Avian Biology, no. 31, p. 239–251.

Sonsthagen, Sarah A., Rodriguez, Ronald L., and White, Clayton M., 2006, Satellite telemetry of Northern Goshawks breeding in Utah—II. Annual habitats: Studies in Avian Biology, v. 31, p. 252–259.

Stabins, Amy J., Raedeke, Kenneth J., and Manuwal, David A., 2006, Productivity of great blue herons in King County, Washington: Northwest Science, v. 80 , no. 2, p. 116–119.

Stapleton, Mary K., and Robertson, Raleigh J., 2006, Female tree swallow home-range movements during their fertile period as revealed by radio-tracking: Wilson Journal of Ornithology, v. 118, no. 4, p. 502–507.

Steenhof, Karen, Bates, Kirk K., Fuller, Mark R., and others, 2006, Effects of radiomarking on prairie falcons: Attachment failures provide insights about survival: Wildlife Society Bulletin, v. 34, no. 1, p. 116–126.

Thorup, Kasper, Fuller, Mark, Alerstam, Thomas, and others, 2006, Do migratory flight paths of raptors follow constant geographical or geomagnetic courses?: Animal Behaviour, v. 72, no. Part 4, p. 875–880.

Tuttle, Elaina M., Jensen, Ryan R., Formica, Vincent A., and others, 2006, Using remote sensing image texture to study habitat use patterns: a case study using the polymorphic white-throated sparrow (*Zonotrichia albicollis*): Global Ecology and Biogeography, v. 15, no. 4, p. 349–357.

Underwood, Jared, White, Clayton M., and Rodriguez, Ronald L., 2006, Winter movement and habitat use of Northern Goshawks breeding in Utah: Studies in Avian Biology, no. 31, p. 228–238.

Vitz, Andrew C., and Rodewald, Amanda D., 2006, Can regenerating clearcuts benefit mature-forest songbirds? An examination of post-breeding ecology: Biological Conservation, v. 127, no. 4, p. 477–486.

Ward, Michael P., Raim, Arlo, Yaremych-Hamer, Sarah, and others, 2006, Does the roosting behavior of birds affect transmission dynamics of West Nile virus?: American Journal of Tropical Medicine and Hygiene, v. 75, no. 2, p. 350–355.

Warnock, N., Bishop, M. A., Takekawa, J., and others, 2006, Connecting the spots—Influences on site use by migratory Pacific Flyway shorebirds: Journal of Ornithology, v. 147, no. 5, Suppl. 1, p. 53.

Wenny, Daniel, Anderson, Lynn, Kirk, D. A. , and others, 2006, Ecology and genetics of an isolated population of Swainson's hawks in Illinois: Journal of Raptor Research, v. 40, no. 4, p. 270–276.

West, Steve, 2006, First winter band recovery of cave swallow from Mexico: North American Bird Bander, v. 31, no. 1, p. 26–27.

Wiebe Robertson, Myra O., and Hines, James E., 2006, Status, distribution, and abundance of black brant on the mainland of the Inuvialuit Settlement Region, Northwest Territories, 1995–1998: Canadian Wildlife Service Occasional Paper, v. 112, p. 9–17.

Wiens, J. David, Reynolds, Richard T., and Noon, Barry R., 2006, Juvenile movement and natal dispersal of northern goshawks in Arizona: Condor, v. 108, no. 2, p. 253–269.

Yackel Adams, Amy A., Skagen, Susan K., and Savidge, Julie A., 2006, Modeling post-fledging survival of lark buntings in response to ecological and biological factors: Ecology (Washington D.C.), v. 87, no. 1, p. 178–188.

Zharikov, Yuri, Lank, David B., Huettmann, Falk, and others, 2006, Habitat selection and breeding success in a forest-nesting Alcid, the marbled murrelet, in two landscapes with different degrees of forest fragmentation: Landscape Ecology, v. 21, no. 1, p. 107–120.

Zimpfer, Nathan L., and Conroy, Michael J., 2006, Modeling movement and fidelity of American black ducks: Journal of Wildlife Management, v. 70, no. 6, p. 1770–1777.

Zimpfer, Nathan L., and Conroy, Michael J., 2006, Models of production rates in American black duck populations: Journal of Wildlife Management, v. 70, no. 4, p. 947–954.

2005

Bald eagles of eastern Idaho Greater Yellowstone ecosystem: 2005 annual productivity report with summary of related research, 2005, Idaho Bureau of Land Management Technical Bulletin, v. 2005–08, 34 p.

Implementation of the Alberta Piping Plover Recovery Plan, 2002–2004: final program report, 2005, Alberta Species at Risk Report, v. 99, 19 p.

Northwest Forest Plan—the first ten years (1994–2003): status and trends of northern spotted owl populations and habitat, 2005, U.S. Forest Service General Technical Report PNW-GTR-648, 176 p.

Abstracts, 2005, Summary of April 15–17 2005 Annual Meeting of the Eastern Bird Banding Association "Partners Across Borders" celebrating Canadian and United States banding research: North American Bird Bander, v. 30, no. 2, p. 76–85.

Anderson, J. G. T., and Anderson, K. B., 2005, An analysis of band returns of the American White Pelican, 1922 to 1981: Waterbirds, v. 28, p. 55–60.

Anderson, Kurt E., Rothstein, Stephen I., Fleischer, Robert C., and others, 2005, Large-scale movement patterns between song dialects in brown-headed cowbirds (*Molothrus ater*): Auk, v. 122, no. 3, p. 803–818.

Anonymous, 2005, Color-banded shorebirds on Long Island, summer 2005: Kingbird, v. 55, no. 4, p. 341–342.

Atkinson, Philip W., Baker, Allan J., Bevan, Richard M., and others, 2005, Unravelling the migration and moult strategies of a long-distance migrant using stable isotopes: red knot *Calidris canutus* movements in the Americas: Ibis, v. 147, no. 4, p. 738–749.

Backlund, Doug, Dowd Stukel, Eileen, Kiesow, Alyssa, and others, 2005, 2004 bird banding report for Farm Island and Fisherman Point, near Pierre, South Dakota: South Dakota Bird Notes, v. 57, no. 1, p. 4–10.

Barber, Colleen A., Edwards, Mandy J., and Robertson, Raleigh J., 2005, A test of the genetic compatibility hypothesis with tree swallows, *Tachycineta bicolor*: Canadian Journal of Zoology, v. 83, no. 7, p. 955–961.

Bartlett, Terri L., Mock, Douglas W., and Schwagmeyer, P. L., 2005, Division of labor: incubation and biparental care in house sparrows (*Passer domesticus*): Auk, v. 122, no. 3, p. 835–842.

Bayard De Volo, Shelley, Reynolds, Richard T., Topinka, J. Rick, and others, 2005, Population genetics and genotyping for mark-recapture studies of northern goshawks (*Accipiter gentilis*) on the Kaibab Plateau, Arizona: Journal of Raptor Research, v. 39, no. 3, p. 286–295.

Bayne, Erin M., Boutin, Stan, Tracz, Boyan, and others, 2005, Functional and numerical responses of ovenbirds (*Seiurus aurocapilla*) to changing seismic exploration practices in Alberta's boreal forest: Ecoscience, v. 12, no. 2, p. 216–222.

Bayne, Erin M., Van Wilgenburg, Steve L., Boutin, Stan, and others, 2005, Modeling and field-testing of ovenbird (*Seiurus aurocapillus*) responses to boreal forest dissection by energy sector development at multiple spatial scales: Landscape Ecology, v. 20, no. 2, p. 203–216.

Blanco, Pedro, and Sanchez, Barbara, 2005, Band recoveries of Nearctic migratory birds of the order Anseriformes in Cuba: Journal of Caribbean Ornithology, v. 18, no. 1, p. 1–6.

Boisvert, Jennifer H., Hoffman, Richard W., and Reese, Kerry P., 2005, Home range and seasonal movements of Columbian sharp-tailed grouse associated with conservation reserve program and mine reclamation: Western North American Naturalist, v. 65, no. 1, p. 36–44.

Brand, Stijn, Lott, Casey A., and Brennan Mulrooney, M., 2005, Two Bicknell's thrushes banded during spring migration on key largo: first accepted records for Florida: Florida Field Naturalist, v. 33, no. 3, p. 102–104.

Brauning, Daniel, 2005, Falcon wanderings: daily movements of five juvenile peregrine falcons: Pennsylvania Birds, v. 18, no. 3, p. 168–171.

Breton, Andre R., Diamond, Antony W., and Kress, Stephen W., 2005, Adult survival estimates from two Atlantic puffin (*Fratercula arctica*) colonies in the Gulf of Maine: Auk, v. 122, no. 3, p. 773–782.

Bronson, C. L., Grubb, Thomas C. Jr., Sattler, Gene D., and others, 2005, Reproductive success across the black-capped chickadee (*Poecile atricapillus*) and Carolina chickadee (*P. carolinensis*) hybrid zone in Ohio: Auk, v. 122, no. 3, p. 759–772.

Brooks, Elizabeth W., 2005, Atlantic flyway review: region III (Western Ridge)—Fall 2004: North American Bird Bander, v. 30, no. 4, p. 179–190.

Calvert, Anna M., Gauthier, Gilles, and Reed, Austin, 2005, Spatiotemporal heterogeneity of greater snow goose harvest and implications for hunting regulations: Journal of Wildlife Management, v. 69, no. 2, p. 561–573.

Casazza, Michael L., Yee, Julie. L., Miller, Michael R., and others, 2005, Evaluation of current population indices for band-tailed pigeons: Wildlife Society Bulletin, v. 33, no. 2, p. 606–615.

Catlin, D. H, Rosenberg, D. K., and Haley, K. L., 2005, The effects of nesting success and mate fidelity on breeding dispersal in burrowing owls: Canadian Journal of Zoology, v. 83, no. 12, p. 1574–1580.

Coleman, J. T. H., Richmond, M. E., Rudstam, L. G., and others, 2005, Six years of double-crested cormorant management on Oneida Lake, New York—Have fish populations responded?: IAGLR Conference Program and Abstracts, v. 48, p. 37.

Coleman, Jeremy T. H., Richmond, Milo E., and Linse, Michael H., 2005, A Programmable Release Device for the Recovery of Avian Telemetry Tags, *in* van Eerden, Mennobart R., and van Rijn, Stef, eds., Proceedings 7th International Conference on Cormorants, 4th Meeting of Wetlands International Cormorant Research Group 23–26 November 2005, Villeneuve, Switzerland: Lelystad, Wetlands International-Iucn Cormorant Research Group, p. 157–161.

Coleman, Jeremy T. H., Richmond, Milo E., Rudstam, Lars G., and others, 2005, Foraging location and site fidelity of the double-crested cormorant on Oneida Lake, New York: Waterbirds, v. 28, no. 4, p. 498–510.

Conroy, Michael J., Fonnesbeck, Christopher J., and Zimpfer, Nathan L., 2005, Modeling regional waterfowl harvest rates using Markov chain Monte Carlo: Journal of Wildlife Management, v. 69, no. 1, p. 77–90.

Conway, Courtney J., and Garcia, Victoria, 2005, Effects of radiotransmitters on natal recruitment of burrowing owls: Journal of Wildlife Management, v. 69, no. 1, p. 404–408.

Cooper, Caren B., Hochachka, Wesley M., and Dhondt, Andre A., 2005, Latitudinal trends in within-year reoccupation of nest boxes and their implications: Journal of Avian Biology, v. 36, no. 1, p. 31–39.

Davies, J. Chris, and Pollard, Bruce, 2005, Ontario cooperative banding program banding results for 2004: Ontario Bird Banding, v. 36, p. 57–59.

Delong, J. P., Meehan, T. D., and Smith, R. B., 2005, Investigating fall movements of hatch-year flammulated owls (*Otus flammeolus*) in central New Mexico using stable hydrogen isotopes: Journal of Raptor Research, v. 39, no. 1, p. 19–25.

Devault, Travis L., Reinhart, Bradley D., Brisbin, I. Lehr Jr, and others, 2005, Flight behavior of black and turkey vultures: implications for reducing bird-aircraft collisions: Journal of Wildlife Management, v. 69, no. 2, p. 601–608.

Dzialak, Matthew R. L, Lacki, Michael J., Larkin, Jeffery L., and others, 2005, Corridors affect dispersal initiation in reintroduced peregrine falcons: Animal Conservation, v. 8, no. Part 4, p. 421–430.

Eimes, John A., Parker, Patricia G., Brown, Jerram L., and others, 2005, Extrapair fertilization and genetic similarity of social mates in the Mexican jay: Behavioral Ecology, v. 16, no. 2, p. 456–460.

Feuerbacher, Charles K., Locke, Shawn L., Lopez, Roel R., and others, 2005, A comparison of brood stock origin for eastern wild turkey restoration in eastern Texas: Texas Journal of Science, v. 57, no. 2, p. 175–186.

Figuerola, J., Green, A. J., and Michot, T. C., 2005, Invertebrate eggs can fly: Evidence of waterfowl-mediated gene flow in aquatic invertebrates: American Naturalist, v. 165, no. 2, p. 274–280.

Frey, Robert I., and Alexander, John D., 2005, The Klamath Bird Observatory 2005 banding report: North American Bird Bander, v. 30, no. 4, p. 212.

Friesen, L., Cheskey, E. D., Cadman, M., and others, 2005, Early impacts of residential development on wood thrushes in an urbanizing forest: U.S. Forest Service General Technical Report PSW-GTR-191, p. 335–344.

Gee, Jennifer M., 2005, No species barrier by call in an avian hybrid zone between California and Gambel's quail (*Callipepla californica* and *C. gambelii*): Biological Journal of the Linnean Society, v. 86, no. 2, p. 253–264.

Ginter, Daniel L., and Desmond, Martha J., 2005, Influence of foraging and roosting behavior on home-range size and movement patterns of Savannah Sparrows wintering in south Texas: Wilson Bulletin, v. 117, no. 1, p. 63–71.

Groh, Terri, and Wernaart, Martin, 2005, Banding in Ontario 2004: Ontario Bird Banding, v. 36, p. 1–16.

Hagen, Christian A., Pitman, James C., Sandercock, Brett K., and others, 2005, Age-specific variation in apparent survival rates of male lesser prairie-chickens: Condor, v. 107, no. 1, p. 78–86.

Harris, Wayne C., Duncan, David D., Franken, Renee J., and others, 2005, Reproductive success of Piping Plovers at Big Quill Lake, Saskatchewan: Wilson Bulletin, v. 117, no. 2, p. 165–171.

Hayward, James L., Henson, Shandelle M., Logan, Clara J., and others, 2005, Predicting numbers of hauled-out harbour seals: a mathematical model: Journal of Applied Ecology, v. 42, no. 1, p. 108–117.

Herring, Garth, and Collazo, Jaime A., 2005, Habitat use, movements and home range of wintering Lesser Scaup in Florida: Waterbirds, v. 28, no. 1, p. 71–78.

Holloran, Matthew J., and Anderson, Stanley H., 2005, Spatial distribution of Greater Sage-Grouse nests in relatively contiguous sagebrush habitats: Condor, v. 107, no. 4, p. 742–752.

Houston, C. S., 2005, Long-eared Owls, Asio otus: A review of North American banding: Canadian Field-Naturalist, v. 119, no. 3, p. 395–402.

Houston, C. Stuart, 2005, Saskatchewan waterfowl banders to 1954: Blue Jay, v. 63, no. 4, p. 175–178.

Houston, C. Stuart, 2005, Swainson's hawk longevity, colour banding and natal dispersal: Blue Jay, v. 63, no. 1, p. 31–39.

Houston, C. Stuart, and Bloom, Peter H., 2005, Turkey vulture marking history: the switch from leg bands to patagial tags: North American Bird Bander, v. 30, no. 2, p. 59–64.

Hull, Buzz, 2005, Golden Gate Raptor Observatory fall 2005: North American Bird Bander, v. 30, no. 4, p. 211.

Husak, Michael S., 2005, Atypical pair-bonding behavior among golden-fronted woodpeckers (*Melanerpes aurifrons*): Southwestern Naturalist, v. 50, no. 1, p. 85–88.

James, R. Andrew, and Krementz, David G., 2005, Dispersal patterns of giant Canada geese in the central United States: Proceedings of the Annual Conference Southeastern Association of Fish and Wildlife Agencies, v. 59, p. 144–154.

Jones, K. L., Krapu, G. L., Brandt, D. A., and others, 2005, Population genetic structure in migratory sandhill cranes and the role of Pleistocene glaciations: Molecular Ecology, v. 14, no. 9, p. 2645–2657.

Jones, Zach F., and Bock, Carl E., 2005, The Botteri's Sparrow and exotic Arizona grasslands: An ecological trap or habitat regained?: Condor, v. 107, no. 4, p. 731–741.

Kassube, Cory M., Restani, Marco, Goetz, Sharon L., and others, 2005, Annual survival and productivity of wild turkey hens transplanted north of their ancestral range in central Minnesota: Minnesota Department of Natural Resources Summaries of Wildlife Research Findings, v. 2004, p. 41–49.

Koczaja, Cathy, Mccall, Laura, Fitch, Elizabeth, and others, 2005, Size-specific habitat segregation and intraspecific interactions in banded sculpin (*Cottus carolinae*): Southeastern Naturalist, v. 4, no. 2, p. 207–218.

Lacroix, Deborah Lise, Boyd, Sean, Esler, Daniel, and others, 2005, Surf Scoters Melanitta perspicillata aggregate in association with ephemerally abundant polychaetes: Marine Ornithology, v. 33, no. 1, p. 61–64.

Lehnen, Sarah E., and Krementz, David G., 2005, Turnover rates of fall-migrating pectoral sandpipers in the lower Mississippi Alluvial Valley: Journal of Wildlife Management, v. 69, no. 2, p. 671–680.

Lewis, Tyler L., Esler, Daniel, Boyd, W. Sean, and others, 2005, Nocturnal foraging behavior of wintering surf scoters and white-winged Scoters: Condor, v. 107, no. 3, p. 637–647.

Lima, Pedro Cerqueira, Hays, Helen, Da Rocha Lima, Rita De Cassia Ferreira, and others, 2005, Recoveries of Sterna hirundo (Linnaeus, 1758) in Bahia, Brazil, between 1995 and 2004: Ararajuba, v. 13, no. 2, p. 177–179.

Lyons, Donald E., Roby, Daniel D., and Collis, K., 2005, Foraging ecology of caspian terns in the Columbia River estuary, USA: Waterbirds, v. 28, no. 3, p. 280–291.

Madden, Elizabeth M., and Restani, Marco, 2005, History and breeding ecology of the American White Pelican at Medicine Lake National Wildlife Refuge, Montana: Waterbirds, v. 28, p. 23–26.

Mazerolle, D. F., Hobson, K. A., and Wassenaar, L. I., 2005, Stable isotope and band-encounter analyses delineate migratory patterns and catchment areas of white-throated sparrows at a migration monitoring station: Oecologia (Berlin), v. 144, no. 4, p. 541–549.

Mcclaren, Erica L., Kennedy, Patricia L., and Doyle, Donald D., 2005, Northern Goshawk (*Accipiter gentilis laingi*) post-fledging areas on Vancouver Island, British Columbia: Journal of Raptor Research, v. 39, no. 3, p. 253–263.

Mcfarlane Tranquilla, Laura, Parker, Nadine R., Bradley, Russell W., and others, 2005, Breeding chronology of marbled murrelets varies between coastal and inshore sites in southern British Columbia: Journal of Field Ornithology, v. 76, no. 4, p. 357–367.

Mcgowan, Conor P., Schulte, Shiloh A., and Simons, Theodore R., 2005, Resightings of marked American oystercatchers banded as chicks: Wilson Bulletin, v. 117, no. 4, p. 382–385.

Mehl, Katherine R., Alisauskas, Ray T., Hobson, Keith A., and others, 2005, Linking breeding and wintering areas of king eiders: Making use of polar isotopic gradients: Journal of Wildlife Management, v. 69, no. 3, p. 1297–1304.

Menu, Stephane, Gauthier, Gilles, and Reed, Austin, 2005, Survival of young greater snow geese (*Chen caerulescens atlantica*) during fall migration: Auk, v. 122, no. 2, p. 479–496.

Miles, John, 2005, Migration monitoring station and banding report for the Fall of 2004 in Selkirk Provincial Park: Ontario Bird Banding, v. 36, p. 41–44.

Miller, Michael R., Takekawa, John Y., Fleskes, Joseph P., and others, 2005, Flight speeds of northern pintails during migration determined using satellite telemetry: Wilson Bulletin, v. 117, no. 4, p. 364–374.

Miller, Michael R., Takekawa, John Y., Fleskes, Joseph P., and others, 2005, Spring migration of Northern Pintails from California's Central Valley wintering area tracked with satellite telemetry: routes, timing, and destinations: Canadian Journal of Zoology, v. 83, no. 10, p. 1314–1332.

Miller, Sherri L., and Ralph, C. John, 2005, A water-scale survey for stream-foraging birds in northern California: U.S. Forest Service General Technical Report PSW-GTR-191, p. 537–540.

Mills, Alexander M., 2005, Changes in the timing of spring and autumn migration in North American migrant passerines during a period of global warming: Ibis, v. 147, no. 2, p. 259–269.

—, 2005, Protogyny in autumn migration: Do male birds "play chicken"?: Auk, v. 122, no. 1, p. 71–81.

Moody, Allison T., Wilhelm, Sabina I., Cameron-Macmillan, Maureen L., and others, 2005, Divorce in common murres (*Uria aalge*): relationship to parental quality: Behavioral Ecology and Sociobiology, v. 57, no. 3, p. 224–230.

Morris, Sara R., Liebner, David A., Larracuente, Amanda M., and others, 2005, Multiple-day constancy as an alternative to pooling for estimating mark-recapture stopover length in Nearctic-Neotropical migrant landbirds: Auk, v. 122, no. 1, p. 319–328.

Morris, Sara R., Turner, Erica M., Liebner, David A., and others, 2005, Problems associated with pooling mark-recapture data prior to estimating stopover length for migratory passerines: U.S. Forest Service General Technical Report PSW-GTR-191, p. 673–679.

Nicolai, Chris A., Flint, Paul L., and Wege, Michael L., 2005, Annual survival and site fidelity of northern pintails banded on the Yukon-Kuskokwim Delta, Alaska: Journal of Wildlife Management, v. 69, no. 3, p. 1202–1210.

Nicoletti, Frank J., Brady, Ryan, and Alexander, David, 2005, The 2004–2005 influx of northern owls. Part III: northern hawk owl banding: Loon, v. 77, no. 4, p. 209–219.

Nisbet, Ian C. T., and Friar, Margaret S., 2005, Hook, line and sinker: a common tern recovers from a bizarre band injury: North American Bird Bander, v. 30, no. 4, p. 169–170.

O'hara, Patrick D., Fernandez, Guillermo, Becerril, Felipe, and others, 2005, Life history varies with migratory distance in western sandpipers Calidris mauri: Journal of Avian Biology, v. 36, no. 3, p. 191–202.

Overton, Cory T., Schmitz, Richard A., and Casazza, Michael L., 2005, Post-precipitation bias in band-tailed pigeon surveys conducted at mineral sites: Wildlife Society Bulletin, v. 33, no. 3, p. 1047–1054.

Paredes, Rosana, Jones, Ian L., and Boness, Daryl J., 2005, Reduced parental care, compensatory behaviour and reproductive costs of thick-billed murres equipped with data loggers: Animal Behaviour , v. 69, no. 1, p. 197–208.

Pearce, J. M., Reed, J. A., and Flint, P. L., 2005, Geographic variation in survival and migratory tendency among North American Common Mergansers: Journal of Field Ornithology, v. 76, no. 2, p. 109–118.

Pearce, J. M., Talbot, S. L., Petersen, M. R., and others, 2005, Limited genetic differentiation among breeding, molting, and wintering groups of the threatened Steller's eider: the role of historic and contemporary factors: Conservation Genetics, v. 6, no. 5, p. 743–757.

Powell, Larkin A., Lang, Jason D., Krementz, David G., and others, 2005, Use of radio-telemetry to reduce bias in nest searching: Journal of Field Ornithology, v. 76, no. 3, p. 274–278.

Priestly, Lisa, 2005, Phenology of three raptor species in central Alberta based on nest banding records: Blue Jay, v. 63, no. 1, p. 26–30.

Proudfoot, Glenn A., Usener, Jessica L., and Teel, Pete D., 2005, Ferruginous Pygmy-Owls: A new host for Protocalliphora sialia and Hesperocimex sonorensis in Arizona: Wilson Bulletin, v. 117, no. 2, p. 185–188.

Reed, Eric T., Gauthier, Gilles, and Pradel, Roger, 2005, Effects of neck bands on reproduction and survival of female greater snow geese: Journal of Wildlife Management, v. 69, no. 1, p. 91–100.

Reese, Kerry P., Beck, Jeffrey L., Zager, Peter, and others, 2005, Nest and brood site characteristics of mountain quail in west-central Idaho: Northwest Science, v. 79, no. 4, p. 254–264.

Rhymer, J. M., Mcauley, D. G., and Ziel, H. L., 2005, Phylogeography of the American woodcock (*Scolopax minor*): Are management units based on band recovery data reflected in genetically based management units?: Auk, v. 122, no. 4, p. 1149–1160.

Rizzolo, Daniel J., Esler, Daniel, Roby, Daniel D., and others, 2005, Do wintering Harlequin Ducks forage nocturnally at high latitudes?: Condor, v. 107, no. 1, p. 173–177.

Roberts, Dan A., Parrish, Jimmie R., and Howe, Frank P., 2005, Repeats, returns, and estimated flight ranges of Neotropical migratory birds in Utah riparian habitat: U.S. Forest Service General Technical Report PSW-GTR-191, p. 690–697.

Roth, T. C., Lima, S. L., and Vetter, W. E., 2005, Survival and causes of mortality in wintering sharp-shinned Hawks and Cooper's Hawks: Wilson Bulletin, v. 117, no. 3, p. 237–244.

Royle, J. Andrew, and Garrettson, Pamela R., 2005, The effect of reward band value on mid-continent mallard band reporting rates: Journal of Wildlife Management, v. 69, no. 2, p. 800–804.

Salinas-Melgoza, Alejandro, and Renton, Katherine, 2005, Seasonal variation in activity patterns of juvenile Lilac-crowned Parrots in tropical dry forest: Wilson Bulletin, v. 117, no. 3, p. 291–295.

Salter, Gregory C., Robel, Robert J., and Kemp, Kenneth E., 2005, Lesser prairie-chicken use of harvested corn fields during fall and winter in southwestern Kansas: Prairie Naturalist, v. 37, no. 1, p. 1–9.

Sandercock, B. K., Szekely, T., and Kosztolanyi, A., 2005, The effects of age and sex on the apparent survival of Kentish Plovers breeding in southern Turkey: Condor, v. 107, no. 3, p. 583–596.

Schiff, Seymour, and Farina, Michael, 2005, Peregrine falcons nesting on Long Island: Kingbird, v. 55, no. 3, p. 228–235.

Shaffer, Scott A., Tremblay, Yann, Awkerman, Jill A., and others, 2005, Comparison of light- and SST-based geolocation with satellite telemetry in free-ranging albatrosses: Marine Biology (Berlin), v. 147, no. 4, p. 833–843.

Sheaffer, Susan E., Kendall, William L., and Bowers, E. Frank, 2005, Impact of special early harvest seasons on subarctic-nesting and temperate-nesting Canada geese: Journal of Wildlife Management, v. 69, no. 4, p. 1494–1507.

Staller, Eric L., Palmer, William E., Carroll, John P., and others, 2005, Identifying predators at northern bobwhite nests: Journal of Wildlife Management, v. 69, no. 1, p. 124–132.

Steenhof, K., Fuller, M. R., Kochert, M. N., and others, 2005, Long-range movements and breeding dispersal of Prairie Falcons from southwest Idaho: Condor, v. 107, no. 3, p. 481–496.

Stenhouse, Iain J., and Robertson, Gregory J., 2005, Philopatry, site tenacity, mate fidelity, and adult survival in Sabine's gulls: Condor, v. 107, no. 2, p. 416–423.

Sung, Ha-Cheol, Miller, Edward H., and Flemming, Stephen P., 2005, Breeding vocalizations of the piping plover (*Charadrius melodus*): structure, diversity, and repertoire organization: Canadian Journal of Zoology, v. 83, no. 4, p. 579–595.

Tallman, Dan A., 2005, Twenty-five years of bird banding in Aberdeen, South Dakota: South Dakota Bird Notes, v. 57, no. 3, p. 49–59.

Tautin, John, 2005, Frederick C. Lincoln and the formation of the North American bird banding program: U.S. Forest Service General Technical Report PSW-GTR-191, p. 813–814.

—, 2005, One hundred years of bird banding in North America: U.S. Forest Service General Technical Report PSW-GTR-191, p. 815–816.

Terhune, T. M., Sisson, D. C., and Stribling, H. L., 2005, Above-ground nesting by Northern Bobwhite: Wilson Bulletin, v. 117, no. 3, p. 315–316.

Thorn, Terri D., Emery, Robert B., Howerter, David W., and others, 2005, Use of radio-telemetry to test for investigator effects on nesting mallards, *Anas platyrhynchos*: Canadian Field-Naturalist, v. 119, no. 4, p. 541–545.

Torchin, M. E., Hechinger, R. F., Huspeni, T. C., and others, 2005, The introduced ribbed mussel (*Geukensia demissa*) in Estero de Punta Banda, Mexico: interactions with the native cord grass, *Spartina foliosa*: Biological Invasions, v. 7, no. 4, p. 607–614.

Walker, Tim, 2005, Alaska Bird Observatory Denali Institute Migration Station: North American Bird Bander, v. 30, no. 4, p. 211.

Wang, Yong, and Moore, Frank R., 2005, Long-distance bird migrants adjust their foraging behavior in relation to energy stores: Acta Zoologica Sinica, v. 51, no. 1, p. 12–23.

Wethington, Susan M., Russell, Stephen M., and West, George C., 2005, Timing of hummingbird migration in southeastern Arizona: implications for conservation: U.S. Forest Service General Technical Report PSW-GTR-191, p. 646–651.

White, Jennifer D., Gardali, Thomas, Thompson, Frank R. III, and others, 2005, Resource selection by juvenile Swainson's Thrushes during the postfledging period: Condor, v. 107, no. 2, p. 388–401.

Whittier, Joanna B., and Leslie, David M. Jr, 2005, Efficacy of using radio transmitters to monitor least tern chicks: Wilson Bulletin, v. 117, no. 1, p. 85–91.

Winkler, David W., Wrege, Peter H., Allen, Paul E., and others, 2005, The natal dispersal of tree swallows in a continuous mainland environment: Journal of Animal Ecology, v. 74, no. 6, p. 1080–1090.

2004

Atlantic Flyway review: Region II (north central) fall 2003, 2004, North American Bird Bander, v. 29, no. 1, p. 27–34.

Aborn, David A., and Moore, Frank R., 2004, Activity budgets of Summer Tanagers during spring migratory stopover: Wilson Bulletin, v. 116, no. 1, p. 64–68.

Abstracts, 2004, 79th Annual Meeting of the Western Bird Banding Association, held jointly with the 29th Annual Meeting of the Western Field Ornithologists and 25th Annual Meeting of the Oregon Field Ornithologists 9–12 September 2004: North American Bird Bander, v. 29, no. 4, p. 212–221.

Ackerman, Joshua T., Adams, Josh, Takekawa, John Y., and others, 2004, Effects of radiotransmitters on the reproductive performance of Cassin's auklets: Wildlife Society Bulletin, v. 32, no. 4, p. 1229–1241.

Ackerman, Joshua T., Takekawa, John Y., Kruse, Kammie L., and others, 2004, Using radiotelemetry to monitor cardiac response of free-living tule greater white-fronted geese (*Anser albifrons elgasi*) to human disturbance: Wilson Bulletin, v. 116, no. 2, p. 146–151.

Amirault, Diane L., Kierstead, Jonathan, Macdonald, Peter, and others, 2004, Sequential polyandry in piping plover, *Charadrius melodus*, nesting in eastern Canada: Canadian Field-Naturalist, v. 118, no. 3, p. 444–446.

Anonymous, 2004, Fall Meeting of the Texas Ornithological Society, Uvalde, TX, USA, October 23 -25, 2003: Bulletin of the Texas Ornithological Society, v. 37, no. 2, p. 33–36.

Ashley, E. Paul, and North, Norman R., 2004, Automated doors for waterfowl banding traps: Wildlife Society Bulletin, v. 32 , no. 1, p. 273–275.

Aversa, Tom, 2004, The role of Woodland Park Zoo keepers in a ferruginous hawl [hawk] satellite telemetry project: Proceedings of the National Conference of the American Association of Zoo Keepers Inc., v. 30, p. 246–249.

Backlund, Doug, Kiesow, Alyssa, Shearer, Jeff, and others, 2004, Banding results on Farm Island 2003: South Dakota Bird Notes, v. 56, no. 2, p. 41–44.

Ballard, Grant, Geupel, Geoffrey R., and Nur, Nadav. 2004, Influence of mist-netting intensity on demographic investigations of avian populations: Studies in Avian Biology, v. 29, p. 21–27.

Barding, E. E., and Nelson, T. A., 2004, Movements and habitat selection by raccoons in a wetland-agriculture landscape: Transactions of the Illinois State Academy of Science, v. 97, p. 36–37.

Barnum, Douglas A., and Johnson, Steven, 2004, The Salton Sea as important waterfowl habitat in the Pacific Flyway: Studies in Avian Biology, v. 27, p. 100–105.

Bell, Tom, 2004, Band-tailed pigeon in Dakota County: Loon, v. 75, no. 4, p. 238.

Bety, Joel, Giroux, Jean-Francois, and Gauthier, Gilles, 2004, Individual variation in timing of migration: causes and reproductive consequences in greater snow geese (*Anser caerulescens atlanticus*): Behavioral Ecology and Sociobiology, v. 57, no. 1, p. 1–8.

Bishop, Mary Anne, Warnock, Nils, and Takekawa, John Y., 2004, Differential spring migration by male and female Western Sandpipers at interior and coastal stopover sites: Ardea, v. 92, no. 2, p. 185–196.

Bridge, Eli S., and Nisbet, Ian C. T, 2004, Wing molt and assortative mating in common terns: A test of the molt-signaling hypothesis: Condor, v. 106, no. 2, p. 336–343.

Brooks, Elizabeth W., 2004, Atlantic Flyway review: region III (Western Ridge)—Fall 2003: North American Bird Bander, v. 29, no. 2, p. 74–87.

Carmen, William J., 2004, Noncooperative breeding in the California scrub-jay: Studies in Avian Biology, v. 28, p. 1–100.

Catry, Paulo, Phillips, Richard A., Phalan, Ben, and others, 2004, Foraging strategies of grey-headed albatrosses Thalassarche chrysostoma: integration of movements, activity and feeding events: Marine Ecology Progress Series, v. 280, p. 261–273.

Cimprich, David A., and Davis, Michelle, 2004, Skull pneumaticization and retained juvenal greater coverts of first-year great crested flycatchers during fall migration: North American Bird Bander, v. 29, no. 1, p. 7–10.

Craig, Gerald R., White, Gary C., and Enderson, James H., 2004, Survival, recruitment, and rate of population change of the peregrine falcon population in Colorado: Journal of Wildlife Management, v. 68, no. 4, p. 1032–1038.

Dale, Brenda C., 2004, Effectiveness of informal banding training at three western Canadian banding stations: Studies in Avian Biology, v. 29, p. 182–186.

Desante, David F., Saracco, James F., O'grady, Danielle R., and others, 2004, Methodological considerations of the Monitoring Avian Productivity and Survivorship (MAPS) Program: Studies in Avian Biology, v. 29, p. 28–45.

Devault, Travis L., Reinhart, Bradley D., Brisbin, I. Lehr Jr, and others, 2004, Home ranges of Sympatric Black and Turkey Vultures in South Carolina: Condor, v. 106, no. 3, p. 706–711.

Dorr, Brian, King, D. Tommy, Tobin, Mark E., and others, 2004, Double-crested cormorant movements in relation to aquaculture in Eastern Mississippi and Western Alabama: Waterbirds, v. 27, no. 2, p. 147–154.

Dugger, K. M., Faaborg, J., Arendt, W. J., and others, 2004, Understanding survival and abundance of overwintering Warblers: Does rainfall matter?: Condor, v. 106, no. 4, p. 744–760.

Dunn, Erica H., Hussell, David J., and Adams, Raymond J., 2004, An investigation of productivity indices derived from banding of fall migrants: Studies in Avian Biology, v. 29, p. 92–96.

Dunn, Erica H., Hussell, David J. T., Francis, Charles M., and others, 2004, A comparison of three count methods for monitoring songbird abundance during spring migration: capture, census, and estimated totals: Studies in Avian Biology, v. 29, p. 116–122.

Dykstra, Cheryl R., Hays, Jeffrey L., Simon, Melinda M., and others, 2004, Dispersal and mortality of red-shouldered hawks banded in Ohio: Journal of Raptor Research, v. 38, no. 4, p. 304–311.

Fearer, Todd M., and Stauffer, Dean F., 2004, Relationship of ruffed grouse *Bonasa umbellus* to landscape characteristics in southwest Virginia, USA: Wildlife Biology, v. 10, no. 2, p. 81–89.

Gabanski, Glenn, 2004, Inland Bird Banding Association. Waterfall Glen Forest Preserve: 2004 report on the MAPS study: North American Bird Bander, v. 29, no. 3, p. 132–141.

Gonzalez, P. M., Carbajal, M., Morrison, R. I. G., and others, 2004, Red Knot (*Calidris canutus rufa*) population trends in southern South America: Ornitologia Neotropical, v. 15, p. 357–365.

Hamel, Nathalie J., Parrish, Julia K., and Conquest, Loveday L., 2004, Effects of tagging on behavior, provisioning, and reproduction in the Common Murre (*Uria aalge*), a diving seabird: Auk, v. 121, no. 4, p. 1161–1171.

Hanneman, Matthew, 2004, The toilet paper bandit: Alberta Naturalist, v. 33, no. 4, p. 92.

Henkel, Laird A., Burkett, Esther E., and Takekawa, John Y., 2004, At-sea activity and diving behavior of a radio-tagged Marbled Murrelet in central California: Waterbirds, v. 27, no. 1, p. 9–12.

Homan, H. J., Linz, G. M., Engeman, R. M., and others, 2004, Spring dispersal patterns of red-winged blackbirds, *Agelaius phoeniceus*, staging in eastern South Dakota: Canadian Field-Naturalist, v. 118, no. 2, p. 201–209.

Houston, C. Stuart, and Zazelenchuk, Dan, 2004, Swainson's hawk productivity in Saskatchewan, 1944–2004: North American Bird Bander, v. 29, no. 4, p. 174–178.

Hussell, David J. T., 2004, Determining productivity indices from age composition of migrants captured for banding: problems and possible solutions: Studies in Avian Biology, v. 29, p. 82–91.

Ibarzabal, Jacques, and Desrochers, Andre, 2004, A nest predator's view of a managed forest: Gray Jay (*Perisoreus canadensis*) movement patterns in response to forest edges: Auk, v. 121, no. 1, p. 162–169.

Johnson, Kristine, Smith, B. Hamilton, Sadoti, Giancarlo, and others, 2004, Habitat use and nest site selection by nesting lesser prairie-chickens in southeastern New Mexico: Southwestern Naturalist, v. 49, no. 3, p. 334–343.

Johnson, Oscar W., and Johnson, Patricia M., 2004, Morphometric features of Pacific and American golden-plovers with comments on field identification: Wader Study Group Bulletin, v. 103, p. 42–49.

Keitt, Bradford S., Tershy, Bernie R., and Croll, Donald A., 2004, Nocturnal behavior reduces predation pressure on Black-vented shearwaters *Puffinus opisthomelas*: Marine Ornithology, v. 32, no. 2, p. 173–178.

Kelly, Elizabeth G., and Forsman, Eric D., 2004, Recent records of hybridization between barred owls (*Strix varia*) and northern spotted owls (*S. occidentalis caurina*): Auk, v. 121, no. 3, p. 806–810.

Kershner, Eric L., Walk, Jeffery W., and Warner, Richard E., 2004, Postfledging movements and survival of juvenile Eastern Meadowlarks (*Sturnella magna*) in Illinois: Auk, v. 121, no. 4, p. 1146–1154.

Knutsen, Alfred D., Carpenter, Thomas W., and Carpenter, Arthur L., 2004, Some evidence of winter site fidelity in Cooper's hawks: North American Bird Bander, v. 29, no. 3, p. 108–110.

Lima, Pedro Cerqueira, Hays, Helen, De Cassia, Rita, and others, 2004, Recoveries of Sterna dougallii (Montagu, 1813) in Bahia, Brazil, between 1995 and 2004: Ararajuba, v. 12, no. 2, p. 147–149.

Lindbloom, Andrew J., Reese, Kerry P., and Zager, Peter, 2004, Seasonal habitat use and selection of Chukars in west central Idaho: Western North American Naturalist, v. 64, no. 3, p. 338–345.

Mehl, Katherine R., Alisauskas, Ray T., Hobson, Keith A., and others, 2004, To winter East or West? Heterogeneity in winter philopatry in a central-Arctic population of King Eiders: Condor, v. 106, no. 2, p. 241–251.

Mennill, Daniel J., and Ratcliffe, Laurene M., 2004, Nest cavity orientation in black-capped chickadees Poecile atricapillus: do the acoustic properties of cavities influence sound reception in the nest and extra-pair matings?: Journal of Avian Biology, v. 35, no. 6, p. 477–482.

Millsap, Brian, Breen, Tim, Mcconnell, Elizabeth, and others, 2004, Comparative fecundity and survival of bald eagles fledged from suburban and rural natal areas in Florida: Journal of Wildlife Management, v. 68, no. 4, p. 1018–1031.

Morrison, R. I. G., Ross, R. K., and Niles, L. J., 2004, Declines in wintering populations of Red Knots in southern South America: Condor, v. 106, no. 1, p. 60–70.

Morrissey, Christy A., Bendell-Young, Leah I., and Elliott, John E., 2004, Seasonal trends in population density, distribution, and movement of American dippers within a watershed of southwestern British Columbia, Canada: Condor, v. 106, no. 4, p. 815–825.

Mulvihill, Robert S., Leberman, Robert C., and Leppold, Adrienne J., 2004, Relationships Among Body Mass, Fat, Wing Length, Age, and Sex for 170 Species of Birds Banded at Powdermill Nature Reserve: Hellentown, Eastern Bird Banding Association, 184 p.

Nguyen, Linh P., Hamr, Josef, and Parker, Glenn H., 2004, Wild Turkey, *Meleagris gallopavo silvestris*, behavior in central Ontario during winter: Canadian Field-Naturalist, v. 118, no. 2, p. 251–255.

Norman, Gary W., Conner, Mary M., Pack, James C., and others, 2004, Effects of fall hunting on survival of male wild turkeys in Virginia and west Virginia: Journal of Wildlife Management, v. 68, no. 2, p. 393–404.

Ortego, Brent, 2004, IBBA annual report 2002. A summary of bandings reported from the IBBA region for 2002 with USFWS/CWS bands: North American Bird Bander, v. 29 , no. 2, p. 88–98.

Otahal, Christopher D., 2004, WBBA annual report of birds banded, 2003, A summary of banding reported from the WBBA area for 2003 with USFWS/CWS bands: North American Bird Bander, v. 29, no. 3, p. 142–153.

Pearce, J. M., Talbot, S. L., Pierson, B. J., and others, 2004, Lack of spatial genetic structure among nesting and wintering King Eiders: Condor, v. 106, no. 2, p. 229–240.

Petersen, Margaret R., and Douglas, David C., 2004, Winter ecology of Spectacled Eiders: Environmental characteristics and population change: Condor, v. 106, no. 1, p. 79–94.

Pyle, P., Mcandrews, A., Velez, P., and others, 2004, Molt patterns and age and sex determination of selected southeastern Cuban landbirds: Journal of Field Ornithology, v. 75, no. 2, p. 136–145.

Ralph, C. John, Hollinger, Kimberly, and Miller, Sherri L., 2004, Monitoring productivity with multiple mist-net stations: Studies in Avian Biology, v. 29, p. 12–20.

Reed, E., Gauthier, G., and Giroux, J. F., 2004, Effects of spring conditions on breeding propensity of greater snow goose females: Animal Biodiversity and Conservation, v. 27, no. 1, p. 35–46.

Reynolds, Richard T., White, Gary C., Joy, Suzanne M., and others, 2004, Effects of radiotransmitters on northern goshawks: Do tailmounts lower survival of breeding males?: Journal of Wildlife Management, v. 68, no. 1, p. 25–32.

Rimmer, Christopher C., Faccio, Steven D., Lloyd-Evans, Trevor L., and others, 2004, A comparison of constant-effort mist netting results at a coastal and inland New England site during migration: Studies in Avian Biology, v. 29, p. 123–134.

Robbins, Chandler S., 2004, Atlantic Flyway review: region IV—Fall 2003: North American Bird Bander, v. 29, no. 3, p. 124–131.

Rothley, Kristina D., Berger, Claire N., Gonzalez, Catherine, and others, 2004, Combining strategies to select reserves in fragmented landscapes: Conservation Biology, v. 18, no. 4, p. 1121–1131.

Roy, W. Kelly, Coombs, Daniel L., and Evans, James W., 2004, Movement and harvest of giant Canada geese in east Tennessee: Migrant, v. 75, no. 4, p. 140–149.

Schamel, Douglas, Tracy, Diane M., and Lank, David B., 2004, Male mate choice, male availability and egg production as limitations on polyandry in the red-necked phalarope: Animal Behaviour, v. 67, no. 5, p. 847–853.

Scott, David P., Berdeen, James B., Otis, David L., and others, 2004, Harvest parameters of urban and rural mourning doves in Ohio: Journal of Wildlife Management, v. 68, no. 3, p. 694–700.

Sheaffer, S. E., Rusch, D. H., Humburg, D. D., and others, 2004, Wildlife monographs: Wildlife Monographs, no. 156, p. 1–54.

Sheaffer, Susan E., Rusch, Donald H., Humburg, Dale D., and others, 2004, Survival, movements, and harvest of eastern prairie population Canada geese: Wildlife Monographs, v. 156, p. 1–54.

Sherman, David E., and Barras, Amy E., 2004, Efficacy of a laser device for hazing Canada geese from urban areas of northeast Ohio: Ohio Journal of Science, v. 104, no. 3, p. 38–42.

Skadsen, Dennis, 2004, Banded Cooper's hawk recovered at Pickerel Lake State Recreation Area: South Dakota Bird Notes, v. 56, no. 1, p. 13.

Slabbekoom, H., 2004, Habitat-dependent ambient noise: Consistent spectral profiles in two African forest types: Journal of the Acoustical Society of America, v. 116, no. 6, p. 3727–3733.

Small, Michael F., Rosales, Randy, Baccus, John T., and others, 2004, A comparison of effects of radiotransmitter attachment techniques on captive white-winged doves: Wildlife Society Bulletin, v. 32, no. 3, p. 627–637.

Sonaiya, E. B., 2004, Direct assessment of nutrient resources in free-range and scavenging systems: Worlds Poultry Science Journal, v. 60, no. 4, p. 523–535.

Stenhouse, Iain J., Robertson, Gregory J., and Gilchrist, H. Grant, 2004, Recoveries and survival rate of ivory gulls banded in Nunavut, Canada, 1971–1999: Waterbirds, v. 27, no. 4, p. 486–492.

Suryan, R. M., Craig, D. P., Roby, D. D., and others, 2004, Redistribution and growth of the Caspian Tern population in the pacific coast region of North America, 1981–2000: Condor, v. 106, no. 4, p. 777–790.

Tallman, Dan, 2004, Aberdeen banding recoveries: South Dakota Bird Notes, v. 56, no. 4, p. 96.

Twedt, Daniel J., 2004, Sex determination of Carolina wrens in the Mississippi Alluvial Valley: North American Bird Bander, v. 29, no. 4, p. 171–174.

Urbina-Torres, Fernando, and Zainhana-Ortiz, Lucila, 2004, [Aspects of the Diet and Nesting of the Banded Quail Philortyx Fasciatus.], Conservation of Quail in the Neotropics: Proceedings of a Symposium Held During the VI Neotropical Ornithology Congress, Monterrey, Mexico, 4–10 October 1999: San Antonio, Center for the Study of Tropical Birds, Miscellaneous Publication No 3, p. 13–14.

Walk, Jeffery W., Wentworth, Kevin, Kershner, Eric L., and others, 2004, Renesting decisions and annual fecundity of female dickcissels (*Spiza americana*) in Illinois: Auk, v. 121, no. 4, p. 1250–1261.

Ward, David H., Schmutz, Joel A., Sedinger, James S., and others, 2004, Temporal and geographic variation in survival of juvenile Black Brant: Condor, v. 106, no. 2, p. 263–274.

Warnock, Nils, Takekawa, John Y., and Bishop, Mary Anne, 2004, Migration and stopover strategies of individual dunlin along the Pacific coast of North America: Canadian Journal of Zoology, v. 82, no. 11, p. 1687–1697.

Waterhouse, F. L., Donaldson, A., and Lank, D. B., 2004, Using airphotos to interpret marbled murrelet nesting habitat in British Columbia: application of a preliminary classification scheme: Research Section, Coast Forest Region, British Columbia Ministry of Forests, Technical Report TR-029, 37 p.

Whitfield, Michael B., Miller, Sue, Rice, Karen, and others, 2004, Bald eagles of eastern Idaho Greater Yellowstone Ecosystem 2004 annual productivity report: Idaho Bureau of Land Management Technical Bulletin, v. 2005–03, 24 p.

Wiltraut, Rick, 2004, Band-rumped storm-petrel Bald Eagle State Park, Centre County: Pennsylvania Birds, v. 17, no. 4, p. 265–266.

Yaremych, Sarah A., Novak, Robert J., Raim, Arlo J., and others, 2004, Home range and habitat use by American Crows in relation to transmission of West Nile Virus: Wilson Bulletin, v. 116, no. 3, p. 232–239.

Yoder, James M., Marschall, Elizabeth A., and Swanson, David A., 2004, The cost of dispersal: predation as a function of movement and site familiarity in ruffed grouse: Behavioral Ecology, v. 15, no. 3, p. 469–476.

Zimmerling, J. Ryan, Craigie, G. Eoin, and Robinson, Andrea E., 2004, A comparison of techniques for marking passerine nestlings: Wilson Bulletin, v. 116, no. 3, p. 240–245.

2003

Atlantic Flyway review: spring 2003, 2003, North American Bird Bander, v. 28, no. 4, p. 179–196.

Abstracts, 2003, Abstracts from papers/presentations at the Eastern Bird Banding Association 80th Annual Meeting: Expanding the World of Banding. Powdermill Nature Reserv. 4–6 Ap. 2003: North American Bird Bander, v. 28, no. 4, p. 175–179.

Ainley, David G., Ford, R. Glenn, Brown, Evelyn D., and others, 2003, Prey resources, competition, and geographic structure of kittiwake colonies in Prince William Sound: Ecology (Washington D C), v. 84, no. 3, p. 709–723.

Alerstam, T., Hedenstrom, A., and Akesson, S., 2003, Long-distance migration: evolution and determinants: Oikos, v. 103, no. 2, p. 247–260.

Anderson, James T., and Haukos, David A., 2003, Breeding ground affiliation and movements of greater white-fronted geese staging in northwestern Texas: Southwestern Naturalist, v. 48, no. 3, p. 365–372.

Bailey, Martin, 2003, Banding Great Horned Owls in farmland in the Weyburn area in 2003: Blue Jay, v. 61, no. 3, p. 140–142.

Bechet, Arnaud, Giroux, Jean-Francois, Gauthier, Gilles, and others, 2003, Spring hunting changes the regional movements of migrating greater snow geese: Journal of Applied Ecology, v. 40, no. 3, p. 553–564.

Beheler, Amanda S., Rhodes, Olin E. Jr, and Weeks, Harmon P. Jr, 2003, Breeding site and mate fidelity in eastern phoebes (*Sayornis phoebe*) in Indiana: Auk, v. 120, no. 4, p. 990–999.

Belthoff, James R., 2003, Monitoring burrowing owls in artificial burrows final report: Idaho Bureau of Land Management Technical Bulletin, v. 03–9, 40 p.

Blancher, Peter, 2003, Importance of Canada's Boreal Forest to Landbirds: The Canadian Boreal Initiative and the Boreal Songbird Initiative, p. 1–42.

Boal, Clint W., Andersen, David E., and Kennedy, Patricia L., 2003, Home range and residency status of Northern Goshawks breeding in Minnesota: Condor, v. 105, no. 4, p. 811–816.

Bronson, C. L., Grubb, Thomas C. Jr, Sattler, Gene D., and others, 2003, Mate preference: A possible causal mechanism for a moving hybrid zone: Animal Behaviour, v. 65, no. 3, p. 489–500.

Brooks, Elizabeth W., 2003, Atlantic flyway review: region III (Western Ridge)—Fall 2002: North American Bird Bander, v. 28, no. 3, p. 134–136.

Bryan, A. Lawrence Jr, Brooks, William B., and Brisbin, I. Lehr Jr, 2003, Satellite telemetry and recovery of the endangered wood stork: how can zoos participate?: American Zoo and Aquarium Association Regional Conference Proceedings, v. 2003, p. 139–142.

Budde, Paul E., and Svingen, Peder H., 2003, The fall season: (1 August to 30 November 2002): Loon, v. 75, no. 2, p. 77–105.

Chartier, Allen, 2003, Holiday Beach Migration Observatory 2002: Ontario Bird Banding, v. 35, p. 20–22.

Clausen, Preben, Green, Martin, and Alerstam, Thomas, 2003, Energy limitations for spring migration and breeding: The case of brent geese Branta bernicla tracked by satellite telemetry to Svalbard and Greenland: Oikos, v. 103, no. 2, p. 426–445.

Craves, Julie A., 2003, "Yellow" palm warbler (*Dendroica palmarum hypochrysea*) banded in Wayne Co: Michigan Birds and Natural History, v. 10, no. 3, p. 99–100.

Davies, J. Chris, and Pollard, Bruce, 2003, Ontario Cooperative Banding Program 2002 banding results: Ontario Bird Banding, v. 35, p. 26–31.

De Solla, Shane R., Martin, Pamela A., Ewins, Peter J., and others, 2003, Productivity and population trends of ospreys in the Kawartha Lakes Region, Ontario, 1978–2001: Journal of Raptor Research, v. 37, no. 4, p. 307–314.

Dean, Tracey, 2003, Atlantic Flyway review: region 1 (northeast)—Fall 2002: North American Bird Bander, v. 28, no. 4, p. 197–202.

Demers, Frederic, Giroux, Jean-Francois, Gauthier, Gilles, and others, 2003, Effects of collar-attached transmitters on behaviour, pair bond and breeding success of snow geese Anser caerulescens atlanticus: Wildlife Biology, v. 9, no. 3, p. 161–170.

Desgranges, Jean-Luc, and Jobin, Benoit, 2003, Knowing, mapping and understanding St. Lawrence biodiversity, with special emphasis on bird assemblages: Environmental Monitoring and Assessment, v. 88, no. 1–3, p. 177–192.

Devault, Travis L., Stephens, Warren L., Reinhart, Bradley D., and others, 2003, Aerial telemetry accuracy in a forested landscape: Journal of Raptor Research, v. 37, no. 2, p. 147–151.

Dinsmore, Stephen J., and Collazo, Jaime A., 2003, The influence of body condition on local apparent survival of spring migrant Sanderlings in coastal North Carolina: Condor, v. 105, no. 3, p. 465–473.

Dosch, Jerald J., 2003, Movement patterns of adult laughing gulls Larus atricilla during the nesting season: Acta Ornithologica (Warsaw), v. 38, no. 1, p. 15–25.

Drost, Charles A., Paxton, Eben H., Sogge, Mark K., and others, 2003, Food habits of the southwestern willow flycatcher during the nesting season: Studies in Avian Biology, v. 26, p. 96–103.

Evans Ogden, Lesley J., Neudorf, Diane L. H., Pitcher, Trevor E., and others, 2003, Female song in the Hooded Warbler: Northeastern Naturalist, v. 10, no. 4, p. 457–464.

Fleskes, Joseph P., 2003, Effects of backpack radiotags on female northern pintails wintering in California: Wildlife Society Bulletin, v. 31, no. 1, p. 213–219.

Flint, Paul L., Reed, John A., Franson, J. Christian, and others, 2003, Monitoring Beaufort Sea waterfowl and marine birds: U.S. Department of Interior, Minerals Management Service, Alaska Outer Continental Shelf Region, Anchorage, Alaska, Final Report, OCS Study MMS 2003-037, 125 p.

Folk, Travis Hayes, and Hepp, Gary R., 2003, Effects of habitat use and movement patterns on incubation behavior of female Wood Ducks (*Aix sponsa*) in southeast Alabama: Auk, v. 120, no. 4, p. 1159–1167.

Fry, Michael D., 2003, Assessment of Lead Contamination Sources Exposing California Condors. Final Report, Assessment of Lead Contamination Sources Exposing California Condors. Final Report: Sacramento, California Department of Fish and Game, p. 1–85.

Garrison, Barrett A., Wachs, Robin L., and Triggs, Matthew L., 2003, Responses of landbirds to group selection logging in the central Sierra Nevada: California Fish and Game, v. 89, no. 4, p. 155–175.

Gaston, Anthony J., 2003, Influence of chick mass and date at departure from the colony on adult characteristics in Ancient Murrelets (*Synthliboramphus antiquus*), a precocial seabird: Auk, v. 120, no. 3, p. 818–826.

Giese, Alan R., and Forsman, Eric D., 2003, Breeding season habitat use and ecology of male Northern Pygmy-Owls: Journal of Raptor Research, v. 37, no. 2, p. 117–124.

Giudice, J. H., 2003, Survival and recovery of Mallards and Gadwalls banded in eastern Washington, 1981–1998: Journal of Field Ornithology, v. 74, no. 1, p. 1–11.

Gleason, Jeffrey S., Jenks, Jonathan A., and Mammenga, Paul W., 2003, Distribution and trends of banded Canada geese in South Dakota: Prairie Naturalist, v. 35, no. 1, p. 19–31.

Gremillet, D., Wright, G., Lauder, A., and others, 2003, Modelling the daily food requirements of wintering great cormorants: a bioenergetics tool for wildlife management: Journal of Applied Ecology, v. 40, no. 2, p. 266–277.

Groh, Terri, and Wernaart, Martin, 2003, Banding in Ontario: 2002: Ontario Bird Banding, v. 35, p. 1–11.

Gutierrez, R. J., Zimmerman, Guthrie S., and Gullion, Gordon W., 2003, Daily survival rates of ruffed grouse *Bonasa umbellus* in northern Minnesota: Wildlife Biology, v. 9, no. 4, p. 351–356.

Haas, Franklin C., 2003, Banding records from Pennsylvania part 5—loons, grebes, and cormorants: Pennsylvania Birds, v. 16, no. 3–4, p. 157–159.

—, 2003, Banding records from Pennsylvania part 6—corvids: Pennsylvania Birds, v. 17, no. 1, p. 41–43.

Haas, William E., and Hargrove, Lori, 2003, A solution to leg band injuries in Willow Flycatchers: Studies in Avian Biology, no. 26, p. 180–184.

Hagelin, Julie C., 2003, A field study of ornaments, body size, and mating behavior of the Gambel's Quail: Wilson Bulletin, v. 115, no. 3, p. 246–257.

Haines, Aaron M., Mcgrady, Mike J., Martell, Mark S., and others, 2003, Migration routes and wintering locations of broad-winged hawks tracked by satellite telemetry: Wilson Bulletin, v. 115, no. 2, p. 166–169.

Hannon, Susan J., Gruys, Rogier C., and Schieck, Jim O., 2003, Differential seasonal mortality of the sexes in willow ptarmigan *Lagopus lagopus* in northern British Columbia, Canada: Wildlife Biology, v. 9, no. 4, p. 317–326.

Hanson, B. A., Stallknecht, D. E., Swayne, D. E., and others, 2003, Avian influenza viruses in Minnesota ducks during 1998–2000: Avian Diseases, v. 47, p. 867–871.

Herbert, Percy N., Carter, Harry R., Golightly, Richard T., and others, 2003, Radio-telemetry evidence of re-nesting in the same season by the marbled murrelet: Waterbirds, v. 26, no. 3, p. 261–265.

Hilton, Bill, and Miller, Mark W., 2003, Annual survival and recruitment in a ruby-throated hummingbird population, excluding the effect of transient individuals: Condor, v. 105, no. 1, p. 54–62.

Houston, C. Stuart, 2003, Rural banders in the Yorkton area: Blue Jay, v. 61, no. 2, p. 94–95.

Houston, C. Stuart, De Smet, Ken D., and Collister, Douglas M., 2003, Loggerhead Shrike banding on the prairies: Blue Jay, v. 61, no. 1, p. 40–42.

Houston, C. Stuart, and Houston, Mary I., 2003, Saskatchewan bird banders: J.A. Briggs of Regina: Blue Jay, v. 61, no. 3, p. 138–139.

Hupp, Jerry W., Ruhl, Gretchen A., Pearce, John M., and others, 2003, Effects of implanted radio transmitters with percutaneous antennas on the behavior of Canada geese: Journal of Field Ornithology, v. 74, no. 3, p. 250–256.

Hyrenbach, K. David, and Dotson, Ronald C., 2003, Assessing the susceptibility of female black-footed albatross (*Phoebastria nigripes*) to longline fisheries during their post-breeding dispersal: An integrated approach: Biological Conservation, v. 112, no. 3, p. 391–404.

Kennamer, Robert A., 2003, Recoveries of ring-necked ducks banded on the U.S. Department of Energy's Savannah River Site, South Carolina: Oriole, v. 68, no. 3–4, p. 8–14.

Krementz, David G., Hines, James E., and Luukkonen, David R., 2003, Survival and recovery rates of American woodcock banded in Michigan: Journal of Wildlife Management, v. 67, no. 2, p. 398–407.

Krijgsveld, Karen L., Reneerkens, Jeroen W. H., Mcnett, Gabriel D., and others, 2003, Time budgets and body temperatures of American Golden-Plover chicks in relation to ambient temperature: Condor, v. 105, no. 2, p. 268–278.

Kruse, Kammie L., Lovvorn, James R., Takekawa, John Y., and others, 2003, Winter distribution and survival of a high-desert breeding population of Canvasbacks: Condor, v. 105, no. 4, p. 791–804.

Lindbloom, Andrew J., Reese, Kerry P., and Zager, Peter, 2003, Nesting and brood-rearing characteristics of Chukars in west central Idaho: Western North American Naturalist, v. 63, no. 4, p. 429–439.

Litzow, Michael A., and Piatt, John F., 2003, Variance in prey abundance influences time budgets of breeding seabirds: evidence from pigeon guillemots *Cepphus columba*: Journal of Avian Biology, v. 34, no. 1, p. 54–64.

Mack, Glenn G., Clark, Robert G., and Howerter, David W., 2003, Size and habitat composition of female mallard home ranges in the prairie-parkland region of Canada: Canadian Journal of Zoology, v. 81, no. 8, p. 1454–1461.

Maimone-Celorio, Maria Rosa, and Mellink, Eric, 2003, Shorebirds and benthic fauna of tidal mudflats in Estero de Punta Banda, Baja California, Mexico: Bulletin Southern California Academy of Sciences, v. 102, no. 1, p. 26–38.

Maisonneuve, Charles, 2003, Importance of large diameter trees and snags for cavity nesting ducks and raptors in the northern forests of Quebec: Vogelwarte, v. 42, no. 1–2, p. 60.

Marino, Cindy, 2003, MacGillivray's warbler banded at Rochester—4 June 2003: second New York State record: Kingbird, v. 53, no. 3, p. 205–206.

Marshall, Matthew R., Dececco, Jennifer A., Williams, Alan B., and others, 2003, Use of regenerating clearcuts by late-successional bird species and their young during the post-fledging period: Forest Ecology and Management, v. 183, no. 1–3, p. 127–135.

Mcfarlane Tranquilla, Laura, Bradley, Russell, Parker, Nadine, and others, 2003, Replacement laying in marbled murrelets: Marine Ornithology, v. 31, no. 1, p. 75–81.

Mennill, Daniel J., Doucet, Stephanie M., Montgomerie, Robert, and others, 2003, Achromatic color variation in black-capped chickadees, *Poecile atricapilla*: Black and white signals of sex and rank: Behavioral Ecology and Sociobiology, v. 53, no. 6, p. 350–357.

Miller, Stanlee M., 2003, First report of a double-brooded Swainson's warbler: Wilson Bulletin, v. 115, no. 1, p. 94–95.

Morris, Sara R., Donovan, Amanda J., Agugliaro, Sara M., and others, 2003, Accuracy of sex determination of hatch-year common yellowthroats (*Geothlypis trichas*) during the fall: North American Bird Bander, v. 28, no. 3, p. 105–110.

Morris, Sara R., Pusateri, Christopher R., and Battaglia, Katherine A., 2003, Spring migration and stopover ecology of common yellowthroats on Appledore Island, Maine: Wilson Bulletin, v. 115, no. 1, p. 64–72.

Morrison, Joan L., 2003, Age-specific survival of Florida's Crested Caracaras: Journal of Field Ornithology, v. 74, no. 4, p. 321–330.

Otahal, Christopher D., 2003, 2002 annual banding report: North American Bird Bander, v. 28, no. 4, p. 203–213.

Paxton, Eben H., Cardinal, Suzanne N., and Koronkiewicz, Thomas J., 2003, Using radiotelemetry to determine home range size, habitat use, and movement patterns of willow flycatchers: Studies in Avian Biology, v. 26, p. 185–189.

Petersen, M. R., Mccaffery, B. J., and Flint, P. L., 2003, Post-breeding distribution of long-tailed ducks *Clangula hyemalis* from the Yukon-Kuskokwim Delta, Alaska: Wildfowl, v. 54, p. 103–113.

Peterson, Jessica L., Bischof, Richard, Krapu, Gary L., and others, 2003, Genetic variation in the midcontinental population of sandhill cranes, *Grus canadensis*: Biochemical Genetics, v. 41, no. 1–2, p. 1–12.

Poole, Richard, and Brown, Christine, 2003, Bird recaptures after scrub restoration: North American Bird Bander, v. 28, no. 3, p. 122–123.

Popham, Gail P., and Gutierrez, R. J., 2003, Greater sage-grouse *Centrocercus urophasianus* nesting success and habitat use in northeastern California: Wildlife Biology, v. 9, no. 4, p. 327–334.

Porneluzi, Paul A., 2003, Prior breeding success affects return rates of territorial male Ovenbirds: Condor, v. 105, no. 1, p. 73–79.

Pyle, Peter, and Desante, David F., 2003, Four-letter and six-letter alpha codes for birds recorded from the American ornithologists' union check-list area: North American Bird Bander, v. 28, no. 2, p. 64–73.

Regehr, Heidi M., 2003, Survival and movement of postfledging juvenile harlequin ducks: Wilson Bulletin, v. 115, no. 4, p. 423–430.

Regehr, Heidi M., and Rodway, Michael S., 2003, Evaluation of nasal discs and colored leg bands as markers for harlequin ducks: Journal of Field Ornithology, v. 74, no. 2, p. 129–135.

Robel, Robert J., Walker, Thomas L. Jr, Hagen, Christian A., and others, 2003, Helminth parasites of lesser prairie-chicken *Tympanuchus pallidicinctus* in southwestern Kansas: incidence, burdens and effects: Wildlife Biology, v. 9, no. 4, p. 341–349.

Rogers, Christopher M., and Heath-Coss, Rejeana, 2003, Effect of experimentally altered food abundance on fat reserves of wintering birds: Journal of Animal Ecology, v. 72, no. 5, p. 822–830.

Sanders, Todd A., and Jarvis, Robert L., 2003, Band-tailed pigeon distribution and habitat component availability in Western Oregon: Northwest Science, v. 77, no. 3, p. 183–193.

Scheuhammer, A. M., Money, S. L., Kirk, D. A., and others, 2003, Lead fishing sinkers and jigs in Canada: review of their use patterns and toxic impacts on wildlife: Canadian Wildlife Service Occasional Paper, v. 108, p. 1–45.

Schroeder, Michael A., and Robb, Leslie A., 2003, Fidelity of greater sage-grouse *Centrocercus urophasianus* to breeding areas in a fragmented landscape: Wildlife Biology, v. 9, no. 4, p. 291–299.

Scribner, Kim T., Malecki, Richard A., Batt, Bruce D. J., and others, 2003, Identification of source population for Greenland Canada Geese: Genetic assessment of a recent colonization: Condor, v. 105, no. 4, p. 771–782.

Sealy, Spencer G., Nero, Robert W., and Duncan, James C., 2003, Additional notes on Manitoba's long-lived great horned owl (band number 568–17752): Blue Jay, v. 61, no. 1, p. 27–30.

Sechrist, Juddson D., and Ahlers, Darrell D., 2003, Movements and home range estimates of female Brown-headed Cowbirds along the Rio Grande, New Mexico: Studies in Avian Biology, no. 26, p. 143–151.

Smith, B. H., Duszynski, D. W., and Johnson, K., 2003, Survey for coccidia and haemosporidia in the lesser prairie-chicken (*Tympanuchus pallidicinctus*) from New Mexico with description of a new Eimeria species: Journal of Wildlife Diseases, v. 39, no. 2, p. 347–353.

Smith, R. B., Meehan, T. D., and Wolf, B. O., 2003, Assessing migration patterns of sharp-shinned hawks *Accipiter striatus* using stable-isotope and band encounter analysis: Journal of Avian Biology, v. 34, no. 4, p. 387–392.

Sodergren, Jason, 2003, Raptor banding at Holiday Beach 2002: Ontario Bird Banding, v. 35, p. 22–25.

Taft, Oriane W., Haig, Susan M., and Kiilsgaard, Chris, 2003, Use of radar remote sensing (RADARSAT) to map winter wetland habitat for shorebirds in an agricultural landscape: Environmental Management, v. 32, no. 2, p. 268–281.

Thorup, Kasper, Alerstam, Thomas, Fuller, Mark, and others, 2003, Are free-flying migrants guided by geomagnetic cues?: Vogelwarte, v. 42, no. 1–2, p. 48.

Timson, Jamie E., and Farley, Greg H., 2003, Intraspecific helping behavior exhibited by hatch-year house wren: Southwestern Naturalist, v. 48, no. 2, p. 300–301.

Vega Rivera, Jorge H., Ayala, Dalia, and Haas, Carola A., 2003, Home-range size, habitat use, and reproduction of the Ivory-billed Woodcreeper (*Xiphorhynchus flavigaster*) in dry forest of western Mexico: Journal of Field Ornithology, v. 74, no. 2, p. 141–151.

Von Proschwitz, Ted, 2003, Faunistical news from the Natural History Museum, Göteborg 2002—snails, slugs and mussels: Goteborgs Naturhistoriska Museum Arstryck, v. 2003, p. 25–42.

Wambach, Ellen J., and Emslie, Steven D., 2003, Seasonal and annual variation in the diet of breeding, known-age Royal Terns in North Carolina: Wilson Bulletin , v. 115, no. 4, p. 448–454.

Wells, Kimberly M. Suedkamp, Washburn, Brian E., Millspaugh, Joshua J., and others, 2003, Effects of radio-transmitters on fecal glucocorticoid levels in captive Dickcissels: Condor, v. 105, no. 4, p. 805–810.

Wethington, Susan M., and Russell, Stephen M., 2003, The seasonal distribution and abundance of hummingbirds in oak woodland and riparian communities in southeastern Arizona: Condor, v. 105, no. 3, p. 484–495.

Yunick, Robert P., 2003, Effectiveness on wing chord/tail length measurements in separating black-capped chickadee from Carolina chickadee: North American Bird Bander, v. 28, no. 2, p. 52–57.

Yunick, Robert P., 2003, Geographical distribution of re-encountered pine siskins captured in eastern New York 1964–1997: North American Bird Bander, v. 28, no. 1, p. 1–9.

Zablan, Marilet A., Braun, Clait E., and White, Gary C., 2003, Estimation of greater sage-grouse survival in North Park, Colorado: Journal of Wildlife Management, v. 67, no. 1, p. 144–154.

2002

Allair, Jody, 2002, Long Point Bird Observatory 2001 Banding summary: Ontario Bird Banding, v. 34, p. 33–34.

Arnold, Todd W., Anderson, Michael G., Sorenson, Michael D., and others, 2002, Survival and philopatry of female redheads breeding in southwestern Manitoba: Journal of Wildlife Management, v. 66, no. 1, p. 162–169.

Arsenault, David P., Stacey, Peter B., and Hoelzer, Guy A., 2002, No extra-pair fertilization in Flammulated Owls despite aggregated nesting: Condor, v. 104, no. 1, p. 197–201.

Balkcom, Gregory D., 2002, Direct band recoveries from wood ducks banded in Georgia in 2000: Oriole, v. 67, no. 3–4, p. 38–42.

Bayne, Erin M., and Hobson, Keith A., 2002, Annual survival of adult American Redstarts and Ovenbirds in the southern boreal forest: Wilson Bulletin, v. 114, no. 3, p. 358–367.

Bennett, R., Mccomb, B., Shin, H. J., and others, 2002, Detection of avian pneumovirus in wild Canada geese (*Branta canadensis*) and blue-winged teal (*Anas discors*): Avian Diseases, v. 46, no. 4, p. 1025–1029.

Bogner, Heidi E., and Baldassarre, Guy A., 2002, Home range, movement, and nesting of Least Bitterns in Western New York: Wilson Bulletin, v. 114, no. 3, p. 297–308.

Bortolotti, Gary R., Dawson, Russell D., and Murza, Gillian L., 2002, Stress during feather development predicts fitness potential: Journal of Animal Ecology, v. 71, no. 2, p. 333–342.

Bradley, Russell W., Mcfarlane Tranquilla, Laura A., Vanderkist, Brett A., and others, 2002, Sex differences in nest visitation by chick-rearing Marbled Murrelets : Condor, v. 104, no. 1, p. 178–183.

Brook, Rodney W., and Clark, Robert G., 2002, Retention and effects of nasal markers and subcutaneously implanted radio transmitters on breeding female Lesser Scaup: Journal of Field Ornithology, v. 73, no. 2, p. 206–212.

Brooks, Elizabeth W., 2002, Atlantic flyway review: region III (Western Ridge)—Fall 2001: North American Bird Bander, v. 27, no. 4, p. 141–154.

Brooks, Elizabeth W., 2002, Atlantic Flyway Review: spring 2001: North American Bird Bander, v. 27, no. 1, p. 19–35.

Budde, Paul E., 2002, The fall season (1 August to 30 November 2001): Loon, v. 74, no. 2, p. 83–110.

Burton, Kenneth M., and Whitehead, Donald R., 2002, Productivity and survival of the loggerhead shrike in Indiana: Bird Populations, v. 6, p. 13–20.

Calvert, Anna M., and Robertson, Gregory J., 2002, Using multiple abundance estimators to infer population trends in Atlantic puffins: Canadian Journal of Zoology, v. 80, no. 6, p. 1014–1021.

Chartier, Allen, 2002, Holiday Beach Migration Observatory—2001. Beach Station (passerine/hummingbird) banding summary: Ontario Bird Banding, v. 34, p. 16–23.

—, 2002, Holiday Beach Migration Observatory—passerine banding summary: Ontario Bird Banding, v. 33, p. 21–24.

Churchill, John B., Wood, Petra Bohall, and Brinker, David F., 2002, Winter home range and habitat use of female Northern Saw-whet Owls on Assateague Island, Maryland: Wilson Bulletin, v. 114, no. 3, p. 309–313.

Cink, Calvin L., 2002, Possible band-induced mortality in a nesting chimney swift: North American Bird Bander, v. 27, no. 4, p. 126–127.

Coluccy, John M., Drobney, Ronald D., Pace, Richard M. III, and others, 2002, Consequences of neckband and legband loss from giant Canada geese: Journal of Wildlife Management, v. 66, no. 2, p. 353–360.

Colwell, Rita R., 2002, Recommended band size for spotted towhees: a suggested revision: North American Bird Bander, v. 27, no. 4, p. 127–129.

Corrigan, Rob, 2002, Peregrine falcon surveys and monitoring in the Parkland Region of Alberta, 1001: Alberta Species at Risk Report, v. 34, 11 p.

—, 2002, Peregrine falcon surveys and monitoring the northeast Boreal region of Alberta, 2001: Alberta Species at Risk Report, v. 57, 12 p.

Cox, Robert R. Jr, Scalf, Joseph D., Jamison, Brent E., and others, 2002, Using an electronic compass to determine telemetry azimuths: Wildlife Society Bulletin, v. 30, no. 4, p. 1039–1043.

Davies, J. Chris, and Pollard, Bruce, 2002, Ontario Cooperative Banding Project 2001 Banding Results: Ontario Bird Banding, v. 34, p. 43–44.

Dean, Tracey, 2002, Atlantic Flyway review: northeast coastal region 1—Fall 2001: North American Bird Bander, v. 27, no. 2, p. 68–73.

Doherty, Paul F. Jr, Nichols, James D., Tautin, John, and others, 2002, Sources of variation in breeding-ground fidelity of mallards (*Anas platyrhynchos*): Behavioral Ecology, v. 13, no. 4, p. 543–550.

Ellison, Kevin, Sykes, Paul W. Jr, and Bocetti, Carol I., 2002, Re-evaluating the Bay-breasted Warbler breeding range: Nine years of presence in Lower Michigan: Wilson Bulletin, v. 114, no. 3, p. 415–416.

Fleishman, E., and Mac Nally, R., 2002, Topographic determinants of faunal nestedness in Great Basin butterfly assemblages: Applications to conservation planning: Conservation Biology, v. 16, no. 2, p. 422–429.

Forsman, Eric D., Anthony, Robert G., Reid, Janice A., and others, 2002, Natal and breeding dispersal of northern spotted owls: Wildlife Monographs, v. 149, p. 1–35.

Franklin, A. B., Anderson, D. R., and Burnham, K. P., 2002, Estimation of long-term trends and variation in avian survival probabilities using random effects models: Journal of Applied Statistics, v. 29, no. 1–4, p. 267–287.

Fraser, Gail S., Jones, Ian L., and Hunter, Fiona M., 2002, Male-female differences in parental care in monogamous crested auklets: Condor, v. 104, no. 2, p. 413–423.

Frost, Roger, 2002, Toronto Bird Observatory Report—2000: Ontario Bird Banding, v. 33, p. 15–16.

Gaston, Anthony J., 2002, Have changes in hunting pressure affected the thick-billed murre populations at Coats Island, Nunavut?: Canadian Wildlife Service Occasional Paper, v. 106, p. 5–12.

Glahder, C., Fox, A., and Walsh, A., 2002, Spring staging areas of white-fronted geese in west Greenland: results from aerial survey and satellite telementry: Wildfowl, v. 53, p. 35–52.

Golden, Elizabeth A., Smith, Henry T., Donlan, Ellen M., and others, 2002, Banded royal terns recovered at Key Biscayne, Florida: Florida Field Naturalist, v. 30, no. 3, p. 91–93.

Golightly, Richard T., Newman, Scott H., Craig, Emilie N., and others, 2002, Survival and behavior of western gulls following exposure to oil and rehabilitation: Wildlife Society Bulletin, v. 30, no. 2, p. 539–546.

Gregoire, John A., 2002, Atlantic Flyway Review: Region II (north central) fall 2001: North American Bird Bander, v. 27, no. 1, p. 35–42.

Groh, Terri, and Wernaart, Martin, 2002, Banding in Ontario: 2000: Ontario Bird Banding, v. 33, p. 1–14.

—, 2002, Banding in Ontario 2001: Ontario Bird Banding, v. 34, p. 1–13.

Guzy, Michael J., Ribic, Christine A., and Sample, David W., 2002, Helping at a Henslow's Sparrow nest in Wisconsin: Wilson Bulletin, v. 114, no. 3, p. 407–409.

Haig, Susan M., Oring, Lewis W., Sanzenbacher, Peter M., and others, 2002, Space use, migratory connectivity, and population segregation among willets breeding in the western Great Basin: Condor, v. 104, no. 3, p. 620–630.

Harmata, Alan R., 2002, Encounters of golden eagles banded in the Rocky Mountain West: Journal of Field Ornithology, v. 73, no. 1, p. 23–32.

Harper, Steven J., Westervelt, James D., and Shapiro, Ann-Marie, 2002, Modeling the movements of cowbirds: Application towards management at the landscape scale: Natural Resource Modeling, v. 15, no. 1, p. 111–131.

Hazlitt, Stephanie L., and Gaston, Anthony J., 2002, Black Oystercatcher natal philopatry in the Queen Charlotte Islands, British Columbia: Wilson Bulletin, v. 114, no. 4, p. 520–522.

Heagy, Audrey, 2002, Cabot Head migration monitoring project: 2000 station report: Ontario Bird Banding, v. 33, p. 28–31.

Hendricks, Paul, and Johnson, Robert F., 2002, Movements and Mortality of American White Pelicans Fledged in Three Montana Colonies, Movements and Mortality of American White Pelicans Fledged in Three Montana Colonies: Helena, Montana Natural Heritage Program, 16 p.

Hepp, Gary R., Folk, Travis Hayes, and Hartke, Kevin M., 2002, Effects of subcutaneous transmitters on reproduction, incubation behaviour, and annual return rates of female wood ducks: Wildlife Society Bulletin, v. 30, no. 4, p. 1208–1214.

Herter, Dale R., Hicks, Lorin L., Stabins, Henning C., and others, 2002, Roost site characteristics of northern spotted owls in the nonbreeding season in central Washington: Forest Science, v. 48, no. 2, p. 437–444.

Hinde, Alan, Grant, Kelly, and Yosef, Reuven, 2002, Banding and Communal Roosts of Wintering Raptors of the Great Basin: 1987–1998, *in* Yosef, Reuven, Miller, Michael, and Pepler, David, eds., Raptors in the New Millennium: Proceedings of the World Conference on Birds of Prey and Owls. Raptors 2000: Joint Meeting of the: Raptor Research Foundation, World Working Group on Birds of Prey. Hosted by the: International Birding and Research Center in Eilat, Israel. Eilat, Israel 2–8 April 2000: Eilat, International Birding and Research Center, p. 112–117.

Hoffman, S. W., Smith, J. P., and Meehan, T. D., 2002, Breeding grounds, winter ranges, and migratory routes of raptors in the mountain west: Journal of Raptor Research, v. 36, no. 2, p. 97–110.

Houston, C. Stuart, 2002, Early Saskatoon city bird banders: Blue Jay, v. 60, no. 2, p. 79–82.

Houston, C. Stuart, and Houston, Mary I., 2002, Rural banders in the Saskatoon area: Blue Jay, v. 60, no. 1, p. 35–37.

Hyrenbach, K. David, Fernandez, Patricia, and Anderson, David J., 2002, Oceanographic habitats of two sympatric North Pacific albatrosses during the breeding season: Marine Ecology Progress Series, v. 233, p. 283–301.

Jenkins, Kendell D., and Cristol, Daniel A., 2002, Evidence of differential migration by sex in White-throated Sparrows (*Zonotrichia albicollis*): Auk, v. 119, no. 2, p. 539–543.

Jones, Edgar T., 2002, Banding report and observations for 2002: Alberta Naturalist, v. 32, no. 3, p. 113.

Jones, Ian L., Rowe, Sherrylynn, Carr, Steve M., and others, 2002, Different patterns of parental effort during chick-rearing by female and male Thick-billed Murres (*Uria lomvia*) at a low-arctic colony: Auk, v. 119, no. 4, p. 1064–1074.

Jones, Kenneth L., Glenn, Travis C., Lacy, Robert C., and others, 2002, Refining the whooping crane studbook by incorporating microsatellite DNA and leg-banding analyses: Conservation Biology, v. 16, no. 3, p. 789–799.

Kenow, Kevin P., Meyer, Michael W., Evers, David C., and others, 2002, Use of satellite telemetry to identify Common Loon migration routes, staging areas and wintering range: Waterbirds, v. 25, no. 4, p. 449–458.

Kroodsma, Donald E., Woods, Robin W., and Goodwin, Elijah A., 2002, Falkland Island sedge wrens (*Cistothorus platensis*) imitate rather than improvise large song repertoires: Auk, v. 119, no. 2, p. 523–528.

Lake, Laura A., Buehler, David A., and Houston, Allan E., 2002, Cooper's hawk non-breeding habitat use and home range in southwestern Tennessee: Proceedings of the Annual Conference Southeastern Association of Fish and Wildlife Agencies, v. 56, p. 229–238.

Lougheed, Cecilia, Vanderkist, Brett A., Lougheed, Lynn W., and others, 2002, Techniques for investigating breeding chronology in Marbled Murrelets, desolation sound, British Columbia: Condor, v. 104, no. 2, p. 319–330.

Machell, Eric A., 2002, Prince Edward Point Bird Observatory: owl banding October 2000: Ontario Bird Banding, v. 33, p. 32–34.

—, 2002, Prince Edward Point Bird Observatory Spring 2000 Report: Ontario Bird Banding, v. 33, p. 17–20.

Martell, Mark S., Englund, Judy Voigt, and Tordoff, Harrison B., 2002, An urban Osprey population established by translocation: Journal of Raptor Research, v. 36, no. 2, p. 91–96.

Mcgrady, Michael J., Maechtle, Thomas L., Vargas, Juan J., and others, 2002, Migration and ranging of Peregrine Falcons wintering on the Gulf of Mexico coast, Tamaulipas, Mexico: Condor, v. 104, no. 1, p. 39–48.

Miller, Stanlee M., 2002, Two white Swainson's warbler nestlings banded in South Carolina: Chat (Raleigh), v. 66, no. 2, p. 62–64.

Morton, Martin L., 2002, The mountain white-crowned sparrow: Migration and reproduction at high altitude: Studies in Avian Biology, no. 24, 236 p.

Mulvihill, Robert S., Cunkelman, Amy, Quattrini, Laura, and others, 2002, Opportunistic polygyny in the Louisiana waterthrush: Wilson Bulletin, v. 114, no. 1, p. 106–113.

Nasution, Marlina D., Brownie, Cavell, and Pollock, Kenneth H., 2002, Optimal allocation of sample sizes between regular banding and radio-tagging for estimating annual survival and emigration rates: Journal of Applied Statistics, v. 29, no. 1–4, p. 443–457.

Nordby, J. Cully, Campbell, S. Elizabeth, and Beecher, Michael D., 2002, Adult song sparrows do not alter their song repertoires: Ethology, v. 108, no. 1, p. 39–50.

Norris, D. Ryan, and Stutchbury, Bridget J. M., 2002, Sexual differences in gap-crossing ability of a forest songbird in a fragmented landscape revealed through radiotracking: Auk, v. 119, no. 2, p. 528–532.

Olmos, Fabio, 2002, Non-breeding seabirds in Brazil: a review of band recoveries: Ararajuba, v. 10, no. 1, p. 31–42.

Ortego, Brent, 2002, IBBA annual report 2001. A summary of bandings reported from the IBBA region for 2001 with USFWS/CWS bands: North American Bird Bander, v. 27 , no. 4, p. 156–166.

Otis, David L., 2002, Survival models for harvest management of mourning dove populations: Journal of Wildlife Management, v. 66, no. 4, p. 1052–1063.

Otis, David L., and White, Gary C., 2002, Re-analysis of a banding study to test the effects of an experimental increase in bag limits of mourning doves: Journal of Applied Statistics, v. 29, no. 1–4, p. 479–495.

Pearce, Rebecca L., Wood, Jesse J., Artukhin, Yuri, and others, 2002, Mitochondrial DNA suggests high gene flow in Ancient Murrelets: Condor, v. 104, no. 1, p. 84–91.

Petersen, Margaret R., and Flint, Paul L., 2002, Population structure of Pacific Common Eiders breeding in Alaska: Condor, v. 104, no. 4, p. 780–787.

Petrie, Scott A., Badzinski, Shannon S., and Wilcox, Kerrie L., 2002, Population trends and habitat use of Tundra Swans staging at Long Point, Lake Erie: Waterbirds, v. 25, no. Special Publication 1, p. 143–149.

Reed, Lisa M., Crans, Wayne J., and Bosak, Peter J., 2002, Seroprevalence of West Nile virus in the wild birds of New Jersey: Proceedings of the New Jersey Mosquito Control Association Inc, v. 89, p. 12–18.

Robb, Joseph R., 2002, Band recovery and recapture rates of American black ducks and mallards: Journal of Wildlife Management, v. 66, no. 1, p. 153–161.

Robert, M., Benoit, R., and Savard, J. P. L., 2002, Relationship among breeding, molting, and wintering areas of male Barrow's Goldeneyes (*Bucephala islandica*) in eastern North America: Auk, v. 119, no. 3, p. 676–684.

Rohwer, Frank C., Richkus, Kenneth D., and Smith, David B., 2002, Effects of backpack radio packages on mass of captive-reared mallards released in Maryland: Proceedings of the Annual Conference Southeastern Association of Fish and Wildlife Agencies, v. 56, p. 365–373.

Roscoe, James W., 2002, Sage grouse movements in southwestern Montana: Intermountain Journal of Sciences, v. 8, no. 2 , p. 94–104.

Rosien, Darwin A., 2002, Ontario Airboat Duck Banding Program—2001: Ontario Bird Banding, v. 34, p. 45–60.

Ruegg, Kristen C., and Smith, Thomas B., 2002, Not as the crow flies: A historical explanation for circuitous migration in Swainson's thrush (*Catharus ustulatus*): Proceedings of the Royal Society Biological Sciences Series B, v. 269, no. 1498, p. 1375–1381.

Salt, Jim, 2002, A magpie band-release project in the Calgary area, 1949: Blue Jay, v. 60, no. 4, p. 213–215.

Salvadori, Antonio, Burger, John, and Frank, Richard, 2002, Some statistics on black-capped chickadees: Ontario Bird Banding, v. 34, p. 61–67.

Sanzenbacher, Peter M., and Haig, Susan M., 2002, Regional fidelity and movement patterns of wintering Killdeer in an agricultural landscape: Waterbirds, v. 25, no. 1, p., 16, 25.

Sibley, Fred, 2002, Bird band recovery: Connecticut Warbler, v. 22, no. 4, p. 160.

Smith, Jim, 2002, Haldimand Bird Observatory 2000: Ontario Bird Banding, v. 33, p. 26–27.

Smith, Larissa, Clark, Kathleen E., and Niles, Lawrence J., 2002, New Jersey Bald Eagle Management Project 2002, New Jersey Bald Eagle Management Project 2002: place of publication not given, New Jersey Division of Fish and Wildlife, p. 1–17.

Sodergren, Jason, 2002, Holiday Beach Migration Observatory. Raptor Banding, September 10–December 8, 2001: Ontario Bird Banding, v. 34, p. 24–26.

Spears, Brian L., Ballard, Warren B., Wallace, Mark C., and others, 2002, Retention times of miniature radiotransmitters glued to wild turkey poults: Wildlife Society Bulletin, v. 30, no. 3, p. 861–867.

St Louis, John, 2002, Raptor banding at Holiday Beach Conservation Area: 2000: Ontario Bird Banding, v. 33, p. 24–25.

Stewart, Rebecca L. M., Francis, Charles M., and Massey, Cheryl, 2002, Age-related differential timing of spring migration within sexes in passerines: Wilson Bulletin, v. 114, no. 2, p. 264–271.

Takekawa, J. Y., Warnock, N., Martinelli, G. M., and others, 2002, Waterbird use of Bayland Wetlands in the San Francisco Bay estuary: Movements of long-billed Dowitchers during the winter: Waterbirds, v. 25, p. 93–105.

Tobin, Mark E., King, D. Tommy, Dorr, Brian S., and others, 2002, Effect of roost harassment on cormorant movements and roosting in the delta region of Mississippi: Waterbirds, v. 25, no. 1, p. 44–51.

Voltura, Karen M., Schwagmeyer, P. L., and Mock, Douglas W., 2002, Parental feeding rates in the house sparrow, Passer domesticus: Are larger-badged males better fathers?: Ethology, v. 108, no. 11, p. 1011–1022.

Whalen, David M., and Watts, Bryan D., 2002, Annual migration density and stopover patterns of northern Saw-whet Owls (*Aegolius acadicus*): Auk, v. 119, no. 4, p. 1154–1161.

Wilson, W. Herbert Jr, 2002, Population and individual responses of red-breasted nuthatches (*Sitta canadensis*) to supplemental food in central Maine: North American Bird Bander, v. 27, no. 2, p. 49–54.

2001

Abstracts from IBBA's 2000 Meeting, 2001, North American Bird Bander, v. 26, no. 4, p. 194–195.

Abstracts from IBBA's 2001 Meeting, 2001, North American Bird Bander, v. 26, no. 4, p. 196–197.

Western Bird Banding Association 76th Annual Meeting 21–23 September 2001, Spokane, WA, 2001, North American Bird Bander, v. 26, no. 3, p. 129–133.

Aldridge, Cameron L., and Brigham, R. Mark, 2001, Nesting and reproductive activities of Greater Sage-Grouse in a declining northern Fringe population: Condor, v. 103, no. 3, p. 537–543.

Anonymous, 2001, 1999 fall banding at the Haldimand Bird Observatory: Ontario Bird Banding, v. 32, p. 17–18.

—, 2001, 1999 spring banding at the Haldimand Bird Observatory: Ontario Bird Banding, v. 32, p. 15–17.

Antolin, Michael F., Van Horne, Beatrice, Berger, Michael D. Jr., and others, 2001, Effective population size and genetic structure of a Piute ground squirrel (*Spermophilus mollis*) population: Canadian Journal of Zoology, v. 79, no. 1, p. 26–34.

Bart, Jonathan, Battaglia, Daniel, and Senner, Nathan, 2001, Effects of color bands on semipalmated sandpipers banded at hatch: Journal of Field Ornithology, v. 72, no. 4, p. 521–526.

Bayne, Erin M., and Hobson, Keith A., 2001, Movement patterns of adult male ovenbirds during the post-fledging period in fragmented and forested boreal landscapes: Condor, v. 103, no. 2, p. 343–351.

Benson, A. M., and Winker, K., 2001, Timing of breeding range occupancy among high-latitude passerine migrants: Auk, v. 118, no. 2, p. 513–519.

Blakesley, Jennifer A., Noon, Barry R., and Shaw, Daniel W., 2001, Demography of the California spotted owl in northeastern California: Condor, v. 103, no. 4, p. 667–677.

Bowman, Reed, and Aborn, David A., 2001, Effects of different radio transmitter harnesses on the behavior of Florida Scrub-Jays: Florida Field Naturalist, v. 29, no. 3, p. 81–86.

Brinkley, Edward S., and Patteson, J. Brian, 2001, Yellow-legged gull (*Larus cachinnans* cf. *michahellis*) at Back Bay National Wildlife Refuge, Virginia Beach: Raven, v. 72, no. 1, p. 66–75.

Carver, A. Vince, Burger, Loren W. Jr, Palmer, William E., and others, 2001, Vegetation characteristics in seasonal-disked fields and at bobwhite brood locations: Proceedings of the Annual Conference Southeastern Association of Fish and Wildlife Agencies, v. 55, p. 436–444.

Chartier, Allen, 2001, Holiday Beach Migration Observatory passerine banding summary—Fall 1999: Ontario Bird Banding, v. 32, p. 19–23.

Chubb, Kit, 2001, Great horned owl band returns: Ontario Bird Banding, v. 32, p. 24–25.

Chubbs, Tony E., Mactavish, Bruce, Oram, Keith, and others, 2001, Unusual Harlequin Duck, *Histrionicus histrionicus*, nest site discovered in central Labrador: Canadian Field-Naturalist, v. 115, no. 1, p. 177, 179.

Coleman, J. T. H., and Richmond, M. E., 2001, Radio-tracking the double-crested cormorants of Oneida Lake, NY: A Study of foraging behavior in a large, temperate lake: IAGLR Conference Program and Abstracts, v. 44, p. 20.

Corrigan, Rob, 2001, Survey of the peregrine falcon (*Falco peregrinus anatum*) in Alberta: Alberta Species at Risk Report, v. 2, 17 p.

Dean, Tracey, 2001, Atlantic flyway review: northeast coastal region I—Fall 2000: North American Bird Bander, v. 26, no. 2, p. 72–77.

Diquinzio, Deborah A., Paton, Peter W., and Eddleman, William R., 2001, Site fidelity, philopatry, and survival of promiscuous saltmarsh sharp-tailed sparrows in Rhode Island: Auk, v. 118, no. 4, p. 888–899.

Dunn, Erica H., 2001, Causes of decline in band encounter rates for small landbirds: North American Bird Bander, v. 26, no. 1, p. 9–15.

Fernandez, Guillermo, De La Cueva, Horacio, and Warnock, Nils, 2001, Phenology and length of stay of transient and wintering western sandpipers at Estero Punta Banda, Mexico: Journal of Field Ornithology, v. 72, no. 4, p. 509–520.

Fernandez, Patricia, Anderson, David J., Sievert, Paul R., and others, 2001, Foraging destinations of three low-latitude albatross (*Phoebastria*) species: Journal of Zoology (London), v. 254, no. 3, p. 391–404.

Friesen, Lyle E., Cadman, Michael D., and Allen, Martha L., 2001, Triple brooding by southern Ontario wood thrushes: Wilson Bulletin, v. 113, no. 2, p. 237–239.

Frost, Roger, 2001, Toronto Bird Observatory report 1999: Ontario Bird Banding, v. 32, p. 15.

Gauthier, Gilles, Pradel, Roger, Menu, Stephane, and others, 2001, Seasonal survival of Greater Snow Geese and effect of hunting under dependence in sighting probability: Ecology (Washington D C), v. 82, no. 11, p. 3105–3119.

Gilbert, William M., and Kwon, Ki-Chung, 2001, Male Wilson's warbler with amputated foot successfully forages and raises brood of young: North American Bird Bander, v. 26, no. 3, p. 93–96.

Giroux, Jean-Francois, Lefebvre, Josee, Belanger, Luc, and others, 2001, Establishment of a breeding population of Canada geese in southern Quebec: Canadian Field-Naturalist, v. 115, no. 1, p. 75–81.

Goguen, Christopher B., and Mathews, Nancy E., 2001, Brown-headed Cowbird behavior and movements in relation to livestock grazing: Ecological Applications, v. 11, no. 5, p. 1533–1544.

Groh, Terri, 2001, Banding in Ontario: 1999: Ontario Bird Banding, v. 32, p. 1–10.

Hagen, Christian A., Kenkel, Norm C., Walker, David J., and others, 2001, Fractal-Based Spatial Analysis of Radiotelemetry Data, Radio Tracking and Animal Populations: San Diego, San Francisco etc., Academic Press, p. 167–187.

Hagen, Cristian, Pitman, James, Robel, Bob, and others, 2001, Use of sandsage habitat by lesser prairie-chickens in southwestern Kansas: a progress report: Grouse News, v. 21, p. 18–20.

Hansrote, Charles, and Hansrote, M., 2001, Orange variant northern cardinal recaptured: North American Bird Bander, v. 26, no. 2, p. 50–52.

Harmata, Alan R., and Montopoli, George J., 2001, Analysis of Bald Eagle spatial use of linear habitat: Journal of Raptor Research, v. 35, no. 3, p. 207–213.

Harmata, Alan R., Restani, Marco, Montopoli, George J., and others, 2001, Movements and mortality of Ferruginous Hawks banded in Montana: Journal of Field Ornithology, v. 72, no. 3, p. 389–398.

Hazlitt, Stephanie L., 2001, Longevity of plastic leg bands on black oystercatchers in British Columbia: North American Bird Bander, v. 26, no. 2, p. 55–56.

Hjertaas, Dale, and Hjertaas, Paule, 2001, Observations from banding house finches in the fall of 1995 at Regina, SK: Blue Jay, v. 59, no. 2, p. 86–89.

Hobson, Keith A., and Wassenaar, Leonard I., 2001, Isotopic delineation of North American migratory wildlife populations: Loggerhead Shrikes: Ecological Applications, v. 11, no. 5, p. 1545–1553.

Hull, Cindy L., Kaiser, Gary W., Lougheed, Cecilia, and others, 2001, Intraspecific variation in commuting distance of Marbled Murrelets (*Brachyramphus marmoratus*): Ecological and energetic consequences of nesting further inland: Auk, v. 118, no. 4, p. 1036–1046.

Hyrenbach, K. David, and Dotson, Ronald C., 2001, Post-breeding movements of a male Black-footed Albatross Phoebastria nigripes: Marine Ornithology, v. 29, no. 1, p. 7–10.

Jones, Edgar T., 2001, Banding records: 1940–2000: Alberta Naturalist, v. 31, no. 1, p. 12–13.

King, D. Tommy, and Grewe, Alfred H. Jr, 2001, Movements and mortality of American white pelicans banded at Marsh Lake, Minnesota: North American Bird Bander, v. 26, no. 2, p. 57–60.

Koronkiewicz, Thomas J., and Sogge, Mark K., 2001, Southwestern willow flycatchers recaptured at wintering sites in Costa Rica: North American Bird Bander, v. 26, no. 4, p. 161–162.

Lahaye, William S., Gutierrez, R. J., and Dunk, Jeffrey R., 2001, Natal dispersal of the spotted owl in southern California: Dispersal profile of an insular population: Condor, v. 103, no. 4, p. 691–700.

Larson, Michael A., Clark, Margaret E., and Winterstein, Scott R., 2001, Survival of ruffed grouse chicks in northern Michigan: Journal of Wildlife Management, v. 65, no. 4, p. 880–886.

Lathrop, Richard G., and Niles, Larry, 2001, Whither the red knot: Mapping and modeling the nesting habitat of an arctic shorebird at both site and regional scales: Ecological Society of America Annual Meeting Abstracts, v. 86, p. 306.

Legare, Michael L., and Eddleman, William R., 2001, Home range size, nest-site selection and nesting success of Black Rails in Florida: Journal of Field Ornithology, v. 72, no. 1, p. 170–177.

Lindberg, M. S., Kendall, W. L., Hines, J. E., and others, 2001, Combining band recovery data and Pollock's robust design to model temporary and permanent emigration: Biometrics, v. 57, no. 1, p. 273–281.

Lowther, Peter, 2001, IBBA Board and General Meetings 7–8 September 2001 Delta Marsh, Manitoba: North American Bird Bander, v. 26, no. 3, p. 126–129.

Machell, Eric A., 2001, Prince Edward Point Bird Observatory: 1999 spring migration report: Ontario Bird Banding, v. 32, p. 11–14.

Malecki, Richard A., Batt, Bruce D. J., and Sheaffer, Susan E., 2001, Spatial and temporal distribution of Atlantic Population Canada geese: Journal of Wildlife Management, v. 65, no. 2, p. 242–247.

Martell, Mark S., Henny, Charles J., Nye, Peter E., and others, 2001, Fall migration routes, timing, and wintering sites of North American Ospreys as determined by satellite telemetry: Condor, v. 103, no. 4, p. 715–724.

Meehan, T. D., Lott, C. A., Sharp, Z. D., and others, 2001, Using hydrogen isotope geochemistry to estimate the natal latitudes of immature Cooper's hawks migrating through the Florida Keys: Condor, v. 103, no. 1, p. 11–20.

Menu, Stephane, Gauthier, Gilles, and Reed, Austin, 2001, Survival of juvenile greater snow geese immediately after banding: Journal of Field Ornithology, v. 72, no. 2, p. 282–290.

Mikaelian, Igor, Ley, David H., Claveau, Raynald, and others, 2001, Mycoplasmosis in evening and pine grosbeaks with conjunctivitis in Quebec: Journal of Wildlife Diseases, v. 37, no. 4, p. 826–830.

Miller, Michael R., Stemler, Casey L., and Blankenship, Daniel S., 2001, Mourning dove productivity in California during 1992–95: Was it sufficient to balance mortality?: Journal of Wildlife Management, v. 65, no. 2, p. 300–311.

Miller, Michael R., Stemler, Casey L., Yee, Julie L., and others, 2001, Differences in mourning dove productivity among three time periods at Gray Lodge Wildlife Area, California: California Fish and Game, v. 87, no. 3, p. 93–101.

Morris, Sara R., and Glasgow, Jamin L., 2001, Comparison of spring and fall migration of American redstarts on Appledore Island, Maine: Wilson Bulletin, v. 113, no. 2, p. 202–210.

Mowbray, Thomas B., Glover, Lex, Whitaker, Abby, and others, 2001, A 20-year record of migratory bird movements in the Black River Swamp of South Carolina: Chat (Raleigh), v. 65, no. 4, p. 123–136.

Nasution, Marlina D., Brownie, Cavell, Pollock, Kenneth H., and others, 2001, Estimating survival from joint analysis of resighting and radiotelemetry capture-recapture data for wild animals: Journal of Agricultural Biological and Environmental Statistics, v. 6, no. 4, p. 461–478.

Otahal, Christopher D., 2001, WBBA annual report 2000. A summary of banding reported from the WBBA area for 2000 with USFWS/CWS bands: North American Bird Bander, v. 26, no. 2, p. 79–88.

Perkins, Dustin W., and Vickery, Peter D., 2001, Annual survival of an endangered passerine, the Florida grasshopper sparrow: Wilson Bulletin, v. 113, no. 2, p. 211–216.

Peterson, Stacy Jon, 2001, Hummingbird Research Group Banding Conference, 15–18 August 2001, Gray Feathers Lodge, Silver City, New Mexico: North American Bird Bander, v. 26, no. 4, p. 201–205.

Pope, Michael D., and Crawford, John A., 2001, Male incubation and biparental care in mountain quail: Condor, v. 103, no. 4, p. 865–870.

Powell, Larkin A., Barry, Irene M., Calvert, Dan J., and others, 2001, Dispersal and survival of juvenile peregrine falcons during a large restoration project: Ecological Society of America Annual Meeting Abstracts, v. 86, p. 181–182.

Ransom, Dean Jr, Honeycutt, Rodney L., and Slack, R. Douglas, 2001, Population genetics of southeastern wood ducks: Journal of Wildlife Management, v. 65, no. 4, p. 745–754.

Restani, Marco, Marzluff, John M., and Yates, Richard E., 2001, Effects of anthropogenic food sources on movements, survivorship, and sociality of common ravens in the Arctic: Condor, v. 103, no. 2, p. 399–404.

Rimmer, Christopher C., and Mcfarland, Kent P., 2001, Known breeding and wintering sites of a Bicknell's thrush: Wilson Bulletin, v. 113, no. 2, p. 234–236.

Robb, Joseph R., Tori, Gildo M., and Kroll, Roy W., 2001, Condition indices of live-trapped American black ducks and mallards: Journal of Wildlife Management, v. 65, no. 4, p. 755–764.

Royle, J. Andrew, and Dubovsky, James A., 2001, Modeling spatial variation in waterfowl band-recovery data: Journal of Wildlife Management, v. 65, no. 4, p. 726–737.

Samuel, Michael D., Goldberg, Diana R., Smith, Arthur E., and others, 2001, Neckband retention for lesser snow geese in the western Arctic: Journal of Wildlife Management, v. 65, no. 4, p. 797–807.

Schmutz, Joel A., 2001, Selection of habitats by Emperor Geese during brood rearing: Waterbirds, v. 24, no. 3, p. 394–401.

Sedinger, James S., Lindberg, Mark S., and Chelgren, Nathan D., 2001, Age-specific breeding probability in black brant: effects of population density: Journal of Animal Ecology, v. 70, no. 5, p. 798–807.

Sissons, Robert A., Scalise, Karyn L., and Wellicome, Troy I., 2001, Nocturnal foraging and habitat use by male Burrowing Owls in a heavily-cultivated region of southern Saskatchewan: Journal of Raptor Research, v. 35, no. 4, p. 304–309.

Skelly, Sharon, Bonter, David, and Semple, David, 2001, An unusual chickadee (*Poecile* species) banded at Braddock Bay, NY: Kingbird, v. 51, no. 2, p. 579–581.

Sloan, Christopher A., 2001, Winter hummingbirds in Tennessee: general comments and summary of 2001–2002 banding efforts: Migrant, v. 72, no. 4, p. 101–104.

Smith, Cyndi M., 2001, Harlequin duck research in Kananaskis Country in 2000: Alberta Species at Risk Report, v. 15, 33 p.

Sordahl, Tex A., 2001, Copulatory behavior of American avocets and black-necked stilts: Auk, v. 118, no. 4, p. 1072–1076.

Stafford, Joshua D., Flake, Lester D., and Mammenga, Paul W., 2001, Evidence for double brooding by a Mallard, *Anas platyrhynchos*, in eastern South Dakota: Canadian Field-Naturalist, v. 115, no. 3, p. 502–504.

Taylor, J. S., Church, K. E., and Rusch, D. H., 2001, Effects of necklace- versus backpack-mounted radiotransmitters on northern bobwhite (*Colinus virginianus*) survival and reproduction: Game and Wildlife Science, v. 18, nos. 3–4, p. 573–579.

Traylor, S. S., Church, K. E., and Draheim, D. L., 2001, Range expansion of grey partridge (*Perdix perdix*) in the central Great Plains, USA: Game and Wildlife Science, v. 18, nos. 3–4, p. 243–252.

Wang, Xiao-Hong, and Trost, Charles H., 2001, Dispersal pattern of black-billed magpies (*Pica hudsonia*) measured by molecular genetic (RAPD) analysis: Auk, v. 118, no. 1, p. 137–146.

Watt, Doris J., 2001, Recapture rate and breeding frequencies of American goldfinches wearing different colored leg bands: Journal of Field Ornithology, v. 72, no. 2, p. 236–243.

Wedeking, Paul, Huie, Janet L., and Suthers, Hannah B., 2001, Utilization of a limited preferred food resource by blue jays (*Cyanocitta cristata*): North American Bird Bander, v. 26, no. 2, p. 41–49.

Wilson, Linda J., and Gaston, Anthony J., 2001, Effects of handling stress on Brunnich's Guillemots *Uria lomvia*: Ringing and Migration, v. 20, no. 4, p. 320–327.

Wilson, W. Herbert Jr, 2001, The effects of supplemental feeding on wintering black-capped chickadees (*Poecile atricapilla*) in central Maine: population and individual responses: Wilson Bulletin, v. 113, no. 1, p. 65–72.

Wood, Douglas R., Vilella, Francisco J., and Burger, L. Wesley Jr, 2001, Red-cockaded woodpecker banding at Bienville National Forest, Mississippi: North American Bird Bander, v. 26, no. 1, p. 16–19.

Woolfenden, Glen E., Monteiro, Luis R., and Duncan, Robert A., 2001, Recovery from the northeastern Gulf of Mexico of a band-rumped storm-petrel banded in the Azores: Journal of Field Ornithology, v. 72, no. 1, p. 62–65.

Yackel Adams, Amy A., Skagen, Susan K., and Adams, Rod D., 2001, Movements and survival of Lark Bunting fledglings: Condor, v. 103, no. 3, p. 643–647.

Western Bird Banding Association 75th Annual Meeting 8–10 September 2000 Fairbanks, Alaska, 2000, North American Bird Bander, v. 25, no. 3, p. 118–121.

2000

Aldridge, Cameron L., 2000, Assessing chick survival of sage-grouse in Canada. Final project report for 2000: Alberta Species at Risk Report, v. 19, 25 p.

Ammon, Elisabeth, and Chisholm, Graham, 2000, Second season of fall migrant banding on the Lower Carson River: Great Basin Birds, v. 3, no. 1, p. 36.

Bolen, Eric G., 2000, Waterfowl management: yesterday and tomorrow: Journal of Wildlife Management, v. 64, no. 2, p. 323–335.

Bolsinger, Jeffrey S., 2000, Use of two song categories by golden-cheeked warblers: Condor, v. 102, no. 3, p. 539–552.

Boyd, W. Sean, Schneider, Saul D., and Cullen, Sean A., 2000, Using radio telemetry to describe the fall migration of Eared Grebes: Journal of Field Ornithology, v. 71, no. 4, p. 702–707.

Brewer, David, Diamond, A., Woodsworth, E., and others, 2000, Canadian Atlas of Bird Banding. Volume 1. Doves, Cuckoos, and Hummingbirds Through Passerines, 1921–1995, Canadian Atlas of Bird Banding. Volume 1. Doves, Cuckoos, and Hummingbirds Through Passerines, 1921–1995: Ottawa, Canadian Wildlife Service, 395 p.

Brooks, Elizabeth W., 2000, Atlantic Flyway Review: Region III (Western Ridge) fall 1999: North American Bird Bander, v. 25, no. 4, p. 148–158.

—, 2000, Atlantic Flyway Review: Spring 2000: North American Bird Bander, v. 25, no. 4, p. 158–170.

Brown, David R., Stouffer, Philip C., and Strong, Cheryl M., 2000, Movement and territoriality of wintering Hermit Thrushes in Southeastern Louisiana: Wilson Bulletin, v. 112, no. 3, p. 347–353.

Carpenter, Thomas W., Carpenter, Arthus L., and Roberts, Phil, 2000, Raptor banding at Holiday Beach Conservation Area, 1997: Ontario Bird Banding, v. 31, p. 35–37.

Clark, William. S., Schultz, Christopher, and Allen, Olin, 2000, Conservation of migrating raptors through banding; results of over 30 years of the Cape May Raptor Banding Project, in Chancellor, R.D., and Meyburg, B.-U., eds., Raptors at risk: World Working Group on Birds of Prey/Hancock House, p. 617–625.

Connelly, John W., Apa, Anthony D., Smith, Randall B., and others, 2000, Effects of predation and hunting on adult sage grouse Centrocercus urophasianus in Idaho: Wildlife Biology, v. 6, no. 4, p. 227–232.

Cupul Magana, and Fabio German, 2000, Aquatic birds of the El Salado estuary, Puerto Vallarta, Jalisco: Huitzil, v. 1, p. 3–8.

Curson, David R., Goguen, Christopher B., and Mathews, Nancy E., 2000, Long-distance commuting by Brown-headed Cowbirds in New Mexico: Auk, v. 117, no. 3, p. 795–799.

Curtis, Paul D., and Braun, Clait E., 2000, Behavior of band-tailed pigeons at feeding sites: Colorado Division of Wildlife Special Report, v. 75, p. 15–20.

Dau, Christian P., Flint, Paul L., and Petersen, Margaret R., 2000, Distribution of recoveries of Steller's eiders banded on the Lower Alaska Peninsula, Alaska: Journal of Field Ornithology, v. 71, no. 3, p. 541–548.

Davis, William E. Jr, 2000, History of the Association of Field Ornithologists (Northeastern Bird Banding Association): Memoirs of the Nuttall Ornithological Club, v. 13, p. 263–309.

Deviche, Pierre, 2000, Timing, pattern, and extent of first prebasic molt of white-winged crossbills in Alaska: Journal of Field Ornithology, v. 71, no. 2, p. 217–226.

Dougill, Steve J., Johnson, Luanne, Banko, Paul C., and others, 2000, Consequences of antenna design in telemetry studies of small passerines: Journal of Field Ornithology, v. 71, no. 3, p. 385–388.

Dugger, Katie M., Ryan, Mark R., and Renken, Rochelle B., 2000, Least tern chick survival on the lower Mississippi River: Journal of Field Ornithology, v. 71, no. 2, p. 330–338.

Esler, Daniel, Mulcahy, Daniel M., and Jarvis, Robert L., 2000, Testing assumptions for unbiased estimation of survival of radiomarked harlequin ducks: Journal of Wildlife Management, v. 64, no. 2, p. 591–598.

Flint, Paul L., Grand, J. Barry, Morse, Julie A., and others, 2000, Late summer survival of adult female and juvenile Spectacled Eiders on the Yukon-Kuskokwim Delta, Alaska: Waterbirds, v. 23, no. 2, p. 292–297.

Friesen, Lyle E., Wyatt, Valerie E., Cadman, Michael D., and others, 2000, Extent of double-brooding and seasonal movement of nesting females in a northern population of wood thrushes: Wilson Bulletin, v. 112, no. 4, p. 505–509.

Gardali, Thomas, Ballard, Grant, Nur, Nadav, and others, 2000, Demography of a declining population of warbling vireos in coastal California: Condor, v. 102, no. 3, p. 601–609.

Hansrote, Charles, 2000, An American goldfinch population study on a July day (1999): North American Bird Bander, v. 25, no. 3, p. 81–86.

Hansrote, Charles, and Hansrote, Melva, 2000, An 'orange variant' northern cardinal: North American Bird Bander, v. 25, no. 1, p. 1–3.

Haramis, G. Michael, and Kearns, Gregory D., 2000, A radio transmitter attachment technique for soras: Journal of Field Ornithology, v. 71, no. 1, p. 135–139.

Harrison, Michael K. Sr, Haramis, G. Michael, Jorde, Dennis G., and others, 2000, Capturing American black ducks in tidal waters: Journal of Field Ornithology, v. 71, no. 1, p. 153–158.

Hartup, Barry K., Kollias, George V., and Ley, David H., 2000, Mycoplasmal conjunctivitis in songbirds from New York: Journal of Wildlife Diseases, v. 36, no. 2, p. 257–264.

Hatch, Scott A., Meyers, Paul M., Mulcahy, Daniel M., and others, 2000, Performance of implantable satellite transmitters in diving seabirds: Waterbirds, v. 23, no. 1, p. 84–94.

Heagy, Audrey, 2000, Cabot Head Bird Migration Study 1998: Ontario Bird Banding, v. 31, p. 33–34.

Houston, C. Stuart, 2000, Migration of common terns banded in western Canada: North American Bird Bander, v. 25, no. 1, p. 4–7.

Hubert, Bob, and Hubert, Fran, 2000, Hawk Cliff raptor banding station—twenty-eighth annual report: 1999: Ontario Bird Banding, v. 31, p. 14–21.

Johnson, L. Scott, and Wise, Joanna, 2000, Wintering grounds of North American House Wrens as revealed by band recoveries: Journal of Field Ornithology, v. 71, no. 3, p. 501–505.

Kautz, J. Edward, and Braun, Clait E., 2000, Feasibility of estimating band-tailed pigeon population parameters using capture-recapture: Colorado Division of Wildlife Special Report, v. 75, p. 1–14.

Keppie, Daniel M., and Braun, Clait E., 2000, Band-tailed pigeon: Columba fasciata: Birds of North America, v. 530, p. 1–28.

King, D. Tommy, Tobin, Mark E., and Bur, Michael, 2000, Capture and telemetry techniques for double-crested cormorants (*Phalacrocorax auritus*): Proceedings of the Vertebrate Pest Conference, v. 19, p. 54–57.

Koenig, Walter D., Hooge, Philip N., Stanback, Mark T., and others, 2000, Natal dispersal in the cooperatively breeding Acorn Woodpecker: Condor, v. 102, no. 3, p. 492–502.

Lariviere, Serge, and Messier, Francois, 2000, Habitat selection and use of edges by striped skunks in the Canadian prairies: Canadian Journal of Zoology , v. 78, no. 3, p. 366–372.

Larson, Michael A., Ryan, Mark R., and Root, Brian G., 2000, Piping Plover survival in the Great Plains: An updated analysis: Journal of Field Ornithology, v. 71, no. 4, p. 721–729.

Lieske, David J., Warkentin, Ian G., James, Paul C., and others, 2000, Effects of population density on survival in merlins: Auk, v. 117, no. 1, p. 184–193.

Lutcavage, M. E., Brill, R. W., Skomal, G. B., and others, 2000, Tracking adult North Atlantic bluefin tuna (*Thunnus thynnus*) in the northwestern Atlantic using ultrasonic telemetry: Marine Biology (Berlin), v. 137, no. 2, p. 347–358.

Machell, Eric A., 2000, Prince Edward Point bird observatory: 1998 spring migration report: Ontario Bird Banding, v. 31, p. 30–32.

Marks, Jeffrey S., and Doremus, John H., 2000, Are Northern Saw-whet Owls nomadic?: Journal of Raptor Research, v. 34, no. 4, p. 299–304.

Martell, Mark S., Goggin, Jane, and Redig, Patrick T., 2000, Assessing rehabilitation success of raptors through band returns, *in* Lumeij, J.T., Remple, J.D., Redig, P.T., Lierz, M., and Cooper, J.E., eds., Raptor biomedicine III, including bibliography of diseases of birds of prey, p. 327–334.

Mcilveen, W., 2000, Banding experiences in reclaimed industrial barrens at Sudbury, Ontario: Ontario Bird Banding, v. 31, p. 44–47.

—, 2000, Banding in Ontario: 1998: Ontario Bird Banding, v. 31, p. 1–10.

—, 2000, Commentary on banding reports from 1984 to 1998: Ontario Bird Banding, v. 31, p. 48–55.

Menu, Stephane, Hestbeck, Jay B., Gauthier, Gilles, and others, 2000, Effects of neck bands on survival of greater snow geese: Journal of Wildlife Management, v. 64, no. 2, p. 544–552.

Morales-Perez, Jose Eduardo, Altamirano Gonzalez-Ortega, Marco A., and Gonzalez Dominguez, Patricia, 2000, Records of the black-banded woodcreeper *Dendrocolaptes picumnus* in Chiapas, Mexico: Bulletin of the British Ornithologists' Club, v. 120, no. 2, p. 133–136.

Mumme, Ronald L., Schoech, Stephan J., Woolfenden, Glen E., and others, 2000, Life and death in the fast lane: demographic consequences of road mortality in the Florida scrub-jay: Conservation Biology, v. 14, no. 2, p. 501–512.

Murphy, Bill, and Petrie, Bill, 2000, Innis Point bird observatory: 1997 in review: Ontario Bird Banding, v. 31, p. 22–26.

——, 2000, Innis Point bird observatory: 1998 spring migration monitoring report: Ontario Bird Banding, v. 31, p. 27–29.

Osborn, Sophie A., 2000, Itinerant breeding and mate switching by an American dipper: Wilson Bulletin, v. 112, no. 4, p. 539–541.

Pace, Richard M., 2000, Winter survival rates of American woodcock in south central Louisiana: Journal of Wildlife Management, v. 64, no. 4, p. 933–939.

Paton, Dale, 2000, Harlequin duck surveys of the Oldman River Basin in 2000: Alberta Species at Risk Report, v. 20, 36 p.

Plissner, Jonathan H., Haig, Susan M., and Oring, Lewis W., 2000, Postbreeding movements of American Avocets and implications for wetland connectivity in the western Great Basin: Auk, v. 117, no. 2, p. 290–298.

Poole, Richard T., 2000, Banding owls in nest boxes—problem of desertion: North American Bird Bander, v. 25, no. 2, p. 48.

Powell, Larkin A., Conroy, Michael J., Hines, James E., and others, 2000, Simultaneous use of mark-recapture and radiotelemetry to estimate survival, movement, and capture rates: Journal of Wildlife Management, v. 64, no. 1, p. 302–313.

Ramey, Craig A., Bourassa, Jean B., and Brooks, Joe E., 2000, Potential risks to ring-necked pheasants in California agricultural areas using zinc phosphide: International Biodeterioration and Biodegradation, v. 45, no. 3–4, p. 223–230.

Reisen, William K., Lundstrom, Jan O., Scott, Thomas W., and others, 2000, Patterns of avian seroprevalence to western equine encephalomyelitis and Saint Louis encephalitis viruses in California, USA: Journal of Medical Entomology, v. 37, no. 4, p. 507–527.

Rimmer, Christopher C., and Mcfarland, Kent P., 2000, Migrant stopover and postfledging dispersal at a montane forest site in Vermont: Wilson Bulletin, v. 112, no. 1, p. 124–136.

Robert, Michel, Bordage, Daniel, Savard, Jean-Pierre L., and others, 2000, The breeding range of the Barrow's Goldeneye in eastern North America: Wilson Bulletin, v. 112, no. 1, p. 1–7.

Roberts, Phil, 2000, Holiday Beach Conservation Area passerine banding station—1998 summary: Ontario Bird Banding, v. 31, p. 40–43.

——, 2000, Raptor banding at Holiday Beach Conservation Area, 1998: Ontario Bird Banding, v. 31, p. 38–39.

Rottenborn, Stephen C., and Morlan, Joseph, 2000, Report of the California Bird Records Committee: 1997 records: Western Birds, v. 31, no. 1, p. 1–37.

Sanders, Todd A., and Jarvis, Robert L., 2000, Do band-tailed pigeons seek a calcium supplement at mineral sites?: Condor, v. 102, no. 4, p. 855–863.

Sanzenbacher, Peter M., Haig, Susan M., and Oring, Lewis W., 2000, Application of modified harness design for attachment of radio transmitters to shorebirds: Wader Study Group Bulletin, v. 91, p. 16–20.

Scharf, William C., 2000, New Michigan tick (Acari: Ixodidae) and flea (Siphonaptera: Ceratophyllidae) records from colonial nesting birds: Great Lakes Entomologist, v. 33, no. 2, p. 155–159.

Schmutz, Joel A., and Morse, Julie A., 2000, Effects of neck collars and radio transmitters on survival and reproduction of emperor geese: Journal of Wildlife Management, v. 64, no. 1, p. 231–237.

Shealer, David A., and Haverland, Jeffrey A., 2000, Effects of investigator disturbance on the reproductive behavior and success of black terns: Waterbirds, v. 23, no. 1, p. 15–23.

Verner, Jared, Breese, Dawn, and Purcell, Kathryn L., 2000, Return rates of banded granivores in relation to band color and number of bands worn: Journal of Field Ornithology, v. 71, no. 1, p. 117–125.

Warner, R. E., Hubert, P., Mankin, P. C., and others, 2000, Disturbance and the survival of female ring-necked pheasants in Illinois: Journal of Wildlife Management, v. 64, no. 3, p. 663–672.

Whitworth, Darrell L., Nelson, S. Kim, Newman, Scott H., and others, 2000, Foraging distances of radio-marked Marbled Murrelets from inland areas in southeast Alaska: Condor, v. 102, no. 2, p. 452–456.

Whitworth, Darrell L., Takekawa, John Y., Carter, Harry R., and others, 2000, Distribution of Xantus' murrelet *Synthliboramphus hypoleucus* at sea in the Southern California Bight, 1995–97: Ibis, v. 142, no. 2, p. 268–279.

Wojnowski, J., 2000, The 1998 Long Point banding summary: Ontario Bird Banding, v. 31, p. 11–13.